ECHOES OF WAR

ROBERT GIDDINGS

ECHOES
OF WAR

PORTRAITS OF WAR
FROM THE FALL OF TROY
TO THE GULF WAR

BCA

LONDON · NEW YORK · SYDNEY · TORONTO

This edition published 1992 by BCA in arrangement with
Bloomsbury Publishing Limited.

CN 2674

First published in Britain 1992
Bloomsbury Publishing Limited
2 Soho Square, London W1V 5DE

A copy of the CIP entry for this book is available from the British Library

Typeset by Hewer Text Composition Services, Edinburgh
Printed in England by Clay Ltd., St. Ives plc.

CONTENTS

'Peace is better than War, because in Peace the sons bury their fathers, but in War the fathers bury their sons.'

Francis Bacon, Baron Verulam of Verulam, Viscount St. Albans (1561)
Apothegms 1625 Number 145.

'Military Glory — that attractive rainbow that rises in showers of blood, that serpent's eye that charms to destroy.'

Abraham Lincoln (1809–1865) Speech Against the War with Mexico, House of Representatives, 12th January 1848.

'Every man thinks meanly of himself for not having been a soldier, or not having been at sea. If Lord Mansfield, the Chief Justice, were in a company of General Officers and Admirals who had been in service, he would shrink; he'd wish to creep under the table.'

Samuel Johnson (1709–1784)

INTRODUCTION

Doughboys were paid a whole dollar a day
and received free burial under the clay.
And movie heroes are paid even more
shooting one another in a Hollywood war.

Alfred Kreyborg (1883–1966) 'What Price Glory?'

This is a collection of writing about war. As far as possible the excerpts
are about real wars. But this is not a history of war, illustrated with
literary gems. The only justification for any example's inclusion is that
of the quality of the writing. This is an anthology first, and whatever
historical value it might have is essentially secondary. Nevertheless, I
found it was impossible when assembling this book to keep out
thoughts about our species' age-old and enduring propensities to inflict
war and suffering on our own kind.

In 1651, looking back over human history and contemplating human
behaviour, Thomas Hobbes wrote in the first part of his *Leviathan* that
the condition of man was a condition of war against everyone. Swift
believed that Hobbes had therefore proved that every creature – man
included – lives in a state of war by nature. It was Edmund Burke who
injected a slight note of optimism into this long-standing discourse
about man's warlike nature by suggesting in *Vindication of Natural
Society* (1756) that Hobbes' meditation on the conduct of political
societies had made him imagine that war was 'the state of nature'. The
Vindication was primarily a satiric imitation of the style of Henry Saint-
John Bolingbroke, First Viscount Bolingbroke, the statesman and
philosopher, and by implication an attack upon Bolingbroke's high Tory
beliefs, with their fundamentally low opinion of human nature.
Nevertheless, Burke does raise a fundamental question; are we to
conclude – from the fact that wherever we look in the history of human
kind, and wherever we cast our attention across the modern world, we

see men at war with each other — that war is our natural condition? Just because it seems we have always done it, and continue to do it, does that mean we cannot help it, because *it is an inescapable part of our nature?* Behind Burke's satiric irony there seems to be a belief in a human goodness we have usually kept from ourselves, and a belief that constant warfare is not part of our nature.

Yet the whole history of human culture as manifested in the creative imagination seems to belie this faith. The earliest evidence we have celebrates war. The *Mahabharata* (Great War of the Bharatas), ascribed to the sage Vyasa ('the arranger'), in its present (late) form dates from between 400 to 200 BC but represents a reworking of vastly older material. In so many important ways it pre-echoes so much later writing on war. It is based on ballads which narrate the adventures of the Aryans during the great migrations on the Ganges plains.

This ancient epic is a heavily upholstered and reworked account of the terrible struggles which resulted from the Aryan invasion of the Indus Valley *circa* 2000—600 BC (comparable with the origins of the Trojan War, *circa* 1184 BC, celebrated by Homer). The written history of South-East Asia begins with the arrival of the Aryan tribes, Indo-European peoples related by language, religion and customs to the Persians (or Iranians). The earlier inhabitants of the Indus Valley, the Dravidians, were pushed southwards by the invading Aryans who came over the Hindu Kush, some of them reaching the tip of India and pushing further into Ceylon. The amalgamation of Dravidian and Aryan cultures formed the basis of Hindu culture, in which tribal wars (wars between different communities or races) are transformed into dynastic wars (power struggles between different family groups) by the bard, or bards, who worked up this original account into the version we know today.

Armies at this time were formed almost entirely of footmen, with the bow as the main weapon. There was no cavalry; horses were rare and were reserved almost exclusively for pulling the war chariots of kings, emperors or nobles. They were not used in organized shock assaults or charges. Warriors were the most honoured class in the social structure. The weapons actually used were probably wooden, as iron did not appear in India until the fifth century BC; war was less technically advanced than in the Middle East.

Dating the *Mahabharata* is not a simple matter. The earliest direct reference we have about the existence of epic material in India is found in a work by Dion Chrysostum (an early bishop of Constantinople, *circa* AD 350—407) who claims that 'even among the Indians, Homer's poetry is sung'. This is usually interpreted to mean not that the Indians enjoyed Homer's epic poetry, but that they had similar epics themselves. It is likely that the public performance – heroic song by bards – at the courts of the princes and kings of India and the Kshatriyas, the knightly order, had been energetically encouraged and richly rewarded, as a means of celebrating the great victories of the past and handing on the legends of the great heroes from one generation to another. The original warlike qualities of the sagas remain even in the version we have today, heavily revised as it clearly has been in the light of the later ascendancy of the Brahmanical code.

The *Mahabharata*, in the form we now have it, is not really a uniform epic in the manner of Homer's *Iliad*, but rather a great collection of poetry. As it stands, it is reckoned to be – with its 100,000 couplets – the longest poem in the world. It is eight times the length of the *Iliad* and *Odyssey* combined. It is a mass of myths and didactic matter, an encyclopaedia of Indian legendary history, worked and woven into a central heroic action divided into eighteen books. The most striking section to modern, especially western, readers must be the portion which narrates the great feud of the rival houses of the Pandavas and the Kauravas, comprising about a fifth of the extant work. This striking section was possibly the original, separate work, called the *Bharata*. The basic plot mechanism is fairly simple. At Kuruksetra, the plain of Kuru, near modern Delhi, the old blind King Dhrtarastra lives in his capital, Hastinapura. He has one hundred sons, the Kauravas, and their five cousins, the Pandavas. The Pandavas leave for the land of the Pancalas, where the beautiful Princess Draupadi is holding a *svayamvara* – a maiden's choice, where local princes will compete for her hand.

The Pandava Prince Arjuna triumphs in an archery contest and wins Draupadi, and she becomes co-wife to the five brothers. They then go back and found the city of Indraprastha (Delhi). The villain of this performance, Kaurava Duryodhana, tempts the eldest of the Pandavas, Yudhisthira, to a game of dice. The result is that the Pandavas lose everything, including even the beautiful Draupadi. She is soon insulted by her new owner.

The Pandavas now plan their revenge. A terrible war ensues, concluding with the great battle. On the eve of the battle Prince Arjuna is struck with terrible remorse by the thought that the next day will certainly involve the slaughter of his kin. His charioteer, the god Krishna in mortal form, comforts him. This section provides the work known as the *Bhagavad Gita* – (the Song of the Lord). Krishna expounds to Arjuna the doctrine of *dharma* – the divinely appointed duties of the four castes.

The *dharma* of the warrior caste is to fight. The body is an illusion, merely the temporary garment of the undying reality, the soul, which is untainted by death. Krishna then reveals himself as the Lord, and Arjuna goes into battle with a steadfast heart.

The battle of Kuruksetra lasts eighteen days in the course of which all the Kauravas perish. Yudhisthira now ascends the throne of Hastinapura in triumph. He eventually abdicates in favour of the grandson, Arjuna. The work ends with the pilgrimage of the five brothers and Draupadi to the Indian Olympus, Mount Meru. One by one the pilgrims fall by the wayside and eventually only Yudhisthira is left, with his dog. When they reach the gates of paradise they are told that dogs are not admitted, but the King refuses to go in without his loyal companion. It is then revealed that the dog is in fact the god of Justice, who had assumed this form to test Yudhisthira's constancy. The old King has survived the test. When he finally enters the gates he is told that he will not find his brothers and the princess in paradise as they are in the nether world to expiate their sins. He then insists on sharing their fate, but is then told that this, too, was a trial, and the Pandavas are all united in everlasting bliss.

It is wholly appropriate that this collection of writings about war should begin with an excerpt from the *Mahabharata*. Not only is this work probably the most ancient example of writing about war to survive in such perfect shape, but it foreshadows much in the tradition of war writing.

In so many ways this massive work is the key to writing about war. It echoes great historical military events which have shaped, textured and conditioned the social experience of succeeding generations. The *Mahabharata* posits something of a permanent theme in war literature – the strange and disturbing paradox which lies at the basis of war, that nationalism and unity constantly refresh themselves in conflict and destruction. The holy quality ascribed to war as a feature of human behaviour is strongly marked in this ancient epic. Themes of attraction, love, union, parting – recurrent in war writing – form striking sections of the *Mahabharata*; the story of princess Draupadi precedes Helen of Troy by several hundred years. Moreover, the epic does not shirk the terrible attrition of war. It is salutary to recall that the word war has its roots in the late Old English word *werre*, from which we also get wear, and wear and tear. The *Mahabharata* shows that when human beings are deeply and covertly ready and prepared for conflict, seemingly trivial and superficial occurrences are enough to precipitate war; a simple matter of punctuation in the Ems telegram sparked off the Franco-

Prussian War. The sacrifices consequent upon such collisions are out of all proportion to the cause apparently being fought for. In the *Mahabharata*, the cause is a game of dice. We then recall that it was a beauty contest which began the process culminating in the terrible Trojan War. Prince Hamlet's words on seeing Fortinbras's army march off to the wars come to mind:

> Witness this army, of such mass and charge,
> Led by a delicate and tender prince,
> Whose spirit, with divine ambition puff'd,
> Makes mouths at the invisible event,
> Exposing what is mortal and unsure
> To all that fortune, death, and danger dare,
> Even for an egg-shell. Rightly to be great
> Is not to stir without great argument,
> But greatly to find quarrel in a straw,
> When honour's at the stake . . .
>   . . . to my shame I see
> The imminent death of twenty thousand men
> That, for a fantasy and a trick of fame,
> Go to their graves like beds, fight for a plot
> Whereon the numbers cannot try the cause,
> Which is not tomb enough and continent
> To hide the slain?

Hamlet, Act IV, Scene 4

This no longer seems remote, from some long-distant and legendary past in which 'honour' and 'great argument' were motives for the actions of nation states, as we recall the trivial beginnings of the Falklands War of 1982. As Mrs Thatcher's press secretary, Bernard Ingham, writes in his memoirs:

> It all began so farcically with a group of Argentine scrap metal merchants landing on South Georgia, an administrative dependency of the Falklands, where Shackleton, the Polar explorer, performed prodigious feats of endurance. Journalists derived some amusement from these Latin Steptoes, as they were called in lobby briefings, and rather saw their illegal landings as imperialist Argentine pinpricks. Then suddenly the Argentine struck. It invaded on Friday 2 April 1982. Nothing was funny any more.

Bernard Ingham, Kill the Messenger (1991), p. 284

Egg-shells. Scrap-metal. There is a continuity.

Personal grief, and the anguish which the duties and obligations of soldiering involve, receive impressive treatment in the *Mahabharata*. These themes are also constant in war writing, and continue to cause considerable controversy — witness the troubles caused by the BBC's decision to screen the drama *Tumbledown*.

Although it is true that the *Mahabharata* is an aristocratic work, and that writing about war has been subject to an extensive process of democratization — through personal letters (which begin early in European history to give a different view of the experience of war) to narrative prose fiction (Smollett with his eye-witness accounts of rank-and-file service life in the 18th century was a trail-blazer here), and on to the attempts made in our times to portray war in film and television — there is a sense in which this ancient Hindu epic is the mother of all war writing. All writing about war is in some measure a series of echoes of the *Mahabharata*, even to that last lingering hope we must all cling to should we wish to retain any hope for our species. For it is the *Mahabharata* which tells us: 'To you I declare the holy mystery: There is nothing nobler than humanity.' When surveying the tensions and conflicts of the modern world, we should resist as well as we can the understandable temptation to say: 'Tell that to the Marines.'

Robert Giddings
Poole, November 1991

I

THE ANCIENT WORLD

2000–600 BC Aryan Invasion of India

The Mahabharata

The Aryan invasion of the Indus valley between 2000 BC and 600 BC, in which the Indo-European tribes waged war on the indigenous population, the Dravidian peoples, forms the substance of the great Hindu epic, The *Mahabharata*.

The poem, although a reworked Brahmin version of the story, in which kings, princes, generals and warriors have been transformed into gods, demons and other supernatural creatures, has an undoubted historical basis. It is a poetic version (eight times as long as Homer's two epics) of the massive wars of succession between two nephews of royal houses, the Kauravas and the Pandavas. The Pandavas eventually succeed, and Prince Arjuna marries Draupadi.

The poem is the greatest early account we have of primitive war, fought almost exclusively by foot soldiers armed with bows and arrows. Horses were rare and used only for royal chariots.

This is the final great battle in which Arjuna eventually triumphs with divine help:

Then those foremost of charioteers (Krishna and Arjuna), riding on their chariots and placing themselves on opposite sides of that forest, began a great slaughter on all sides, of the creatures dwelling in Khāndava. And at whatever point any of the creatures residing in Khāndava could be seen attempting to escape, thither rushed those mighty heroes (for preventing its flight). And the chariots themselves were moving so fast around that forest that the inmates of Khāndava saw not an interval of space (between them). Indeed, those two excellent cars seemed to be but one, and the two warriors also on them but one individual. And while the forest was burning, hundreds and thousands of living creatures, uttering frightful yells, began to run about in all directions. And some had particular limbs burnt and some were scorched with excessive heat and some were withered therewith. And the eyes of some came out, and some ran about in fear. And some clasping their children and some their parents and brothers, died calmly without, from excess of affection, being able to abandon those that were dear unto them. And many there were who biting their nether lips rose upwards and soon fell whirling into the blazing element below. And some were seen to roll on the ground with wings, eyes, and feet scorched and burnt. And these creatures were all seen to perish there almost soon enough. And the tanks and ponds within that forest, heated with the fire around, began to boil, and the fishes and the tortoises in them were all seen to perish. And during that great slaughter of living creatures in that forest, the burning bodies of various animals looked as if fire itself had assumed many forms. And the birds that took to their wings for escaping from that conflagration were pierced by Arjuna with his shafts, and cut into pieces they fell down into the burning element below. And pierced all over with Arjuna's shafts, the birds dropped down upon the burning forest, uttering loud cries. And the dwellers of the forest, struck with those shafts, began to roar and yell. And the clamour they caused was like unto the frightful uproar that had been heard during the churning of the ocean (in days of yore). And the mighty flames of the blazing fire, reaching the firmament, caused great anxiety amongst the celestials themselves. Then all the illustrious dwellers of heaven went in a body unto him of an hundred sacrifices and thousand eyes, *viz*, their chief, that grinder of Asuras. And approaching Indra, the celestial said, 'Why, O lord of the immortals, doth Agni burn these creatures below? Hath the time come for the destruction of the worlds?'

Hearing these words of the gods, and himself beholding what Agni was doing, the slayer of Vritrā set out for the protection of the forest of Khāndava. And Vāsava — the chief of the celestials — soon covering the sky with masses of clouds of every kind, began to shower upon the burning forest. And these masses of clouds by hundreds and thousands, commanded by Indra, began to pour rain upon Khāndava in showers thick as the flag-staffs of chariots. But the showers were all dried up in the sky itself by the heat of the fire and could not, therefore, reach the fire at all. Then the slayer of Namuchi, getting angry with Agni, collected more masses of clouds and caused them to yield a heavy down-pour. Then with the flames contending with

2

those heavy showers, and with masses of clouds overhead, that forest, filled with smoke and flashes of lightning, became terrible to behold.

The Mahabharata of Krishna-Dwaipayana Vyasa,
translated by Protap Chandra Roy (1884)

1380 BC *Trojan War*

In Hittite records from around 1380 to 1340 BC there is the first reference to a people of some consequence, the 'Ahhiyawa' – usually considered to be the Homeric *Achaiwoi* or Achaeans. These are the Mycenaean Greeks.

The celebrated accounts of the Trojan War and the Hittite references to the 'Ahhiyawa' have led to the conclusion that the Mycenaeans' policy of punishing women-stealing, together with their attempts by conquest to gain commercial control at the entrance of the Black Sea, are the basic material so magnificently elaborated in Homer's *Iliad*.

The legend reflects an historical war of trade between the Achaeans and the inhabitants of the Troad. In the Homeric version the Achaeans, under Agamemnon, fight to regain Helen, the wife of Menelaus.

Helen, the most beautiful of all women, was wooed by the major chieftains of Greece. Odysseus suggested they abide by her choice. She chose Menelaus, king of Sparta, Agamemnon's brother. She was then abducted by Paris, a son of Priam and Hecuba, king and queen of Troy. The Greek chieftains, under Agamemnon, embarked on an expedition and besieged Troy.

Homer's *Iliad* is centred on the tenth year of the siege. A plague ravages the Greek camp and the seer Calchas decrees it will only be ended when the maiden Chryseis, who has been abducted by Agamemnon, is returned to her father, a priest of Apollo.

The truth of war as a terrible human experience animates the entire work. Homer's subject is the wrath of Achilles, a chieftain in Agamemnon's army.

We are presented with a brilliant picture of an army, composed of various groups and factions, impatient with each other, united mainly by collective danger, pinned down on a narrow shore, on which lie dead dogs, mules and piles of burning corpses. Their own means of sustenance is provided by raiding parties sent into the neighbouring countryside. Homer does not flinch from showing us an army almost at war with itself, whose *casus belli* is a squabble over a captured woman, who are near to mutiny and ready to sell anything – arms, armour, cattle, captives — for liquor to drink themselves into delirium.

Agamemnon is persuaded to appease the anger of the gods by returning Chryseis. He takes in her place Briseis, who belongs to Achilles, who now retires sulking to his tent with his friend Patroclus. All attempts to reconcile Achilles and Agamemnon fail.

In Book III it is hoped that a single combat between Paris and Menelaus will resolve the war. When Menelaus comes forward, Paris visibly blanches. Hector, his brother, then admonishes him (fortunately at the moment when Paris seemed about to be defeated, Aphrodite spirited him away).

> 'Accursed, made but in beauty's scorn,
> Impostor, woman's man! Oh heaven, that thou hadst ne'er been born,
> Or, being so manless, never lived to bear man's noblest state,
> The nuptial honor! Which I wish, because it were a fate
> Much better for thee than this shame. This spectacle doth make
> A man a monster. Hark! how loud the Greeks laugh, who did take
> Thy fair form for a continent of parts as fair. A rape
> Thou mad'st of nature, like their queen. No soul, an empty shape,
> Takes up thy being; yet how spite to every shade of good
> Fills it with ill! For as thou art, thou couldst collect a brood
> Of others like thee, and far hence fetch ill enough to us,
> Even to thy father; all these friends make those foes mock them thus
> In thee, for whose ridiculous sake so seriously they lay
> All Greece, and fate, upon their necks. Oh wretch! Not dare to stay
> Weak Menelaus? But 'twas well; for in him thou hadst tried
> What strength lost beauty can infuse, and with the more grief died
> To feel thou robb'dst a worthier man, to wrong a soldier's right.
> Your harp's sweet touch, curled locks, fine shape, and gifts so
>   exquisite,
> Given thee by Venus, would have done your fine dames little good,
> When blood and dust had ruffled them, and had as little stood
> Thyself in stead; but what they care of all these in thee flies
> We should inflict on thee ourselves. Infectious cowardice
> In thee hath terrified our host; for which thou well deserv'st
> A coat of tombstone, not of steel in which, form, thou serv'st.'
> To this thus Paris spake (for form, that might inhabit heaven),
> 'Hector, because thy sharp reproof is out of justice given,
> I take it well; but though thy heart, inured to these affrights,
> Cuts through them as an ax through oak, that more used more excites
> The workman's faculty, whose art can make the edge go far,
> Yet I, less practised than thyself in these extremes of war,

4

May well be pardoned, though less bold; in these your worth exceeds,
In others mine. Nor is my mind of less force to the deeds
Required in war, because my form more flows in gifts of peace.
Reproach not, therefore, the kind gifts of golden Cyprides.
All heaven's gifts have their worthy price; as little to be scorned
As to be won with strength, wealth, state; with which to be adorned
Some men would change state, wealth, or strength. But, if your
    martial heart
Wish me to make my challenge good, and hold it such a part
Of shame to give it over thus, cause all the rest to rest,
And, 'twixt both hosts, let Sparta's king and me perform our best
For Helen and the wealth she brought; and he that overcomes
Or proves superior any way, in all your equal dooms,
Let him enjoy her utmost wealth, keep her, or take her home,
The rest strike leagues of endless date, and hearty friends become;
You dwelling safe in gleby Troy, and Greeks retire their force
T' Achaia, that breeds fairest dames, and Argos, fairest horse.'

Homer, *The Iliad*, Book III, translated by George Chapman (1611)

Achilles refuses all entreaties to make him return to the war. His friend
Patroclus is stung into action by witnessing the continued suffering of
the Greeks. He gets Achilles's permission to take part in the fighting,
and borrows Achilles's armour. The Trojans are driven back, but
Patroclus is slain by Hector. Achilles is now also stung into action. He
has a new shield made by Hephaestos and returns to battle to avenge
his friend by facing Hector.

Achilles and Hector meet in hand-to-hand combat. Hector accepts
that matters between them must be settled. In the fight Hector is
mortally wounded and begs Achilles not to deface his body, nor to
leave him to be ravaged by dogs, but to give him sacred burial and thus
to spare his mother and father, Hecuba and Priam, distress. Achilles
swears that these respectful rites will be denied him. Hector dies and
Achilles gloats over his victory, and drags the Trojan hero's body
behind his chariot for all to see:

Then his fell soul a thought of vengeance bred;
(Unworthy of himself, and of the dead;)
The nervous ankles bored, his feet he bound
With thongs inserted through the double wound;
These fix'd up high behind the rolling wain,
His graceful head was trail'd along the plain.
Proud on his car the insulting victor stood,

5

And bore aloft his arms, distilling blood.
He smites the steeds; the rapid chariot flies;
The sudden clouds of circling dust arise.
Now lost is all that formidable air;
The face divine, and long-descending hair,
Purple the ground, and streak the sable sand;
Deform'd, dishonour'd in his native land,
Given to the rage of an insulting throng,
And, in his parents' sight, now dragg'd along!
    The mother first beheld with sad survey;
She rent her tresses, venerable grey,
And cast, far off, the regal veils away.
With piercing shrieks his bitter fate she moans,
While the sad father answers groans with groans;
Tears after tears his mournful cheeks o'erflow,
And the whole city wears one face of woe
No less than if the rage of hostile fires,
From her foundations curling to her spires,
O'er the proud citadel at length should rise,
And the last blaze send Ilion to the skies.
The wretched monarch of the falling state,
Distracted, presses to the Dardan gate.
Scarce the whole people stop his desperate course,
While strong affliction gives the feeble force:
Grief tears his heart, and drives him to and fro,
In all the raging impotence of woe.
At length he roll'd in dust, and thus begun,
Imploring all, and naming one by one:
'Ah! let me, let me go where sorrow calls;
I, only I, will issue from your walls
(Guide or companion, friends! I ask ye none),
And bow before the murderer of my son.
My grief perhaps his pity may engage;
Perhaps at least he may respect my age.
He has a father too; a man like me;
One, not exempt from age and misery
(Vigorous no more, as when his young embrace
Begot this pest of me, and all my race).
How many valiant sons, in early bloom,
Has that cursed hand sent headlong to the tomb!
Thee, Hector! last; thy loss (divinely brave)
Sinks my sad soul with sorrow to the grave.

Oh had thy gentle spirit pass'd in peace,
The son expiring in the sire's embrace,
While both thy parents wept the fatal hour,
And, bending o'er thee, mix'd the tender shower!
Some comfort that had been, some sad relief,
To melt in full satiety of grief!'
  Thus wail'd the father, grovelling on the ground,
And all the eyes of Ilion stream'd around.

Homer, The Iliad, Book XXII, translated by Alexander Pope (1720)

The story of the Wooden Horse, by means of which the Greeks gain access to Troy and sack it, is told by the Trojan hero, Aeneas, to Dido, Queen of Carthage, in Book II of Virgil's *Aeneid*. Cassandra, the seer, has prophesied the fall of Troy, and the ghost of Hector appears to give additional warning, but the enemy is already within the city walls and the dreadful work of the night begins apace.

'Twas in the dead of night, when sleep repairs
Our bodies worn with toils, our minds with cares,
When Hector's ghost before my sight appears,
A bloody shroud he seemed, and bathed in tears.
Such as he was when, by Pelides slain,
Thessalian coursers dragged him o'er the plain.
Swollen were his feet, as when the thongs were thrust
Through the bored holes, his body black with dust.
Unlike that Hector who returned from toils
Of war triumphant, in Æacian spoils,
Or him who made the fainting Greeks retire,
And launched against their navy Phrygian fire.
His hair and beard stood stiffened with his gore,
And all the wounds he for his country bore,
Now streamed afresh, and with new purple ran;
I wept to see the visionary man;
And, while my trance continued, thus began.
'O light of Trojans, and support of Troy,
Thy father's champion and thy country's joy!
O long expected by thy friends, from whence
Art thou so late returned for our defence?
Do we behold thee, wearied as we are
With length of labours and with toils of war?
After so many funerals of thy own,
Art thou restored to thy declining town?
But say, what wounds are these? What new disgrace

Deforms the manly features of thy face?
To this the spectre no reply did frame,
But answered to the cause for which he came;
And, groaning from the bottom of his breast,
This warning in these mournful words expressed:
'O goddess-born, escape by timely flight
The flames and horrors of this fatal night;
The foes already have possessed the wall,
Troy nods from high, and totters to her fall;
Enough is paid to Priam's royal name,
More than enough to duty and to fame.
If by a mortal hand my father's throne
Could be defended, 'twas by mine alone;
Now Troy to thee commends her future state,
And gives her gods companions of thy fate;
From their assistance happier walls expect,
Which, wandering long, at last thou shalt erect.'
He said, and brought me, from their blest abodes,
The venerable statues of the gods,
With ancient Vesta from the sacred choir,
The wreaths and relics of the immortal fire.

   Now peals of shouts come thundering from afar,
Cries, threats, and loud laments, and mingled war.
The noise approaches, though our palace stood
Aloof from streets, encompassed with a wood.
Louder, and yet more loud, I hear the alarms
Of human cries distinct, and clashing arms;
Fear broke my slumbers; I no longer stay,
But mount the terrace, thence the town survey,
And hearken what the fruitful sounds convey.
Thus when a flood of fire by wind is born,
Crackling it rolls, and mows the standing corn;
Or deluges, descending on the plains,
Sweep o'er the yellow year, destroy the pains
Of labouring oxen, and the peasant's gains;
Unroot the forest oaks, and bear away
Flocks, folds, and trees, an undistinguished prey.
The shepherd climbs the cliff, and sees from far
The wasteful ravage of the watery war.
Then Hector's faith was manifestly cleared,
And Grecian frauds in open light appeared.

Virgil, *The Aeneid*, Book II, translated by John Dryden (1694)

509 BC Rome: The Republican Revolt

Between 600 BC and 509 BC Rome seems to have flourished under the
rule of the line of Etruscan kings, the Tarquins. Tradition has it that the
throne was then seized by one Servius Tullius, a politician of lowly
birth, who married into the royal family. For several years the Tarquins,
supported by their Etruscan relatives, tried to regain rule. During the
Republican Revolt of 509 BC the legendary hero Horatius Cocles held
the bridge over the Tiber against an Etruscan army, led by Lars Porsena.
This incident has become celebrated through the schoolroom classic by
Thomas Babington Macaulay.

> Meanwhile the Tuscan army,
>   Right glorious to behold,
> Came flashing back the noonday light,
> Rank behind rank, like surges bright
>   Of a broad sea of gold.
> Four hundred trumpets sounded
>   A peal of warlike glee,
> As that great host, with measured tread,
> And spears advanced, and ensigns spread,
> Rolled slowly towards the bridge's head,
>   Where stood the dauntless Three.
>
> The Three stood calm and silent,
>   And looked upon the foes,
> And a great shout of laughter
>   From all the vanguard rose:
> And forth three chiefs came spurring
>   Before that deep array;
> To earth they sprang, their swords they drew,
> And lifted high their shields, and flew
> To win the narrow way;
>
> Aunus from green Tifernum,
>   Lord of the Hill of Vines;
> And Seius, whose eight hundred slaves
>   Sicken in Ilva's mines;
> And Picus, long to Clusium
>   Vassal in peace and war,
> Who led to fight his Umbrian powers
> From that grey crag where, girt with towers,
> The fortress of Nequinum lowers
>   O'er the pale waves of Nar.

Stout Lartius hurled down Aunus
   Into the stream beneath:
He reeled, and on Herminius
   He leaned one breathing space;
Then, like a wild cat mad with wounds,
   Sprang right at Astur's face.
Through teeth, and skull, and helmet
   So fierce a thrust he sped,
The good sword stood a hand-breadth out
   Behind the Tuscan's head.

And the great Lord of Luna
   Fell at that deadly stroke,
As falls on Mount Alvernus
   A thunder-smitten oak.
Far o'er the crashing forest
   The giant arms lie spread;
And the pale augurs, muttering low,
   Gaze on the blasted head.

On Astur's throat Horatius
   Right firmly pressed his heel,
And thrice and four times tugged amain,
   Ere he wrenched out the steel.
'And see,' he cried, 'the welcome,
   Fair guests, that waits you here!
What noble Lucumo comes next
   To taste our Roman cheer?'

But at his haughty challenge
   A sullen murmur ran,
Mingled of wrath, and shame, and dread,
   Along that glittering van.
There lacked not men of prowess,
   Nor men of lordly race;
For all Etruria's noblest
   Were round the fatal place.

But all Etruria's noblest
   Felt their hearts sink to see
On the earth the bloody corpses,
   In the path the dauntless Three:
And, from the ghastly entrance
   Where those bold Romans stood,

All shrank, like boys who unaware,
Ranging the woods to start a hare,
Come to the mouth of the dark lair
Where, growling low, a fierce old bear
    Lies amidst bones and blood.

Was none who would be foremost
    To lead such dire attack:
But those behind cried 'Forward!'
    And those before cried 'Back!'
And backward now and forward
    Wavers the deep array;
And on the tossing sea of steel,
To and fro the standards reel;
And the victorious trumpet-peal
    Dies fitfully away.

Thomas Babington Macaulay, 'Horatius',
Lays of Ancient Rome (1842)

492 BC *Corioli*

Gnaeus Marcius Coriolanus was a legendary Roman military hero, a patrician and General. The name Coriolanus was bestowed upon him after his brilliant victory in capturing Corioli from the Volscians.

This account is from Plutarch:

Corioli was the capital of the country of the Volscians, with whom the Romans were at war. And as it was besieged by the consul Cominius, the rest of the Volscians were much alarmed, and assembled to succour it, intending to give the Romans battle under the walls, and to attack them on both sides. But after Cominius had divided his forces, and with part went to meet the Volscians . . . who were marching against him . . . the inhabitants of Corioli despised the body that were left, and sallied out to fight them.

The Romans were at first obliged to give ground . . . But Marcius with a small party flew to their assistance, killed the foremost of the enemy, and stopping the rest in their career, with a loud voice called the Romans back . . . Many Romans then crowding about him, and being ready to second him, the enemy retired in confusion . . . he pressed hard upon their rear, and pursued them quite up to the gates.

There he perceived that his men discontinued the pursuit, by reason of the shower of arrows which fell from the walls . . . nevertheless he exhorted and encouraged them to press forward,

11

crying out 'That fortune had opened the gates, rather to the victors, than to the vanquished.' But as few were willing to follow him, he broke through the enemy, and pushed into the town with the crowd . . . he summoned all his force, and performed the most incredible exploits . . . he overpowered all that were in his way, forcing some to seek refuge in the furthest corners of the town, and others to give out and throw down their arms . . . The city thus taken, most of the soldiers fell to plundering, which Marcius highly resented; crying out, 'That it was a shame for them to run about after plunder . . . while the consul and the Romans under his command were, perhaps, engaged with the enemy.' He put himself at the head of such as offered to follow him, and took the route he knew would lead to the consul's army . . . Some were startled at his first appearance, covered as he was with blood and sweat. But when he ran cheerfully up to the consul, took him by the hand and told him that Corioli was taken, the consul clasped him to his heart . . .

Next day, Marcius waiting upon the consul, and the army being assembled, Cominius mounted the rostrum; and having returned due thanks to the gods for such extraordinary success, addressed himself to Marcius. He began with a detail of his gallant actions . . . Then out of the great quantity of treasure, the many horses and prisoners they had taken, he ordered him to take a tenth . . . besides making him a present of a fine horse, with noble trappings, as a reward for his valour.

The army received this speech with great applause; and Marcius, stepping forward, said: 'That he accepted of the horse, and was happy in the consul's approbation; but, as for the rest, he considered it rather as a pecuniary reward than as a mark of honour, and therefore, desired to be excused, being satisfied with his single share of the booty . . .'

These words were followed with still louder acclamations . . . when the multitude were silent again Cominius subjoined: 'You cannot, indeed, my fellow soldiers, force these gifts of yours upon a person so firmly resolved to refuse them; let us then give him what it is not in his power to decline, let us pass a vote that he be called CORIOLANUS, if his gallant behaviour at Corioli has not already bestowed that name upon him.'

Plutarch, *Parallel Lives*, translated by John Langhorne and William Langhorne (1770)

490 BC Marathon

The Battle of Marathon was fought in September 490 BC during the Persian–Greek Wars between the Athenian and Plataean armies (totalling 11,000 under Miltiades) and the Persian armies of Darius Hystaspes (60,000 commanded by Datis). In order to compensate for being so considerably outnumbered, Miltiades extended his army line the entire width of the valley so as to escape the danger of being outflanked. As the Persians advanced in the middle, the weakest part of the line, and penetrated so deeply, they were enclosed by the two outer wings of the Greek army and the Persian centre was completely routed. The Persians fled back to their ships to escape but lost 6,400 men. Greek losses were 192. The victory stiffened Greek resistance. This account is from the *Histories* of Herodotus:

. . . Now, as they marshalled the host upon the field of Marathon, in order that the Athenian front might be of equal length with the Median, the ranks of the centre were diminished, and it became the weakest part of the line, while the wings were made both strong with a depth of many ranks.

So when the battle was set in array, and the victims showed themselves favourable, instantly the Athenians, so soon as they were let go, charged the barbarians at a run. Now the distance between the two armies was little short of eight furlongs. The Persians, therefore, when they saw the Greeks coming on at speed, made ready to receive them, although it seemed to them that the Athenians were bereft of their senses, and bent upon their own destruction; for they saw a mere handful of men coming on at a run without either horsemen or archers. Such was the opinion of the barbarians; but the Athenians in close array fell upon them, and fought in a manner worthy of being recorded. They were the first of the Greeks . . . who introduced the custom of charging the enemy at a run, and they were likewise the first who dared to look upon the Median garb . . . Until this time the very name of the Medes had been a terror to the Greeks to hear.

The two armies fought together on the plain of Marathon for a length of time; and in the mid battle, where the Persians themselves and the Sacae had their place, the barbarians were victorious, and broke and pursued the Greeks into the inner country; but on the two wings the Athenians and the Plataeans defeated the enemy. Having so done, they suffered the routed barbarians to fly at their ease, and joining the two wings in one, fell upon those who had broken their own centre, and fought and conquered them. These likewise fled, and now the Athenians hung upon the runaways and cut them down, chasing them all the way to the shore, on reaching which they laid hold of their ships and called for fire . . .

The remainder of the barbarians pushed off . . . doubled Cape

Sunium, hoping to reach Athens before the return of the Athenians
. . . The Persians accordingly sailed round Sunium. But the Athenians
with all possible speed marched away to the defence of their city, and
succeeded in reaching Athens before the appearance of the barbarians
. . . The barbarian fleet arrived, and lay off Phalerum, which was at
that time the haven of Athens; but after resting a while upon their
oars, they departed and sailed away to Asia . . .

History of Herodotus, Book VI, Chapters 108−9,
translated by George Rawlinson (1880)

480 BC *The Persian Wars: Thermopylae*

In the spring of 480 BC a huge Persian army under Xerxes crossed the
Hellespont and invaded the Thracian and Macedonian coast. They then
marched southwards into Thessaly. A supporting fleet of fifteen
hundred ships and three thousand transport vessels shadowed their
movements. The main Greek defence was at the pass at Thermopylae.
King Leonidas with an army of 7,000 and a Spartan elite bodyguard of
300 arrived to organize the defence.

Leonidas's main army of 6,000 held the middle position, with a
support of 1,000 on the mountains to his left, to cover any advances
from the enemy.

For three days the Greeks held the Persian host back, but then a
traitor told Xerxes about a track through to the rear of the Greek forces.
The Persian Immortals (Xerxes's elite troops) slaughtered the Greek
army; Leonidas and the main body of the army surrendered after terrible
losses, but the 300 Spartans fought to the last man.

The Greeks, knowing that death awaited them at the hands of those
who were going round the mountain, being desperate, and regardless
of their own lives, displayed the utmost possible valour against the
barbarians. Already were most of their javelins broken, and they had
begun to despatch the Persians with their swords. In this part of the
struggle fell Leonidas, fighting valiantly, and with him other eminent
Spartans, whose names, seeing they were deserving men, I have
ascertained: indeed I have ascertained the names of the whole three
hundred. On the side of the Persians, also, many other eminent men
fell on this occasion, and amongst them two sons of Darius,
Abrocomes and Hyperanthes, born to Darius of Phrataguna, daughter
of Artanes; but Artanes was brother to king Darius, and son of
Hystaspes, son of Arsames. He, when he gave his daughter to Darius,

14

gave him also all his property, as she was his only child. Accordingly, two brothers of Xerxes fell at this spot, fighting for the body of Leonidas, and there was a violent struggle between the Persians and Lacedæmonians, until at last the Greeks rescued it by their valour, and four times repulsed the enemy. Thus the contest continued until those with Ephialtes came up. When the Greeks heard that they were approaching, from this time the battle was altered. For they retreated to the narrow part of the way, and passing beyond the wall, came and took up their position on the rising ground, all in a compact body, with the exception of the Thebans: the rising ground is at the entrance where the stone lion now stands to the memory of Leonidas. On this spot, while they defended themselves with swords, such as had them still remaining, and their hands and teeth, the barbarians overwhelmed them with missiles, some of them attacking them in front, and having thrown down the wall; and others surrounding and attacking them on every side.

Though the Lacedæmonians and Thespians behaved in this manner, yet Dieneces, a Spartan, is said to have been the bravest man. They relate that he made the following remark, before they engaged with the Medes, having heard a Trachinian say, that when the barbarians let fly their arrows, they would obscure the sun by the multitude of their shafts, so great were their numbers: but he, not at all alarmed at this, said, holding in contempt the numbers of the Medes, that 'their Trachinian friend told them every thing to their advantage, since if the Medes obscure the sun, they would then have to fight in the shade, and not in the sun.' This and other sayings of the same kind they relate that Dieneces, the Lacedæmonian, left as memorials. Next to him, two Lacedæmonian brothers, Alpheus and Maron, sons of Orisiphantus, are said to have distinguished themselves most; and of the Thespians, he obtained the greatest glory whose name was Dithyrambus, son of Harmatides. In honour of the slain, who were buried on the spot where they fell, and of those who died before they who were dismissed by Leonidas went away, the following inscription has been engraved over them: 'Four thousand from Peloponnesus once fought on this spot with three hundred myriads.' This inscription was made for all; and for the Spartans in particular: 'Stranger, go tell the Lacedæmonians, that we lie here, obedient to their commands.'

Herodotus, *Histories*, Book VII, translated by Henry Carey (1847)

480 BC The Persian Wars: Battle of Salamis

After their victory at Thermopylae, the Persians continued the war against the Greeks. The Greek fleet withdrew to Salamis to reinforce a second line of defence at Corinth, as all Central Greece was lost to the enemy. The Persians advanced into Attica where the Acropolis was captured and ransacked.

The Greeks then forced a sea battle on the Persian fleet. The Greeks had 370 sailing-ships and the Persians a huge fleet of 1,000 galleys. Initially Greek tactics were cautious, but an Athenian trireme pushed forward and the rest of the Athenian and Aeginetan vessels followed, and the Persian fleet was smashed – half of them sunk. Xerxes watched the entire engagement from a throne on the shore. This victory caused him to postpone the Persian invasion, and helped foster a Greek sense of nationality and patriotism. This account is taken from the Messenger's speech in Aeschylus's drama *The Persians*, in which the news of the disaster at Salamis reaches the Persian court:

Some fiend it was, O mistress, or evil spirit that appeared from somewhere, who began all the mischief. A Greek, who came from the Athenian host, told thy son Xerxes that if the darkness of black night should come the Greeks would not stand fast, but, leaping on to the thwarts of their vessels, would, each taking his own direction, endeavour to save their lives by stealthy flight. And he, as soon as he heard this, not realising the wile of the Greek nor the jealousy of the gods, publishes to all the captains the following order – when the sun should have ceased to illumine the earth with his rays and darkness should have laid hold on the temple of the sky, then to draw up vessels in close order arranged in three lines to guard the sea-exits and the murmuring straits; and [to station] other vessels in a circle round about the isle of Aias; understanding that, if the Greeks shall escape an evil fate by finding some means of escape for their ships, without being discovered, it has been decreed that they shall all be deprived of their heads. Such were his words, prompted by much confidence of mind, since he knew not what was appointed by the gods to come to pass. And the Persian troops in orderly fashion and disciplined spirit set about preparing an evening meal, and each seaman saw to the lashing of his oar about the nicely fitted thole-pin. Then, when the light of the sun had waned and night was coming on, every master of an oar went to his ship, and every master of weapons. And one line of warships kept cheering on another line and [the Persians] make sail even as each man had orders, and the livelong night ship-captains kept all the crews working their vessels backwards and forwards. But though night began to draw off, yet the Greek host made nowhere any kind of attempt at a stealthy escape. When, however, day with its white steeds, radiant to behold, had occupied all the earth, first of all a cheer from the Greeks rang loudly like a chant of triumph, and shrill and clear from the island crags Echo returned the cry. And fear was in the hearts of all the barbarians, finding themselves mistaken; for the Greeks were then chanting a solemn pæan not as seeking to escape, but as advancing to battle with daring courage. Next a bugle with its call fired all their line to action, and at once with foaming dash of oars in unison they smote, to the word of command, the resounding brine. And rapidly the whole of them came plain into view. The right wing in good order led on foremost, and after that their whole armament was coming on against us, and at the same time a mighty shout could be heard, 'Sons of the Greeks, advance! Deliver your country, deliver your children and your wives, the temples of your fathers' gods, the tombs of your ancestors. Now is the contest which decides all!' And then a confused noise of Persian tongues met them from our line, and no longer was it a time for inaction, but forthwith ship against ship struck its armoured prow. A Greek vessel commenced the charge, and breaks off the whole stern part of a Phœnician ship, and each [captain] then steered his bark against some other vessel. At first indeed the torrent of the Persian armament held its own. But since the multitude of our ships was crowded in the narrows, and they could give no assistance the one to the other but [on the contrary] were rammed by the brazen-pointed beaks of their friends, they splintered their whole equipment of oars, − the Greek ships, too, all around them noting their opportunity, kept charging them on every side, slaughtered men; and the shores and the reefs were full of them. Then in rout and confusion every ship, as many as there were of the barbarian armament, sought to row away. But the Greeks kept striking and hewing, as though we were tunnies or some draught of fish, with fragments of broken oars and splinters of wreckage; and cries of anguish filled the open sea with shrieks, until the appearance of dark night broke off [the combat]. Now the total of our misfortunes, not even were I to recite the list of them for ten days, could I complete for thee; for be well assured that never on a single day died so great a number of men . . .

An island there is, lying off Salamis − insignificant in size, a dangerous anchorage for ships . . .

Thither Xerxes sends these [chosen warriors] in order that,

whenever their foes wrecked from out their ships should attempt to win safe to the island, they might make an easy prey of the Greek soldiery and slay them; and help their own comrades to safety from out the sea-way – sadly at fault in his opinion of the future: for when some god had given the glory of [victory in] the sea-fight to the Greeks, that same day having secured their bodies with brazen armour they set to leaping out of their ships and forming a circle round about the entire island, so that [the Persian band] were at a loss whither to turn. For oft they were struck by stones thrown by hand and arrows from the bow-string fell upon and destroyed them; and at last [the Greeks] charging upon them with a simultaneous cheer strike them down, and hack in pieces the limbs of the unhappy men, till they had utterly destroyed the life in all of them. And Xerxes groaned aloud when he saw the depth of his calamities, for he had a seat in full view of all the army – a high knoll close to the ocean brine; and, having rent his garments and uttered a shrill cry of wailing and issued orders rapidly to the land-force, he dismisses them in flight all disorderly.

Aeschylus, *The Persians*, translated by C. E. S. Headlam (1909)

431 BC–404 BC *The Peloponnesian War: Pericles's Oration over the Athenian War Dead*

At the conclusion of the Peloponnesian war Sparta emerged as the dominant power over Athens.

Pericles, ruler of Athens, placed emphasis on Athenian cultural identity and patriotism which strikes us today – after the Second World War and the Falklands engagement – as surprisingly modern.

This is well demonstrated by his celebrated funeral oration for the Athenian dead. The proper burial of the fallen, observed with due ceremony, is traditionally a means of creating and fostering collective endeavours. Pericles here stands at the beginning of the same tradition in which Abraham Lincoln speaking at Gettysburg consciously placed himself over two thousand years later.

This, then, is the kind of city for which these men, who could not bear the thought of losing her, nobly fought and nobly died. It is only natural that every one of us who survive them should be willing to undergo hardships in her service. And it was for this reason that I have spoken at such length about our city, because I wanted to make it clear that for us there is more at stake than there is for others who lack our advantages; also I wanted my words of praise for the dead to be set in the bright light of evidence. And now the most important of these words has been spoken. I have sung the praises of our city; but it was the courage and gallantry of these men, and of people like them, which made her splendid . . . Some of them, no doubt, had their faults; but what we ought to remember first is their gallant conduct against the enemy in defence of their native land. They have blotted out evil with good, and done more service to the commonwealth than they ever did harm in their private lives . . .

I shall not commiserate with those parents of the dead, who are present here. Instead I shall try to comfort them. They are well aware that they have grown up in a world where there are many changes and chances. But this is good fortune – for men to end their lives with honour, as these have done, and for you honourably to lament them: their life was set to a measure where death and happiness went hand in hand. I know that it is difficult to convince you of this. When you see other people happy you will often be reminded of what used to make you happy too. One does not feel sad at not having some good thing which is outside one's experience: real grief is felt at the loss of something which one is used to. All the same, those of you who are of the right age must bear up and take comfort in the thought of having more children. In your own homes these new children will prevent you from brooding over those who are no more, and they will be a help to the city, too, both in filling the empty places, and in assuring her security. For it is impossible for a man to put forward fair and honest views about our affairs if he has not, like everyone else, children whose lives may be at stake. As for those of you who are now too old to have children, I would ask you to count as gain the greater part of your life, in which you have been happy, and remember that what remains is not long, and let your hearts be lifted up at the thought of the fair fame of the dead. One's sense of honour is the only thing that does not grow old, and the last pleasure, when one is worn out with age, is not, as the poet said, making money, but having the respect of one's fellow men.

As for those of you here who are sons or brothers of the dead, I can see a hard struggle in front of you. Everyone always speaks well of the dead, and, even if you rise to the greatest heights of heroism, it will be a hard thing for you to get the reputation of having come near, let alone equalled, their standard. When one is alive, one is always liable to the jealousy of one's competitors, but when one is out of the way, the honour one receives is sincere and unchallenged.

Thucydides, *The Peloponnesian War*, translated by Rex Warner (1954)

401 BC The Revolt of Cyrus: Battle of Cunaxa

The battle of Cunaxa occurred during the revolt organized against the Emperor Artaxerxes II of Persia by his brother, Cyrus. The rebel army of 50,000 contained 13,000 Spartan veterans of the Peloponnesian war.

The revolt was severely defeated at Cunaxa, near Babylon. Xenophon, who served in Cyrus's forces, gives a celebrated account of this battle in the first book of *The Anabasis*. Although routed by Artaxerxes's forces – over 100,000 Persians – the Greek veterans stood their ground heroically. After the battle Artaxerxes held a banquet to which all the Greek commanders were invited, where they were beheaded by the Persians. The Greeks then made their famous march – the Anabasis – to safety at Trebizond, on the Black Sea, a thousand miles away.

This records the first sight of Artaxerxes's army:

And now it was midday, and the enemy were not yet in sight; but when afternoon was coming on, there was seen a rising dust, which appeared at first like a white cloud, but some time later like a kind of blackness in the plain, extending over a great distance. As the enemy came nearer and nearer, there were presently flashes of bronze here and there, and spears and the hostile ranks began to come into sight. There were horsemen in white cuirasses on the left wing of the enemy, under the command, it was reported, of Tissaphernes; next to them were troops with wicker shields and, farther on, hoplites with wooden shields which reached to their feet, these latter being Egyptians, people said; and then more horsemen and more bowmen. All these troops were marching in national divisions, each nation in a solid square. In front of them were the so-called scythe-bearing chariots, at some distance from one another; and the scythes they carried reached out sideways from the axles and were also set under the chariot bodies, pointing towards the ground, so as to cut to pieces whatever they met; the intention, then, was that they should drive into the ranks of the Greeks and cut the troops to pieces. As for the statement, however, which Cyrus made when he called the Greeks together and urged them to hold out against the shouting of the barbarians, he proved to be mistaken in this point; for they came on, not with shouting, but in the utmost silence and quietness, with equal step and slowly.

The Death of Cyrus

He knew that the King held the centre of the Persian army; in fact, all the generals of the barbarians hold their own centre when they are in command, for they think that this is the safest position, namely, with their forces on either side of them, and also that if they want to pass along an order, the army will get it in half the time; so in this instance the King held the centre of the army under his command, but still he found himself beyond the left wing of Cyrus. Since, then, there was no one in his front to give battle to him or to the troops drawn up before him, he proceeded to wheel round his line with the intention of encircling the enemy.

Thereupon Cyrus, seized with fear lest he might get in the rear of the Greek troops and cut them to pieces, charged to meet him; and attacking with his six hundred, he was victorious over the forces stationed in front of the King and put to flight the six thousand, slaying with his own hand, it is said, their commander Artagerses. But when they turned to flight, Cyrus' six hundred, setting out in pursuit, became scattered also, and only a very few were left about him, chiefly his so-called table companions. While attended by these only, he caught sight of the King and the compact body around him; and on the instant he lost control of himself and, with the cry 'I see the man,' rushed upon him and struck him in the breast and wounded him through his breastplate.

While Cyrus was delivering his stroke, however, some one hit him a hard blow under the eye with a javelin; and then followed a struggle between the King and Cyrus and the attendants who supported each of them. The number that fell on the King's side is stated by Ctesias, who was with him; on the other side, Cyrus himself was killed and eight of the noblest of his attendants lay dead upon him. Of Artapates, the one among Cyrus' chamberlains who was his most faithful follower, it is told that when he saw Cyrus fallen, he leaped down from his horse and threw his arms about him. And one report is that the King ordered someone to slay him upon the body of Cyrus, while others say that he drew his dagger and slew himself with his own hand; for he had a dagger of gold, and he also wore a necklace and bracelets and all the other ornaments that the noblest Persians wear; for he had been honoured by Cyrus because of his affection and fidelity.

Xenophon, *The Anabasis*, Book I, translated by Carleton L. Brownson (1924)

331 BC *Alexander the Great's Victory at Arbela*

After making himself supreme ruler in his own land following the death of his father, Philip of Macedon, Alexander was chosen to lead the expedition against Persia. His victory over Darius and the Persians, at Arbela, beyond the Tigris, in October 331 BC, finally crushed the power of the Persian empire, which had previously threatened all the nations in the known world with subjection. Darius fled the field, after the failure of his cavalry and charioteers.

In the early part of the battle, Darius had showed skill and energy; and he now for some time encouraged his men, by voice and example, to keep firm. But the lances of Alexander's cavalry, and the pikes of the phalanx now gleamed nearer and nearer to him. His charioteer was struck down by a javelin at his side; and at last Darius's nerve failed him; and, descending from his chariot, he mounted on a fleet horse and galloped from the plain, regardless of the state of the battle in other parts of the field, where matters were going on much more favourably for his cause, and where his presence might have done much towards gaining a victory . . .

At length the Macedonian discipline and valour again prevailed, and a large number of the Persian and Indian horsemen were cut down; some few only succeeded in breaking through and riding away. Relieved of these obstinate enemies, Alexander again formed his horse-guards, and led them towards Parmenio; but by this time that general also was victorious. Probably the news of Darius's flight had reached Mazæus, and had damped the ardour of the Persian right wing; while the tidings of their comrades' success must have proportionally encouraged the Macedonian forces under Parmenio. His Thessalian cavalry particularly distinguished themselves by their gallantry and persevering good conduct; and by the time that Alexander had ridden up to Parmenio, the whole Persian army was in full flight from the field.

It was of the deepest importance to Alexander to secure the person of Darius, and he now urged on the pursuit. The river Lycus was between the field of battle and the city of Arbela, whither the fugitives directed their course, and the passage of this river was even more destructive to the Persians than the swords and spears of the Macedonians had been in the engagement. The narrow bridge was soon choked up by the flying thousands who rushed towards it, and vast numbers of the Persians threw themselves, or were hurried by

22

others, into the rapid stream, and perished in its waters. Darius had crossed it, and had ridden on through Arbela without halting. Alexander reached that city on the next day, and made himself master of all Darius's treasure and stores; but the Persian king, unfortunately for himself, had fled too fast for his conqueror: he had only escaped to perish by the treachery of his Bactrian satrap, Bessus.

A few days after the battle Alexander entered Babylon, 'the oldest seat of earthly empire' then in existence, as its acknowledged lord and master.

Sir Edward Creasy, *Fifteen Decisive Battles of the World from Marathon to Waterloo* (1851)

327–326 BC *Alexander Conquers India*

After defeating Darius, Alexander occupied Phoenicia and Tyre, and founded Alexandria. He was now master of Asia. In 329 BC he crossed the Hindu Kush and invaded India, where his conquests were to extend as far as the south-west of the Punjab.

He then had to contend with unrest caused by the increasing homesickness of his troops. He was glad to turn one conquest to his advantage when the surrendering Nysa tribesmen claimed his clemency, saying they were akin to Dionysos and the Greeks as the vine grew in their country and Mount Meros overshadowed their land too:

Alexander, who found such fancies useful as a stimulant to his home-sick troops, did not examine the evidence for the kinship with Dionysos in too critical a spirit, but was glad to accept the Nysaean appeals and to exercise a gracious clemency.

In order to gratify his own curiosity, and to give some of his best troops a pleasant holiday, he paid a visit to the mountain, probably that now known as the Koh-i-Mor, accompanied by an adequate escort of the companion cavalry and foot guards. The chants and dances of the natives, the ancestors of the Kafirs of the present day, bore sufficient resemblance to the Bacchanalian rites of Hellas to justify the claims made by the Nysaeans, and to encourage the soldiers in their belief that, although far from home, they had at last found a people who shared their religion and might be regarded as kinsmen. Alexander humoured the convenient delusion and allowed his troops to enjoy, with the help of their native friends, a ten days' revel in the jungles. The Nysaeans, for their part, showed their gratitude for the clemency which they had experienced by contributing a contingent of three hundred horsemen, who remained with Alexander throughout the whole period of his advance and were not sent home until October 326 BC.

Arrian, *Anabasis Alexandri*, Book I, translated by E. I. Robson (1921)

Alexander was a ruthless military commander. Learning that some Indian mercenaries who had changed sides to fight in his ranks had resolved to slip away during the night, Alexander exacted a terrible penalty for their treachery.

The mercenaries, being unwilling to aid the foreigner in the subjugation of their countrymen, desired to evade the unwelcome obligation which they had incurred, and proposed to slip away by night and return to their homes. Alexander, having received information of their design, suddenly attacked the Indians while they reposed in fancied security and inflicted severe loss upon them. Recovering from their surprise, the mercenaries formed themselves into a hollow circle, with the women and children in the centre, and offered a desperate resistance, in which the women took an active part. At last, the gallant defenders were overpowered by superior numbers, and, in the words of an ancient historian (Arrian) 'met a glorious death which they would have disdained to exchange for a life with dishonour'. The unarmed camp followers and the women were spared.

This incident, which has been severely condemned by various writers, ancient and modern, as a disgraceful breach of faith by Alexander, does not seem to have been . . . the outcome of implacable enmity felt by the king against the mercenaries. The slaughter of the contingent was rather . . . the tremendous penalty for a meditated breach of faith on the part of the Indians . . .

Vincent Smith, *The Early History of India from 600 BC to the Muhammadan Conquest Including the Invasion of Alexander the Great* (1908)

265 BC – 146 BC *The Punic Wars*

Hannibal crosses the Alps (218 BC)

The Punic Wars between Rome and Carthage (in North Africa) were motivated by political and trade rivalry. By 241 BC the Romans had secured Sicily, Sardinia and Corsica.

Hannibal, commanding the armies of Carthage, resolved to invade

Rome over land, thus circumventing Roman control of the sea, taking his armies through southern Gaul, over the Alps and into the Po Valley.

He was harassed by appalling weather and hostile tribes. Although his long-term war against Rome was unsuccessful, his brilliantly planned campaign retains its place in military history.

His men, beasts of burden and elephants suffered terrible hardships:

Though the elephants were driven through steep and narrow roads with great loss of time, yet wherever they went they rendered the army safe from the enemy, because men unacquainted with such animals were afraid of approaching too nearly. On the ninth day they came to a summit of the Alps, chiefly through places trackless; and after many mistakes of their way, which were caused either by the treachery of the guides, or, when they were not trusted, by entering valleys at random, on their own conjectures of the route. For two days they remained encamped on the summit; and rest was given to the soldiers, exhausted with toil and fighting: and several beasts of burden, which had fallen down among the rocks, by following the track of the army arrived at the camp. A fall of snow, it being now the season of the setting of the constellation of the Pleiades, caused great fear to the soldiers, already worn out with weariness of so many hardships.

Eventually they had advanced to the extent that Hannibal was able to point out to his soldiers Italy and the plains of the Po, assuring them the rest of the journey would be smooth and downhill. But snow and rain made their journey hazardous in the extreme, and they had to force their way down untrodden and pathless routes, hampered by further ice and snow whilst almost starving.

At length, after the men and beasts of burden had been fatigued to no purpose, the camp was pitched on the summit, the ground being cleared for that purpose, with great difficulty, so much snow was there to be dug out and carried away. The soldiers being then set to make a way down the cliff, by which alone a passage could be effected, and it being necessary that they should cut through the rocks, having felled and lopped a number of large trees which grew around, they make a huge pile of timber; and as soon as a strong wind fit for exciting the flames arose, they set fire to it, and, pouring vinegar on the heated stones, they render them soft and crumbling. They then open a way with iron instruments through the rock thus heated by the fire, and soften its declivities by gentle windings, so that not only the beasts of burden, but also the elephants could be led down it. Four days were spent about this rock, the beasts nearly perishing through hunger: for the summits of the mountains are for the most part bare, and if there is any pasture the snows bury it. The lower parts contain valleys, and some sunny hills, and rivulets flowing beside woods, and scenes more worthy of the abode of man. There the beasts of burden were sent out to pasture, and rest given for three days to the men, fatigued with forming the passage: they then descended into the plains, the country and the dispositions of the inhabitants being now less rugged.

In this manner chiefly they came to Italy in the fifth month (as some authors relate) after leaving New Carthage, having crossed the Alps in fifteen days.

Livy, *History of Rome*, Book 21, translated by Richard Church and
William Broadribb (1890)

101 BC *Roman victory at Vercellae*

Vercellae (30 July 101 BC) – one of the most celebrated battles of ancient history – was a Roman victory which demonstrated the efficacy of the army reforms instigated by Gaius Marius. He increased the legions from 5,000 to 6,000 each, numbered them and made them carry identifying standards. He also created closer and more flexible formations, lightened equipment and weaponry, and opened up promotion to all ranks of society. The Roman army was thus rendered more democratic and wholly professional.

This account of the engagement between the armies of the Germanic tribe, the Cimbri, numbering 140,000 (including women and children) and 42,000 Romans at Vercellae (Borgo Vercelli; north-east of Turin) is from Plutarch. Such a dust was raised that at first both armies were hidden, and the heat and sun worked against the Cimbri:

> Those barbarians . . . could bear the severest cold, but were not proof against heat. Their bodies soon ran down with sweat; they drew their breath with difficulty, and were forced to hold their shields to shade their faces . . . The dust, too, which hid the enemy, helped to encourage the Romans. For, as they could have no distinct view of the vast numbers of their antagonists, they ran to the charge, and were come to close engagement before the sight of such multitudes could give them any impression of terror. Besides, the Romans were so strengthened by labour and exercise, that not one of them was observed to sweat or be out of breath . . . The greatest part of the

enemy's troops were cut to pieces upon the spot; those who fought in the front fastened themselves together, by long cords run through their belts, to prevent their ranks from being broken. The Romans drove the fugitives back to their camp, where they found the most shocking spectacle. The women standing in mourning by the carriages, killed those that fled; some their husbands, some their brothers, others their fathers. They strangled their little children with their own hands . . . Last of all they killed themselves . . . But though they were so industrious to destroy themselves, above 60,000 were taken prisoners, and the killed were said to be twice that number.

Plutarch, *Parallel Lives*, translated by John Langhorne and William Langhorne (1770)

57 BC The Gallic Wars: Battle of Sabis

Julius Caesar served as a staff officer under Sulla and then was a member of the First Triumvirate with Pompey and Crassus. He has left his own account of the provincial wars in Northern Italy and France.

In July 57 BC he fought the Nervii at Sabis (Sambre) when his army was taken by surprise in their camp by the Nervii army of 75,000. The legions withstood this assault and Caesar went from legion to legion to fight alongside his men:

After haranguing the Tenth Legion Caesar started for the right wing. There he beheld his troops hard driven, and the men of the Twelfth Legion, with their standards collected in one place, so closely packed that they hampered each other for fighting. All the centurions of the fourth cohort had been slain, and the standard-bearer likewise, and the standard was lost; almost all the centurions of the other cohorts were either wounded or killed, among them the chief centurion, Publius Sextius Baculus, bravest of the brave, who was overcome by many grievous wounds, so that he could no longer hold himself upright. The rest of the men were tiring, and some of the rearmost ranks, abandoning the fight, were retiring to avoid the missiles; the enemy were not ceasing to move upwards in front from the lower ground, and were pressing hard on either flank. The condition of affairs, as he saw, was critical indeed, and there was no support that could be sent up. Taking therefore a shield from a soldier of the rearmost ranks, as he himself was come thither without a shield, he went forward into the first line, and, calling on the centurions by name, and cheering on the rank and file, he bade them advance and extend the companies, that they might ply swords more easily. His coming brought hope to

27

the troops and renewed their spirit; each man of his own accord, in sight of the commander-in-chief, desperate as his own case might be, was fain to do his utmost. So the onslaught of the enemy was checked a little.

Perceiving that the Seventh Legion, which had formed up near at hand, was also harassed by the enemy, Caesar instructed the tribunes to close the legions gradually together, and then, wheeling, to advance against the enemy. This was done; and as one soldier supported another, and they did not fear that their rear would be surrounded by the enemy, they began to resist more boldly and to fight more bravely.

Caesar, The Gallic War, translated by H. J. Edwards (1917)

31 BC *Wars of the Second Triumvirate: Battle of Actium*

Antony was finally defeated at sea when his fleet of 480 galleys was overcome by Octavius Caesar's fleet of 400. The battle was fiercely contested but at a critical stage Cleopatra gave orders to her 60 Egyptian vessels to withdraw. Antony followed and his fleet surrendered. Within a few days his army of 120,000 also surrendered. This account of the last moments is from Plutarch, in North's translation on which Shakespeare based *Antony and Cleopatra*:

When Antonius saw that his men did forsake him and yielded unto Caesar, and that his footmen were broken and overthrown, he then fled into the city, crying out that Cleopatra had betrayed him unto them with whom he had made war for her sake. Then she, being afraid of his fury, fled into the tomb which she had caused to be made, and there locked the doors unto her and shut all the springs of the locks with great bolts and in the meantime sent unto Antonius to tell him that she was dead. Antonius believing it, said unto himself, 'What dost thou look for further, Antonius, sith spiteful fortune hath taken from thee the only joy thou hadst for whom thou yet reservedst thy life?' When he had said these words, he went into a chamber and unarmed himself, and being naked said thus, 'O Cleopatra, it grieveth me not that I have lost thy company, for I will not be long from thee; but I am sorry that having been so great a captain and emperor, I am indeed condemned to be judged of less courage and noble mind than a woman.' Now he had a man of his called Eros, whom he loved and trusted much, and whom he had long before caused to swear unto him that he should kill him when he did command him, and then he willed him to keep his promise. His man drawing his sword, lift it up as though he had meant to have stricken his master, but turning his head at one side, he thrust his sword into himself and fell down dead at his master's foot. Then said Antonius, 'O noble Eros, I thank thee for this, and it is valiantly done of thee, to show me what I should do to myself, which thou couldst not do for me.' Therewithal he took his sword and thrust it into his belly and so fell down upon a little bed. The wound he had killed him not presently, for the blood stinted a little when he was laid, and when he came somewhat to himself again he prayed them that were about him to dispatch him. But they all fled out of the chamber and left him crying out and tormenting himself, until at last there came a secretary unto him called Diomedes, who was commanded to bring him into the tomb or monument where Cleopatra was. When he heard that she was alive, he very earnestly prayed his men to carry his body thither, and so he was carried in his men's arms into the entry of the monument. Notwithstanding, Cleopatra would not open the gates, but came to the high windows and cast out certain chains and ropes in the which Antonius was trussed; and Cleopatra her own self, with two women only, which she had suffered to come with her into these monuments, triced Antonius up. They that were present to behold it, said they never saw so pitiful a sight. For they plucked up poor Antonius all bloody as he was, and drawing on with pangs of death, who holding up his hands to Cleopatra, raised up himself as well as he could. It was a hard thing for these women to do, to lift him up, but Cleopatra stooping down with her head, putting to all her strength to her uttermost power, did lift him up with much ado, and never let go her hold, with the help of the women beneath that bade her be of good courage and were as sorry to see her labor so as she herself. So when she had gotten him in after that sort, and laid him on a bed, she rent her garments upon him, clapping her breast and scratching her face and stomach. Then she dried up his blood that had berayed his face, and called him her lord, her husband, and emperor, forgetting her own misery and calamity, for the pity and compassion she took of him. Antonius made her cease her lamenting and called for wine, either because he was athirst or else that he thought thereby to hasten his death. When he had drunk, he earnestly prayed her, and persuaded her, that she would seek to save her life, if she could possible without reproach and dishonor, and that chiefly she should trust Proculeius above any man else about Caesar. And as for himself, that she should not lament nor sorrow for the miserable change of his fortune at the end of his days, but rather, that she should think him the more fortunate, for the former triumphs and honors he had received, considering that while he lived he was the noblest and greatest prince of the world, and that now he was overcome, not cowardly, but valiantly, a Roman by another Roman. As Antonius gave the last gasp, Proculeius came that was sent from Caesar. For after Antonius had thrust his sword in himself, as they carried him into the tombs and monuments of Cleopatra, one of his guard, called Dercetaeus, took his sword with the which he had stricken himself and hid it. Then he secretly stale away and brought Octavius Caesar the first news of his death and showed him his sword that was bloodied. Caesar hearing these news, straight withdrew himself into a secret place of his tent and there burst out with tears, lamenting his hard and miserable fortune that had been his friend and brother-in-law, his equal in the Empire, and companion with him in sundry great exploits and battles.

Plutarch, *Parallel Lives*, translated by Sir Thomas North (1579)

II

FROM TEUTOBURG TO HASTINGS

AD 9 Battle of Teutoburg Forest: Hermann's victory over the Roman legions under Varius

The Germanic warrior, Hermann, has assumed importance in his nation's consciousness at various stages of history. His victory at Teutoburg was one of the decisive battles of history — Roman expansion in North Germany was at an end for ever. The numbers of the legions lost were never made up again in the Roman army. Interest in Teutoburg was revived to draw strength and inspiration during the struggle against Napoleon, and again during Bismarck's unification of Germany from 1866 to 1870. Nourishment was once more drawn from the story during the Nazi regime. There are several interesting poetic and dramatic treatments of the story.

Arminius (the Latinized form of Hermann) was a native of North Germany who served as an officer in the Roman army. He returned to his homeland, and as tribal chief of the Cherusci he led a revolt against the Romans.

The battle of the Teutoburg Forest was fought near the site of modern Detmold, between the rivers Ems and Lippe. The local place-names retained associations of this great battle — *das Winnefeld* (field of victory), *die Knochenbahn* (bone lane), *die Knochenleke* (bone stream) and *der Mordkessel* (kettle of slaughter).

During the reign of the Emperor Augustus, a series of revolts in Germany was put down by Quintilius Varus. Early in these campaigns an auxiliary unit of the Cherusci tribe was under the command of Arminius. At the end of the summer in AD 9 Varus intended to march his three legions and auxiliary warriors, totalling 20,000, back to winter quarters near the Lippe. Arminius planned an attack which took place during terrible rain storms while the legions were harassed and attacked by tribal parties en route through the marshy wooded area of the Teutoburg. At this stage Arminius and his auxiliaries deserted and turned on the Romans, who had little time to deploy themselves defensively.

The battle lasted several days, and the Roman force was almost annihilated. Varus and his fellow officers took their own lives. Legend has it that Augustus was reduced to tears at the news and throughout the rest of his life would lament the disaster, exclaiming: 'Varus! Varus! Give back my legions!'

Hermann first appears in literature in the sixteenth century, but interest in him really revived two hundred years later. Friedrich Gottlob Klopstock wrote three dramas and an epic based on his life. Hermann Kleist's *Die Hermannsschlacht* (1809) was deliberately composed to encourage the effort against Napoleon.

This triumphal bardic chorus is from Klopstock's *Hermann und die Fürsten* (1784):

> Sister of Cannae[1]! Winfield's[2] fight!
> We saw thee with thy streaming bloody hair,
> With fiery eye, bright with the world's despair,
> Sweep by Walhalle's bards from out our sight.
> Hermann outspake: 'Now Victory or Death!'
> The Romans: 'Victory!'
> And onward rushed their eagles with the cry.
> So ended the first day. 'Victory or Death!' began
> Then, first, the Roman chief; and Hermann spake
> Not, but home struck; the eagles fluttered – brake.
> So sped the second day.
> And the third came. The cry was 'Flight or Death!'
> Flight left they not for them who'd make them slaves.
> Men who stab children! Flight for them! No! Graves!
> 'Twas their last day.
> Yet spared they messengers: two came to Rome.
> How drooped the plume! The lance was left to trail
> Down in the dust behind: their cheek was pale:
> So came the messengers to Rome.
> High in his hall the Imperator sate –
> Octavius Caesar Augustus sate.
> They filled up wine cups, wine cups filled they up
> For him the highest, Jove of all their state.
> The flutes of Lydia hushed before their voice.

Before the messengers – the 'Highest' sprung –
The god[3] against the marble pillars, wrung
By the dread words, striking his brow, and thrice
Cried he aloud in anguish: 'Varus! Varus!
Give back my legions, Varus!'
And now the world-wide conquerors shrunk and feared
For fatherland and home
The lance to raise; and 'mongst those false to Rome
The death-lot rolled[4] and still they shrunk and feared;
'For she her face hath turned,
The victor goddess,' cried these cowards – (for aye
Be it!) 'from Rome and Romans, and her day
Is done!' And still he mourned,
And cried aloud in anguish – 'Varus! Varus!
Give back my legions, Varus!'

> Friedrich Gottlob Klopstock, 'Triumphenlied of Hermann, the Saviour of Germany
> From the Romans', from *Hermann und die Fürsten*, anonymous translation,
> *Fraser's Magazine* (1849)

1. The battle of Cannae was Hannibal's victory over the Romans in 216 BC.
2. Winfield is another name for the site of Arminius's victory.
3. Augustus was worshipped as a god.
4. A lottery was used for drafting unwilling conscripts into the Roman army.

AD 73 The Jewish Revolt, Judea: Siege of Masada

Dealing with the Jewish Revolt eventually required four Roman legions and 25,000 auxiliary troops. The last Jewish stronghold was Masada, which was besieged in AD 72–3.

The rebels were finally burned out and as the fortress burst into flames around them the Jewish leader, Eleazar ben Yair, decided that the entire population – men, women and children – should seek their own deaths rather than fall into Roman hands. This account of their last moments and of Eleazar's address is by Flavius Josephus, who was a Jewish commander during the Revolt, and was held in Roman captivity for much of its duration.

'But we hoped, forsooth, to survive alone of all the Jewish race, preserving our freedom, as if we had been guiltless towards God, and had participated in no crime; – we who had even instructed others to transgress. Observe, therefore, how He exposes the vanity of our expectations, involving us in difficulties and distress which exceed all that we could anticipate. The impregnable nature of the fortress has not availed for our security . . . all this is but the vengeance for the many injuries which we have, in madness, ventured to commit against our fellow-countrymen; for which let us not await punishment from our bitterest foes the Romans, but receive it from God through ourselves. It will be milder than they would inflict. For let our wives die undishonoured; our children, ere they know what slavery is . . .

But, first, let us destroy with fire our property and the fortress. For I know well the Romans will be grieved to lose at once our persons and our goods. Our provisions alone let us spare; for these will testify, when we are dead, that we were not subdued from want; but that, as we had resolved from the beginning, we preferred death to servitude.'

Thus spoke Eleazar; not, however, in accordance with the sentiments of those present. Some there were, indeed, who were eager to obey, and deeming death honourable, were all but filled with delight; but others, of softer mould, were moved with compassion for their wives and families; and especially when their own dissolution was thus set before them, the tears that flowed as they looked at one another testified the disinclination of their minds.

They went their way, like men possessed, each ambitious to outstrip the other, and thinking that not to be found among the last would be an evidence of their fortitude and wise determination: − so ardent a desire had seized upon them to slaughter their wives, their children, and themselves. Nor were their spirits damped, as might have been expected, when they came to the work: they adhered inflexibly to the resolution they had formed while listening to Eleazar's address; − natural affection and a love of kindred still alive in every breast, but the reflection that they had consulted best for those dearest to them prevailing over everything else. For, while they clasped and fondly embraced their wives, and took their children in their arms, clinging to them and weeping as they kissed them for the last time, at that very moment, as if executing it with strangers' hands, they completed their design; deriving consolation, under the necessity of killing them, from the consideration of the evils they would endure, if they came into the power of their enemies. And, in fine, no one was found to waver in so stern an undertaking; all going through the work with their nearest relatives. Wretched victims of necessity, to whom it seemed the lightest of evils with their own hands to kill their wives and children!

Unable, therefore, longer to support the anguish they felt for what they had done, and thinking that they wronged those whom they had put to death, by surviving them even but for a moment, they quickly heaped together all their effects, and set fire to them; and then, having chosen by lot ten of their number to slay the rest, they laid themselves down, each beside his fallen wife and children, and throwing their arms around them, made ready their throats for those who discharged the mournful office. These, having slaughtered all without flinching, adopted the same plan of drawing lots with one another, that he on whom it fell should, after killing the nine, destroy himself on the bodies of his companions. Such confidence had all in themselves, that neither in acting, nor in suffering, would one excel another. At length, the nine underwent the slaughter; whereupon he who stood single and last, having inspected the prostrate multitude, to see whether haply in so wide a murder any were left still requiring his hand, and having ascertained that all were dead, set fire to the palace; and then driving his sword with one collected effort completely through his body, fell down beside his family.

They died under the impression that nothing among them drawing the breath of life remained in the power of the Romans. An elderly woman, however, and another, related to Eleazar, in understanding and education superior to most of her sex, together with five children, escaped by concealing themselves in the subterraneous aqueducts, while the rest were intent on slaughter. Nine hundred and sixty persons, including women and children, perished on this occasion.

Flavius Josephus, *Jewish War*, translated by Revd Robert Traill (1862)

AD 778 Roncevalles: Death of Roland

At the pass of Roncevalles, in the Pyrenees, the rearguard of Charlemagne's army, returning from a campaign in Spain, was attacked and defeated by a mountain force of Basque and Gascon soldiers, commanded by Loup II, in August 778.

This celebrated ambush was worked up by numerous medieval poets to become the subject matter of the *Chanson de Roland*. The ambush becomes an attack by an army of 400,000 warriors from Saragossa commanded by King Marsile. Charlemagne's troops are betrayed by one of their own knights.

Roland is based on the historical paladin, Hruotland of Brittany, traditionally the nephew of Charlemagne. He is brave and loyal but trusting – almost naive. His close friend, Olivier, is rather more sage and perceptive.

During seven years' fighting, Charlemagne has conquered all Spain except Saragossa. King Marsile asks for a truce to discuss Charlemagne's leaving Spain on agreed terms. Roland warns of a trap but Charlemagne agrees, taking the advice of the treacherous Ganelon. Roland insists that Ganelon bear the message to Saragossa. Ganelon is bribed to betray Charlemagne's movements, resulting in the terrible ambush at Roncevalles [Roncevaux] pass. Olivier begs Roland to sound his ivory horn, Olivant, to summon help, but Roland is too proud. At last when only sixty men remain alive Roland sounds the horn, bursting veins in the process.

> The oliphant[1] is set to Roland's lips;
> He holds it firm and sounds it with great power.
> High are the hills, and the call carries far:
> They heard its echoes at full thirty leagues.
> Charles heard it sound, and all his company.
> 'Our men are doing battle', said the king.
> And Ganelon flung back these words at him:
> 'From other lips great falsehood this would seem!'

> Count Roland spares no effort and no pains;
> With agony he sounds his oliphant,
> And from his mouth the bright blood gushes forth,
> And at at the temple he has burst his skull.

But it now too late to save anyone. When Charlemagne arrives with help they are all dead. The death of Roland is one of the key moments in chivalric literature.

> Now Roland finds that all his sight is gone.
> He struggles to his feet as best he may;
> And all the colour from his face is fled.
> Before him stands a dark and swarthy stone:
> On it he strikes ten blows in bitter grief.
> Loud grates the steel, but does not break or breach.
> 'Ah,' said the count, 'sweet Mary, help me now!
> Ah, my good Durendal, alas for you!
> With life, I'll leave my mastery of you.
> With you I've won such battles in the field,
> And so many vast lands I've brought to heel
> That are now held by hoary-bearded Charles!
> May no man hold you who would flee in fight!
> So fine a vassal held you for so long!
> In blessed France your like will not be found.'

Roland strikes hard on the sardonyx stone;
Loud grates the steel, but does not break or notch.
Then, when he saw he could not shiver it,
Soft to himself he started this lament:
'Ah Durendal, how fair and white you shine,
And with what fire you glitter in the sun!
Charles once was in the vales of Maurienne
When, through an angel He sent from above,
God bade him give you to a captain count:
The great and noble king girt you on me.
With you I conquered Anjou, Brittany,
With you I won for him Poitou and Maine
And for him conquered Normandy the free
And overcame Provence and Aquitaine,
The whole of the Romagna, Lombardy,
And won all Flanders and Bavaria,
Burgundy and Apulia entire,
Constantinople that he held in fee,
And Saxony, where he does what he will;
With you I won Scotland and Ireland too;
And England, which he held as his domain;
With you so many lands and realms I've won
That now white-bearded Charles holds in his sway.
Sorely I grieve and sorrow for this sword:
I'd die to save it from the infidel.
Our Father, God above, spare France this shame!'

Roland strikes hard upon a swarthy stone,
Cuts more of it away than I could tell.
Loud grates the sword, but does not break or snap:
Instead it flies rebounding to the sky.
When the count sees he cannot shatter it,
In soft tones to himself he makes lament:
'Ah, Durendal, holy and fair you are!
Relics in plenty fill your gilded hilt:
Saint Peter's tooth, some of Saint Basil's blood,
Hairs from the head of my lord Saint Denis,
Part of a garment blessed Mary wore.
For infidels to wield you would be wrong:
Your service is for Christian men alone;
And may no craven coward take you up!
So many vast lands I have won with you
That now are held by grizzle-bearded Charles

And bring the emperor riches and might.'

Now Roland feels that death closes its grip,
Descending from his head down to his heart.
Running, he makes his way beneath a pine,
And on the green grass he prostrates himself,
Placing beneath him sword and oliphant.
His head he turns towards the infidel,
Because he wishes from his very soul
That Charles and all his company shall say:
'This noble count has died a conqueror!'
Then, beating many times upon his breast,
He offers for his sins his glove to God.

Now Roland feels his life is at an end.
Upon a steep hilltop he faces Spain,
And with his hand he beats against his breast:
'God, I confess my sins before your might.
Forgive me for the faults both great and small
That I've committed since I first drew breath
Until this day, when I am stricken down!'
Then his right glove he held aloft to God.
Angels descend from Heaven to his side.

Roland the count lies there beneath a pine;
His face he's set toward the realm of Spain.
His mind began to turn on divers things:
The many lands he had with valour won,
Fair France, the men of his own lineage,
And Charlemagne, his patron and his lord.
He could but weep and sigh with heavy heart;
But he was not forgetful of himself
And begged God to have mercy for his sins:
'Our rightful Father, fountain of all truth,
Who from the dead raised holy Lazarus
And guarded Daniel in the lions' den,
Protect my soul from every peril now
And from the sins committed while I lived!'
Then his right glove he offered up to God:
Saint Gabriel received it from his hand.
He held his head bowed down upon his arm,
Folded his hands, and went to meet his end.
To him God sent His angel Cherubim
Together with Saint Michael du Peril;

And with them both there came Saint Gabriel
To bear the count's soul up to Paradise.

Roland is dead, his soul with God in Heaven.
The emperor is come to Roncevaux.

The Song of Roland, translated by D. D. R. Owen (1972)

1. Oliphant: an ivory horn, from the Old French *olifant*, a corruption of elephant.

AD 991 Battle of Maldon

During the Danish invasions of Britain, an Anglo-Saxon force, commanded by Byrhnoth, was defeated by a Viking army under Olaf Triggvason, at Maldon in Essex. The event probably is of minor historical importance, but is significant in the national consciousness. It is preserved in imperishable form in the anonymous Anglo-Saxon poem, *The Battle of Maldon*. Here, only moments before his own death, Byrhnoth urges his men forward:

> Then there was breaking of shields; the seamen advanced, enraged by war. Often the spear pierced the body of a fated man. Then Wistan went forth, the son of Thurstan; he fought with the men; he slew three of them in the press ere Wigelin's son was laid low among the slain. There was a stern meeting; the warriors stood firm in the struggle; fighters fell, wearied with wounds; the slaughtered dropped to the earth. Oswold and Ealdwold, both the brothers, exhorted the men all the while; they bade their kinsmen with words to bear up there in the stress, use their weapons resolutely. Byrhtwold spoke; he grasped his shield; he was an old companion; he shook his ash spear; full boldly he exhorted the warriors: 'Thought shall be the harder, heart the keener, courage the greater, as our might lessens. Here lies our leader all hewn down, the valiant man in the dust; may he lament for ever who thinks now to turn from this war-play. I am old in age; I will not hence, but I purpose to lie by the side of my lord, by the man so dearly loved.' Godric, the son of Æthelgar, likewise exhorted them all to fight. Often he let fly the spear, the deadly dart, against the Vikings, as he went foremost in the host. He hewed and struck down until he fell in the battle; that was not the Godric who fled from the fight.

The Battle of Maldon, translated by R. K. Gordon (1926)

1066 Battle of Hastings

The Battle of Hastings in 1066 was a decisive engagement in a long-standing dynastic struggle. In 1064 King Harold, who was to die so memorably with an arrow in his eye, was shipwrecked off the Normandy coast. Duke William of Normandy took advantage of his predicament to make Harold promise his support for William's claim to the English throne when Edward the Confessor died. Edward died in 1066 and after a few local wars and scuffles Harold was proclaimed King. In September he had to cope with a Norwegian invasion, and a few weeks later William landed in Sussex.

William believed it would be a dangerous policy to bring his feudal lords and leave his home territory unprotected, so he came over with an army of mercenaries, greedy for the spoils of land and titles. It has been estimated that his army may have comprised as many as 12,000 horsemen and 20,000 infantrymen.

The army was assembled and the shipping ready for midsummer, but the weather was not propitious. They finally sailed in good weather at the end of September. William waited until he believed Harold's armies would be exhausted by their conflict with the Norsemen. Harold brought his troops down from the North to Senlac (Hastings). He deployed his army (estimated strength 25,000) defensively on a ridge eight miles from Hastings.

At dawn, 14 October 1066, the Normans advanced:

From nine o'clock in the morning, when the combat began, till three o'clock came, the battle was up and down, this way and that, and no one knew who would conquer and win the land. Both sides stood so firm and fought so well, that no one could guess which would prevail. The Norman archers with their bows shot thickly upon the English; but they covered themselves with their shields, so that the arrows could not reach their bodies, nor do any mischief, how true soever was their aim, or however well they shot. Then the Normans determined to shoot their arrows upwards into the air, so that they might fall on their enemies' heads, and strike their faces. The archers adopted this scheme, and shot up into the air towards the English; and the arrows in falling struck their heads and faces, and put out the eyes of many; and all feared to open their eyes, or leave their faces unguarded.

The arrows now flew thicker than rain before the wind; fast sped the shafts that the English called 'wibetes'. Then it was that an arrow, that had thus been shot upwards, struck Harold above his right eye, and put it out. In his agony he drew the arrow and threw it away, breaking it with his hands: and the pain to his head was so great, that he leaned upon his shield. So the English were wont to say, and still say to the French, that the arrow was well shot which was so sent up against their king; and that the archer won them great glory, who thus put out Harold's eye.

The Normans saw that the English defended themselves well, and were so strong in their position that they could do little against them. So they consulted together privily, and arranged to draw off, and pretend to flee, till the English should pursue and scatter themselves over the field; for they saw that if they could once get their enemies to break their ranks, they might be attacked and discomfited much more easily. As they had said, so they did. The Normans by little and little fled, the English following them. As the one fell back, the other pressed after; and when the Frenchmen retreated, the English thought and cried out, that the men of France fled, and would never return.

Thus they were deceived by the pretended flight, and great mischief thereby befell them; for if they had not moved from their position, it is not likely that they would have been conquered at all; but like fools they broke their lines and pursued.

The Normans were to be seen following up their stratagem, retreating slowly so as to draw the English further on. As they still flee, the English pursue; they push out their lances and stretch forth their hatchets: following the Normans, as they go rejoicing in the success of their scheme, and scattering themselves over the plain. And the English meantime jeered and insulted their foes with words. 'Cowards,' they cried, 'you came hither in an evil hour, wanting our lands, and seeking to seize our property, fools that ye were to come! Normandy is too far off, and you will not easily reach it. It is of little use to run back; unless you can cross the sea at a leap, or can drink it dry, your sons and daughters are lost to you.'

The Normans bore it all, but in fact they knew not what the English said; their language seemed like the baying of dogs, which they could not understand. At length they stopped and turned round, determined to recover their ranks; and the barons might be heard crying DEX AIE! for a halt. Then the Normans resumed their former position, turning their faces towards the enemy; and their men were to be seen facing round and rushing onwards to a fresh *mêlée*; the one party assaulting the other; this man striking, another pressing onwards. One hits, another misses; one flies, another pursues: one is aiming a stroke, while another discharges his blow. Norman strives with Englishman again, and aims his blows afresh. One flies, another pursues swiftly: the combatants are many, the plain wide, the battle and the *mêlée* fierce. On every hand they fight hard, the blows are heavy, and the struggle becomes fierce . . .

Where the throng of the battle was greatest, the men of Kent and Essex fought wondrously well, and made the Normans again retreat, but without doing them much injury. And when the duke saw his men fall back, and the English triumphing over them, his spirit rose high, and he seized his shield and his lance, which a vassal handed to him, and took his post by his standard.

Then those who kept close guard by him and rode where he rode, being about a thousand armed men, came and rushed with closed ranks upon the English; and with the weight of their good horses, and the blows the knights gave, broke the press of the enemy, and scattered the crowd before them, the good duke leading them on in front. Many pursued and many fled; many were the Englishmen who fell around, and were trampled under the horses, crawling upon the earth, and not able to rise. Many of the richest and noblest men fell in that rout, but the English still rallied in places; smote down those whom they reached, and maintained the combat the best they could; beating down the men and killing the horses. One Englishman watched the duke, and plotted to kill him; he would have struck him with his lance, but he could not, for the duke struck him first, and felled him to the earth.

Loud was now the clamour, and great the slaughter; many a soul then quitted the body it inhabited. The living marched over the heaps of dead, and each side was weary of striking. He charged on who could, and he who could no longer strike still pushed forward. The strong struggled with the strong; some failed, others triumphed; the cowards fell back, the brave pressed on; and sad was his fate who fell in the midst, for he had little chance of rising again; and many in truth fell, who never rose at all, being crushed under the throng.

And now the Normans pressed on so far, that at last they had reached the standard. There Harold had remained, defending himself to the utmost; but he was sorely wounded in his eye by the arrow, and suffered grievous pain from the blow. An armed man came in the throng of the battle, and struck him on the ventaille of his helmet, and beat him to the ground; and as he sought to recover himself, a knight beat him down again, striking him on the thick of his thigh, down to the bone.

The standard was beaten down, the golden standard was taken, and Harold and the best of his friends were slain; but there was so much eagerness, and throng of so many around, seeking to kill him, that I know not who it was that slew him.

The English were in great trouble at having lost their king, and at the duke's having conquered and beat down the standard; but they still fought on, and defended themselves long, and in fact till the day drew to a close. Then it clearly appeared to all that the standard was lost, and the news had spread throughout the army that Harold for certain was dead; and all saw that there was no longer any hope, so they left the field, and those fled who could.

Robert Wace, *Le Roman de Rou, ou Geste des Normands* (1174), translated by
Edgar Taylor (1836)

THE MIDDLE AGES

1094 Conquest of Valencia by El Cid Campeador

Rodrigo Diaz de Bivar, who earned the title 'El Cid' ('Sidi' = Lord) from his Muslim opponents, assisted Alfonzo VI, King of Castile, against the Moors. He was exiled by Alfonzo and went over to the Moors, conquering Aragón and Barcelona. Eventually Muslim Spain was conquered by the Almoravid dynasty, Berber invaders from the Sahara. At the battles of Cuarte in 1094 and Bairen in 1097, El Cid, commanding a combined army of Moors and Christians, recovered Valencia.

These wars form the substance of the celebrated Spanish epic, *El Cid*. This section describes the hero's greatest military triumphs:

Sleeping by day and marching by night, My Cid spends three years in the lands of the Moors, seizing and sacking their cities. Those of Valencia learn caution and no longer dare sally forth to meet him. He fells their orchards and does them much hurt in each of these three years, cutting off their food. Those of Valencia are troubled and know not what to do, for nowhere can they find bread. Parents cannot help their children, nor children their parents, and friends have no comfort for friends. Ah, my lords, it is a bitter thing to have no bread and see your wives and children perishing of hunger!

Their misery is upon them and they cannot help themselves. They appeal to the King of Morocco, but he is engaged in a great war with the King of the Atlas and can give them neither aid nor counsel.

My Cid hears of their plight and likes it well. So he sets forth from Murviedro, marching by night, and dawn finds him in the land of Monreal. Thence he sends criers to Aragón and Navarre, and envoys to Castile, bearing this message:

'Those who would no longer be poor but rich, let them come and join My Cid, who plans to take the field and lay siege to Valencia and win her for Christendom. Let them come freely and unforced. I shall tarry three days at Celfa del Canal.'

Thus said My Cid, the loyal Campeador, and turned back to Murviedro, which was now his.

His message, know you, sped throughout the land, and many men from noble Christendom, thirsting after spoils, hastened to join him. The word was everywhere noised about, and many joined him and deserted him not.

My Cid, he of Bivar, grew in wealth, and when he saw all his men gathering he was pleased.

My Cid Don Rodrigo tarries no longer, but sets out for Valencia and falls upon it, investing it so closely that none can escape, for he stops all who would leave or enter. He gives those of Valencia nine months in which to yield or find help. Nine full months, know you, he lies there, and at the tenth they yield.

Ah, how great was the rejoicing when My Cid won Valencia and entered the city! Those who had been on foot may now ride, and the gold and silver, who can count it? All his men are rich!

My Cid Don Rodrigo commands that his fifth be set apart. Thirty thousand marks fall to his lot, and other booty beyond the telling! Happy is My Cid, and happy are his men, when his standard is raised above the citadel!

While My Cid and his companies were resting, the King of Seville heard that Valencia had fallen defenseless, and he came to her aid with thirty thousand men. A battle was fought beyond the Garden of Valencia and My Cid, he of the great beard, put them to flight and pursued them well into Játiva. Ah, you should have seen the Moors as they fought against the current of the Júcar. And how they drank the water, although they thirsted not! The King of Seville escaped, thrice wounded.

My Cid returned with all his booty. What he took when he won the city was great, but this victory, know you, was more gainful still, for even the lowest ranks received a hundred marks of silver! You can see how the fame of our knight spread everywhere.

Poema De Mio Cid (1200), translated by Lesley Byrd Simpson (1957)

A version of El Cid's victory over the Moors is to be found in the fourth act of Pierre Corneille's *Le Cid* (*The Cid*) (1636), where the hero relates his triumphs to the King of Spain:

> Sire, under me these troops advance,
> Bearing themselves with manly confidence.
> We started scarce five hundred. Reinforced,

We were, reaching the port, three thousand strong.
To see so many marching, resolute,
Even those who panicked now took heart again.
I hid two thirds of them when we arrived
Deep in the ships we found at anchor there.
The rest whose number constantly increased
Remain around me with impatience fired,
Lie on the ground and, keeping silence, spend
The better part of such a splendid night.
By my command the guard does likewise, and,
Remaining hid, they aid my stratagem.
I boldly feign to have been given by you
The orders which I follow and impart.
This darkling light that from the stars descends
At last shows us the tide with thirty sails.
The waters swell beneath them. Moors and sea,
Moving together, sweep into the port.
We let them pass. Everything seems asleep.
No soldiers in the port; none on the walls.
This silence so profound leads them astray.
Now they are sure they've stolen a march on us.
They heave to, unsuspecting, anchor, land,
And throw themselves into our waiting hands.
Our soldiers rise, and all as if one man,
We rend the welkin with a thousand cries.
Our men echo this clamour from the ships.
They sally forth. The Moors in disarray
Are seized by terror, not yet disembarked.
Before they fight, they deem themselves undone;
They come to pillage and encounter war.
We press them hard on water and on land;
We shed whole rivers of their Moorish blood,
Before they can resist or close their ranks.
But soon their kings despite us rally them;
Morale revives; their terrors are forgot.
The shame of dying without fighting back
Halts the stampede and gives them heart again.
Against us, resolute, they draw their swords,
Mingling our blood most horribly with theirs.
The earth, the river's banks, the fleet, the port,
Are fields of carnage for triumphant death.
How many feats, how many famous deeds

Remain unheralded amid the dark,
In which each man, sole witness of his blows,
Can not discern which way the fates incline!
I scour the field, encouraging our men,
Ord'ring some forward, giving some support,
Directing and inspiring new recruits.
We do not learn the outcome till the dawn.
At last it shows us we have won the day.
The Moor, defeated, sudden loses heart,
And, seeing reinforcements marching up,
The urge to win yields to the fear of death.
Back in their ships, they cut themselves adrift,
And utter to the heavens fearful shrieks
In wild confusion. Now they give no thought
Whether their kings can flee along with them.
The voice of duty's silenced by their fear.
The tide that brought them bears them back again.
Meanwhile, their kings, at grips with our brigade,
With the sore-wounded remnants of their force
Resist courageously, sell their life dear.
I urge them to surrender, but in vain;
Their scimitar in hand, they listen not.
But, at their feet seeing their soldiers fall,
And that henceforth in vain alone they fight,
They ask who is our chief and yield to me.
I sent them both to you together, Sire.
The combat ceased for lack of combatants.

Pierre Corneille, *Le Cid* (1636), Act IV Scene 5,
translated by John Carincross (1975)

1187 Fall of Jerusalem

'Jerusalem is the Navel of the World, a land fruitful above all others,
like a second Paradise of Delights. This Royal City is now held
captive by her enemies . . . so she asks and prays to be liberated, and
calls on you unceasingly to come to her aid.'

(Pope Urban II, Council of Clermont, November 1095)

The Crusades (1095–1291) were a series of wars fought by Europeans
to recover the Holy Lands from the Muslims. Pope Urban II exhorted
the Christians to war at the Council of Clermont. Religious motives

were initially proclaimed but eventually these were overtaken by the nobles' ambitions in land, plunder and loot, and the Italian cities' hopes to increase trade with the Near and Middle East.

The First Crusade (1096−99) ended with the capture of Jerusalem, where 70,000 Muslims died. The Second Crusade, which ended in 1149, was disastrous. Saladin captured Acre, Beirut and Sidon, and following a siege of two weeks he also took the Holy City on 15 July 1187, after a final assault. The Christians were given forty days to evacuate Jerusalem.

With the omens prophesying success, the victorious Saladin made for Jerusalem full of haste, and hate. He set up his engines, laid siege to the city, and, with his usual unholy insolence, broke into the holy places. Long ago, when our troops took Jerusalem after their victory at Antioch in 1099, they had raised a stone cross above the wall to commemorate the event. This the savage horde demolished with a heavy missile, bringing down a great part of the wall with it. The citizens put up what barriers they could, but everything our people tried was fruitless and unsuccessful. In vain they wielded bows, catapults and slings. It was as though both weapons and engines were clearly proclaiming the wrath of the Lord and foretelling the doom of the city.

People from surrounding fortresses flocked into Jerusalem from every side, putting their trust in the holiness of the place rather than in its defences. But in that great multitude of men scarcely a dozen soldiers were to be found. Priests and clerics, though fighting was forbidden to their Orders, became warriors, battling for the home of the Lord.

The terrified and craven mob kept running to the patriarch Heraclius and the queen Sibylla, who were at that time in charge of Jerusalem. They complained tearfully and urged that negotiations be started with Saladin immediately about handing over the city. The pact which followed was more to be deplored than commended. For each person a ransom was paid: twelve sovereigns for a man, five for a women, one for a child. Anyone who could not pay was taken captive. So it happened that while a good many people were able to find the payment for their safety, fourteen thousand who could not pay went under the yoke of perpetual slavery.

Those who could buy their freedom had a choice: they could either make the journey to Antioch, or sail under safe-conduct to Alexandria. A bitter day it was indeed, the day on which the people left their holy place and went their different ways into exile. On that day, 2 October 1187, the queen of all the world's cities was taken into bondage, and the inheritance of her sons brought under the yoke of strangers.

This holiest of cities had been held for about eighty-nine years by our people, from the time when the Christians took it, along with Antioch, in a mighty victory. But Saladin drove the Christians out and re-took it, in 1187.

After Jerusalem had been handed over, a muezzin climbed the high mount of Calvary and there, where Christ on his cross put an end to the law of death, the proclamation of a bastard law rang out.

Another shocking deed of this cruel foe was as follows: they pulled down with ropes the cross surmounting the church of the Hospitallers, smashed it and spat upon it, then dragged it through the city dungheap as an insult to our faith.

W. Stubbs, *Chronicles and Memorials of the Reign of Richard I* (1865)

The Third Crusade (1188–92) led by the Emperor Frederick I, Philip II of France and Richard I of England, did not succeed in recapturing Jerusalem, but a three-year truce gave the Christians access to the Holy City. The Fourth Crusade (1202–4) and the pitiful Children's Crusade (1212) cost thousands of lives. The Latin Empire of Constantinople (1204–61) was founded as a result of the Fourth Crusade.

The Fifth Crusade (1217–21) was directed at Egypt but failed. A Sixth Crusade (1228–9) gained nothing. Frederick II undertook a Crusade in 1228 and gained Jerusalem, by diplomacy rather than conquest, and access to the South of Palestine. In 1238 his gains were lost to the Muslims.

Louis IX of France ('St Louis') embarked on a Crusade in 1249 against Egypt but was captured, together with his army, and ransomed for 800,000 pieces of gold. Louis started another Crusade in 1270 but died at Carthage. He was accompanied by Edward (later Edward I, King of England), who attempted, unsuccessfully, to gain Acre.

In 1291 Acre fell to Sultan-al-Ashraf Khalil, and European influence in the Holy Land was at an end.

Sultan al-Ashraf Khalil had his tents and pavilions set up very close together; they stretched from Toron towards Samaria so that the whole plain was covered with them. The sultan's tent was high up on a hillock, where there were a fine tower and gardens and vines belonging to the Templars. This tent was bright vermilion all over, and had one door open towards Acre.

It is the custom of the sultans that in whatever direction the sultan's tent door is open, then all men know that the sultan must go that way. He remained inactive for a week, except that now and then our men skirmished with theirs and a few died on both sides.

Then at the end of the week, they got their siege-engines set up and ready. One of these weapons was called *Haveben*, which means 'Furious', and was aimed at the Templars' quarter of the city, and another, called *Mansur*, 'Victorious', was directed against the Pisans' quarter. The other big one attacked the Hospitallers' quarter and the machine on wheels shot at a tall tower called the Accursed Tower, which is at a salient point on the walls.

Henry II of Lusignan, king of Jerusalem and Cyprus, had summoned his forces in Cyprus; he collected them, left Famagusta, and arrived in Acre on 4 May 1291.

A few days after King Henry arrived, envoys were sent to the sultan. The sultan left his tent and went to the gate in the town called the Legate's Gate; all shooting was forbidden.

The envoys came unarmed into the sultan's presence. He asked, 'Have you brought me the keys of the town?' But the envoys replied that this was not a city to be surrendered so easily and they had come to ask him to show some sort of mercy to the poor people. To this Sultan al-Ashraf Khalil answered, 'I will do you this much grace: give me nothing but the stones; take everything else and go out and go away. I do this for the sake of your king who is young, as I am myself.'

The envoys told him that this was not possible and he said, 'Then go away, for I will not do anything else for you.' And as he was saying this, by some unknown chance one of the crusaders' weapons at the Legate's Gate loosed off its stone, and it fell so near the tent where the sultan and the envoys were that the sultan – out of youth, not meaning to do wrong – stood up and put his hand to his sword, drew it at least a hand's breadth and said, 'Ah, you flea-ridden swine, what is to stop me cutting your heads off?' But Emir Shujai said to him, 'My lord, God forbid we should soil the iron of your swords with the blood of swine! The men who shot behaved like traitors, but you will let these go, as men who are in your power.' The envoys went back into Acre and both sides resumed shooting at each other with mangonels, and behaving like enemies. When the new tower, known as the King's Tower, was taken, most men sent their wives and children out to sea in ships. In the morning of Thursday 17 May, the weather was so bad and the sea so rough that the women and children could not bear it and went back to their homes.

Then on Friday 18 May 1291, before daybreak, there came the

loud and terrible sound of a kettledrum, and as the drum sounded, the Saracens assaulted the city of Acre on every side. The place where they first got in was through this damned tower which they had taken.

They came in countless numbers, all on foot; in front came men with great tall shields, after them men throwing Greek fire, and then men who shot bolts and feathered arrows so thickly that they seemed like rain falling from the sky.

When Henry of Lusignan, king of Jerusalem and Cyprus, witnessed this disaster, he went to the master of the Hospitallers; they saw clearly that no advice or help could do any good, so they fled and went aboard the galleys.

That day was appalling, for nobles and citizens, women and girls were frantic with terror; they went running through the streets, their children in their arms, weeping and desperate; they fled to the sea-shore to escape death, and when the Saracens caught them one would take the mother and the other the child, they would drag them from place to place and pull them apart; and sometimes two Saracens would quarrel over a woman and she would be killed; or a woman was taken and her sucking child flung to the ground where it died under the horses' hooves.

'Chronicle of the Templar of Tyre', from Philip of Novara, *Les Gestes des Chiprois*,
edited by Guillaume Raynaud (1887)

1314 Battle of Bannockburn

At Bannockburn on 24 June 1314, Edward II's invading English army was defeated. This great Scottish victory made Robert the Bruce a national hero and guaranteed Scottish independence for generations.

ROBERT BRUCE'S
MARCH TO BANNOCKBURN

Scots, wha hae wi Wallace bled,
Scots, wham Bruce has aften led;
Welcome to your gory bed,
    Or to victorie.

Now's the day, and now's the hour;
See the front o' battle lower,
See approach proud Edward's power —
    Chains and slaverie!

Wha will be a traitor knave?
Wha can fill a coward's grave?
Wha sae base as be a slave?
    Let him turn and flee!

Wha for Scotland's King and law
Freedom's sword will strongly draw,
Free-man stand, or free-man fa'?
    Let him follow me!

By oppression's woes and pains!
By your sons in servile chains!
We will drain our dearest veins,
    But they shall be fee!

Lay the proud usurpers low!
Tyrants fall in every foe!
Liberty's in every blow!
    Let us do, or die!

Robert Burns

1388 Battle of Otterbourne

Sir Philip Sidney wrote that he could never hear the old song of Percy and Douglas without finding 'my heart moved more than with a trumpet'.

The incident was a border dispute during the Border Wars. It was fought on 15 August 1388 when 9,000 soldiers under Henry Percy (Hotspur) and a much smaller Scottish force under the Earls of Douglas and Murray fought a pitched battle. Scottish losses totalled 2,000.

The story is related in a traditional ballad:

At last these two stout erles did meet,
    Like captains of great might:
Like lions would, they laid on lode,
    And made a cruel fight:

They fought until they both did sweat,
    With swords of tempered steel;
Until the blood, like drops of rain,
    They trickling down did feel.

Yield thee, Lord Percy, Douglas said,
  In faith I will thee bring,
Where thou shalt high advancèd be
  By James our Scottish king:

Thy ransom I will freely give,
  And this report of thee,
Thou art the most courageous knight,
  That ever I did see.

No, Douglas, quoth Erle Percy then,
  Thy proffer I do scorn;
I will not yield to any Scot,
  That ever yet was born.

With that, there came an arrow keen
  Out of an English bow,
Which struck Erle Douglas to the heart,
  A deep and deadly blow:

Who never spake more words than these,
  Fight on, my merry men all;
For why, my life is at an end; .
  Lord Percy sees my fall.

Then leaving life, Erle Percy took
  The dead man by the hand;
And said, Erle Douglas, for thy life
  Would I had lost my land.

O God! my very heart doth bleed
  With sorrow for thy sake;
For sure, more redoubted knight
  Mischance could never take.

A knight amongst the Scots there was
  Which saw Erle Douglas die,
Who straight in wrath did vow revenge
  Upon the Lord Percye:

Sir Hugh Mountgomery was he call'd,
  Who, with a spear most bright,
Well mounted on a gallant steed,
  Ran fiercely through the fight;

And past the English archers all,
> Without all dread or fear;
And through Erle Percy's body then
> He thrust his hateful spear;

With such a vehement force and might
> He did his body gore,
The staff ran through the other side
> A large cloth-yard, and more.

> Traditional, excerpt from
> 'The Chevy Chase (The Hunting of the Cheviot)'

1403 Battle of Shrewsbury

After Henry Bolingbroke seized the throne, forcing the abdication of his cousin Richard II, he had to deal with various rebel factions — in particular the Northern nobles, led by Henry Percy (Hotspur) and the Welsh under Owen Glendower. The Percies came deep into south-west England with 4,000 men, but Henry was able to defeat them at Shrewsbury on 21 July 1403, before they met up with the Welsh under Glendower.

> The next day in the morning early, being the even of Mary Magdalene, they set their battles in order on both sides, and now whilst the warriors looked when the token of battle should be given, the Abbot of Shrewsbury and one of the Clerks of the Privy Seal were sent from the King unto the Percies to offer them pardon if they would come to any reasonable agreement.
>
> By their persuasions, the Lord Henry Percy began to give ear unto the King's offers, and so sent with them his uncle the Earl of Worcester to declare unto the King the causes of those troubles and to require some effectual reformation in the same.
>
> It was reported for a truth that now when the King had condescended unto all that was reasonable at his hands to be required and seemed to humble himself more than was meet for his estate, the Earl of Worcester upon his return to his nephew made relation clean contrary to that the King had said, in such sort that he set his nephew's heart more in displeasure towards the King than ever it was before, driving him by that means to fight whether he would or not. Then suddenly blew the trumpets, the King's part cried 'St. George! Upon them!', the adversaries cried 'Esperance! Percy!', and so the two armies furiously joined. The archers on both sides shot for the best

game, laying on such load with arrows that many died, and were driven down, that never rose again.

*　　　*　　　*

The Prince that day holp his father like a lusty young gentleman, for although he was hurt in the face with an arrow so that divers noblemen that were about him would have conveyed him forth of the field, yet he would in no wise suffer them so to do, lest his departure from among his men might haply have stricken some fear into their hearts; and so, without regard of his hurt, he continued with his men and never ceased either to fight where the battle was most hottest or to encourage his men where it seemed most need. This battle lasted three long hours, with indifferent fortune on both parts, till at length the King crying 'St. George! Victory!', brake the array of his enemies and adventured so far that, as some write, the Earl Douglas strake him down, and at that instant slew Sir Walter Blunt and three other appareled in the King's suit and clothing, saying, 'I marvel to see so many kings thus suddenly to arise, one in the neck of another.' The King indeed was raised, and did that day many a noble feat of arms, for as it is written, he slew that day with his own hands six-and-thirty persons of his enemies. The other on his part encouraged by his doings, fought valiantly and slew the Lord Percy, called Sir Henry Hotspur. To conclude, the King's enemies were vanquished and put to flight, in which flight the Earl of Douglas, for haste, falling from the crag of a mountain, brake one of his genitals, and was taken, and for his valiantness, of the King frankly and freely delivered.

Raphael Holinshed, Chronicles of Englande, Scotlande and Irelande (1577)

1327–1453 *The Hundred Years War*

Historians attribute the institution of the Round Table to Arthur, the son of Uter Pendragon, a celebrated British hero, whose achievements are so disguised with legendary wonders, that it has been doubted if such a person ever existed . . . In the eighth year of Edward I Roger de Mortemer . . . established a Round Table at Kenilworth for the encouragement of military pastimes . . . The fame of this institution occasioned . . . a great influx of foreigners who came either to initiate themselves, or maker some public proof of their powers. About seventy years after Edward III erected a splendid table of the same kind at Windsor, but on a more extensive scale. It contained the area of a circle two hundred feet in diameter, and the weekly expense for the maintenance of this table . . . amounted to a hundred pounds, which afterwards was reduced to twenty, on account of the large sums of money required for the prosecution of the war with France. This receptacle of military men gave continual occasion for the exercise of arms, and afforded to the young nobility an opportunity of learning, by way of pastime, all the requisites of a soldier. The example of King Edward was followed by Philip of Valois, King of France, who also instituted a Round Table at his court, and by that means drew thither many German and Italian knights who were coming to England. The contest between the two monarchs seems to have had the effect of destroying the establishment of the round table in both kingdoms, for after this period we hear no more concerning it. In England the Round Table was succeeded by the Order of the Garter . . .

Joseph Strutt, *Sport and Pastimes of the People of England* (1801)

The Hundred Years War was waged between England and France, from 1327 to 1453. It was initiated by Edward III's attempts to claim the throne of France when Charles IV of France died without issue. Edward III claimed the throne through his mother Isabella, who was Charles IV's sister — in spite of the fact that according to the Salic Law women were excluded from the French succession. At first Edward III seemed to accept the French claimant, Philip of Valois, only beginning war after Philip supported David II, King of Scotland, against Edward. The English king then assumed the title 'King of France' and invaded the country with an army. The economic imperatives of the war were England's endeavours to maintain control of the Flemish wool trade.

The major engagements of the Hundred Years War were the Battle of Sluys in which the French fleet was defeated, the Battle of Crècy in 1346, the Siege of Calais, the Battle of Poitiers in 1356, Henry V's campaign culminating at Agincourt in 1415, and the victories of Joan of Arc between 1429 and 1431.

This series of battles brought economic ruin upon both countries, ravaged the continental theatres of the conflict, slew thousands and resolved very little. Nevertheless, these barbaric events fostered the idea and the ideals of chivalry. The military forays inspired a vast literature of chronicles — notably the work of Sir John Froissart, in which chivalry found its historian. The epoch saw the revival of the Round Table, which serves as an emblem of the Hundred Years War, providing both the military training and economic subsistence for the continuance of wars of such duration. It seems appropriate that as both major powers exhausted themselves in so long a war effort, so the Round Table, too, died, to be replaced by a ceremonial order.

1346 Battle of Crècy

On 26 August 1346, a force of 9,000 under Edward III defeated a vastly superior army of 30,000 under Philip VI. English foot-soldiers here demonstrated the superiority of massed archery over heavy cavalry. French losses: eleven princes, 1,200 knights and 10,000 soldiers.

The French troops did not advance in any regular order, and that as soon as their king came in sight of the English his blood began to boil, and he cried out to his marshals, 'Order the Genoese forward and begin the battle in the name of God and St. Denis.' There were about 15,000 Genoese cross-bow men; but they were quite fatigued, having marched on foot that day six leagues, completely armed and carrying their cross-bows, and accordingly they told the constable they were not in a condition to do any great thing in battle. The Earl of Alençon hearing this, said, 'This is what one gets by employing such scoundrels, who fall off when there is any need for them.' During this time a heavy rain fell, accompanied by thunder and a very terrible eclipse of the sun; and, before this rain, a great flight of crows hovered in the air over all the battalions, making a loud noise; shortly afterwards it cleared up, and the sun shone very bright; but the French had it in their faces, and the English on their backs. When the Genoese were somewhat in order they approached the English and set up a loud shout, in order to frighten them; but the English remained quite quiet and did not seem to attend to it. They then set up a second shout, and advanced a little forward; the English never moved. Still they hooted a third time, advancing with their cross-bows presented, and began to shoot. The English archers then advanced one step forward, and shot their arrows with such force and quickness, that it seems as if it snowed. When the Geneose felt these arrows, which pierced through their armour, some of them cut the strings of their cross-bows, others flung them to the ground, and all turned about and retreated quite discomfited.

The French had a large body of men-at-arms on horseback to support the Genoese, and the king, seeing them thus fall back, cried out, 'Kill me those scoundrels, for they stop up our road without any reason.' The English continued shooting, and some of their arrows falling among the horsemen, drove them upon the Genoese, so that they were in such confusion, they could never rally again.

In the English army there were some Cornish and Welsh men on foot, who had armed themselves with large knives; these advancing through the ranks of the men-at-arms and archers, who made way for them, came upon the French when they were in this danger, and falling upon earls, barons, knights, and squires, slew many.

This battle, which was fought on Saturday, between La Broyes and Cressy, was murderous and cruel; and many gallant deeds of arms were performed that were never known: towards evening, many knights and squires of the French had lost their masters, and, wandering up and down the plain, attacked the English in small parties; but they were soon destroyed, for the English had determined that day to give no quarter, nor hear of ransom from any one.

The Earl of Blois, nephew to the King of France, and the Duke of Lorraine, his brother-in-law, with their troops, made a gallant defence; but they were surrounded by a troop of English and Welsh, and slain in spite of their prowess. The Earl of St. Pol, and the Earl of Auxerre, were also killed, as well as many others. Late after vespers, the King of France had not more about him than sixty men, every one included. Sir John of Hainault, who was of the number, had once remounted the king, for his horse had been killed under him by an arrow: and seeing the state he was in, he said, 'Sir, retreat whilst you have an opportunity, and do not expose yourself so simply; if you have lost this battle, another time you will be the conqueror.' After he had said this he took the bridle of the king's horse and led him off by force, for he had before entreated him to retire.

Sir John Froissart, Chronicles of England, France and Spain (1930), translated by
Thomas Johnes (1810)

1415 Battle of Agincourt

Henry V waged war on France to retain certain dukedoms he had been assured were rightfully his. He was dispatched to the wars with the full financial backing of the Church as the bishops were anxious to have him out of the way while they scuppered the Lollard Bill then before Parliament. Henry waged war like a professional. His brutal speech to the besieged citizens of Harfleur, often cut in stage productions of Shakespeare's masterpiece *Henry V*, presents the true barbarities of warfare as practised in the Middle Ages:

KING   How yet resolves the Governor of the town?
   This is the latest parle we will admit;
   Therefore to our best mercy give yourselves
   Or, like to men proud of destruction,
   Defy us to our worst; for, as I am a soldier,
   A name that in my thoughts becomes me best,

If I begin the batt'ry once again,
I will not leave the half-achieved Harfleur
Till in her ashes she lie buried.
The gates of mercy shall be all shut up,
And the flesh'd soldier, rough and hard of heart,
In liberty of bloody hand shall range
With conscience wide as hell, mowing like grass
Your fresh fair virgins and your flow'ring infants.
What is it then to me if impious war,
Array'd in flames, like to the prince of fiends,
Do, with his smirch'd complexion, all fell feats
Enlink'd to waste and desolation?
What is't to me when you yourselves are cause,
If your pure maidens fall into the hand
Of hot and forcing violation?
What rein can hold licentious wickedness
When down the hill he holds his fierce career?
We may as bootless spend our vain command
Upon th' enraged soldiers in their spoil,
As send precepts to the Leviathan
To come ashore. Therefore, you men of Harfleur,
Take pity of your town and of your people
Whiles yet my soldiers are in my command;
Whiles yet the cool and temperate wind of grace
O'erblows the filthy and contagious clouds
Of heady murder, spoil, and villainy.
If not – why, in a moment look to see
The blind and bloody soldier with foul hand
Defile the locks of your shrill-shrieking daughters;
Your fathers taken by the silver beards,
And their most reverend heads dash'd to the walls;
Your naked infants spitted upon pikes,
Whiles the mad mothers with their howls confus'd
Do break the clouds, as did the wives of Jewry
At Herod's bloody-hunting slaughtermen.
What say you? Will you yield, and this avoid?
Or, guilty in defence, be thus destroy'd?
GOV   Our expectation hath this day an end:
The Dauphin, whom of succours we entreated,
Returns us that his powers are yet not ready
To raise so great a siege. Therefore, great King,
We yield our town and lives to thy soft mercy.

Enter our gates; dispose of us and ours;
For we no longer are defensible.

William Shakespeare, *Henry V*, Act III, Scene 3 (*c.*1599)

According to the English chronicler Holinshed, King Henry V reacted strongly when he heard one of his soldiers wish for just some of the men they had left at home in England:

It is said, that as he heard one of the host vtter his wish to another thus: 'I would to God there were with vs now so manie good soldiers as are at this houre within England!' the king answered: 'I would not wish a man more here than I haue; we are indeed in comparison to the enimies but a few, but if God of his clemencie doo fauour vs, and our iust cause, (as I trust he will,) we shall speed well inough. But let no man ascribe victorie to our owne strength and might, but onelie to Gods assistance; to whome I haue no doubt we shall worthilie haue cause to giue thanks therefore. And if so be that for our offenses sakes we shall be deliuered into the hands of our enimies, the lesse number we be, the less damage shall the realme of England susteine; but if we should fight in trust of multitude of men, and so get the victorie, (our minds being prone to pride,) we should thervpon peraduenture ascribe the victorie not so much to the gift of God, as to our own puissance, and thereby prouoke his high indignation and displeasure against vs: and if the enimie get the vpper hand, then should our realme and countrie suffer more damage and stand in further danger. But be you of good comfort, and shew your selues valiant! God and our iust quarrell shall defend vs, and deliuer these our proud aduersaries with all the multitude of them which you see (or at the least the most of them) into our hands.'

Raphael Holinshed, *Chronicles of Englande, Scotlande and Ireland* (1577)

Henry then went on to tell his soldiers they would never forget this day:

This day is call'd the feast of Crispian.
He that outlives this day, and comes safe home,
Will stand a tip-toe when this day is nam'd,
And rouse him at the name of Crispian.
He that live this day, and see old age,
Will yearly on the vigil feast his neighbours,
And say 'To-morrow is Saint Crispian'.
Then will he strip his sleeve and show his scars,
And say 'These wounds I had on Crispian's day'.

Old men forget; yet all shall be forgot,
But he'll remember, with advantages,
What feats he did that day. Then shall our names,
Familiar in his mouth as household words –
Harry the King, Bedford and Exeter,
Warwick and Talbot, Salisbury and Gloucester –
Be in their flowing cups freshly rememb'red.
This story shall the good man teach his son;
And Crispin Crispian shall ne'er go by,
But we in it shall be remembered –
We few, we happy few, we band of brothers;
For he today that sheds his blood with me
Shall be my brother; be he ne'er so vile,
This day shall gentle his condition;
And gentlemen in England now a-bed
Shall think themselves accurs'd they were not here,
And hold their manhoods cheap while any speaks
That fought with us upon Saint Crispin's day.

William Shakespeare, *Henry V*, Act IV, Scene 3 (*c.*1599)

1429 Joan of Arc Delivers France from the English

Jeanne d'Arc, 'La Pucelle d'Orléans', was an illiterate peasant girl born in
the Meuse valley in 1412. At the age of 17 she claimed that voices had
told her she had been born to deliver France from her enemies. She
joined Charles VII and led the French in raising the siege of Orléans
from the English, begun in October 1428. Orléans was relieved on 8
May 1429.

She conducted Charles to his coronation at Rheims. She was later
captured by the Burgundians and sold to the English. After being
condemned for heresy by a French ecclesiastical court she was burned
on 30 May 1431.

This account of her first appearance is from the contemporary
Burgundian chronicler Waurin:

> In that year, which was then reckoned one thousand four hundred and
> twenty-eight, while Orléans was besieged, there came to King
> Charles of France, at Chinon where he was then staying, a young girl
> who described herself as a maid of twenty years of age or thereabout
> named Joan, who was clothed and habited in guise of a man, born in

the parts between Burgundy and Lorraine at a town named Domrémy very near Vaucoulleurs. This Joan had remained a long time at an inn and she was very bold in riding horses and leading them to drink and also in performing others feats and exercises which young girls are not accustomed to do; and she was sent to the king of France by a knight named Sir Robert de Baudricourt, captain of the place of Vaucoulleurs appointed on behalf of King Charles. This sir Robert gave her horses and five or six companions, and likewise instructed her, and taught her what she ought to say and do, and the way in which she could conduct herself, since she asserted that she was a maid inspired by divine providence, and sent to King Charles to restore him and bring him back into the possession of all his kingdom generally, from which he was, as she said, wrongfully driven away and put out. And the maid was, at her coming, in very poor estate; and she was about two months in the house of the king, whom she many times admonished by her speeches, as she had been instructed, to give her troops and aid, and she would repel and drive away his enemies, and exalt his name, enlarging his lordships, certifying that she had had a sufficient revelation concerning this; but whatever she could say at this beginning neither the king nor those of his council put much faith in her words or admonitions. And she was then considered at court only as one deranged and deluded, because she boasted herself as able to achieve so great an enterprise, which seemed to the great princes a thing impossible, considering that all they together could not effect it; and so her words were turned into folly and derision, for it seemed indeed to the princes that it was a perilous thing to believe on account of the blasphemy which might follow upon it from the speeches or scoffs of the people, as it is a great reproach to a wise man to fall into deception through believing too readily, especially in perilous matters. Nevertheless, after the maid had remained a good space at the king's court in the state that I have mentioned, she was brought forward and aided, and she raised a standard whereon she had painted the figure and representation of Our Lord Jesus Christ; indeed, all her words were full of the name of God, wherefore a great part of those who saw her and heard her speak, like fools, had great belief that she was inspired by God as she said, or hesitated about it; and she was many times examined by famous clerks and men of great authority in order to inquire and know more fully her intention, but she always held to her purpose, saying that if the king would believe her she would restore him to his dominion. Maintaining this purpose she accomplished some operations successfully, whereby she acquired great renown, fame, and exaltation, about which it shall be more fully declared hereafter.

Now when she came to the king there were at court the Duke of Alençon, the Marshal de Raiz, and many other great lords and captains, with whom the king had held council concerning the matter of the siege of Orléans; and this maid went with him soon after from Chinon and Poitiers, where he ordered that the marshall should take provisions and artillery and other necessary things to Orléans in force, with whom the maid Joan wished to go; and she made request that they would give her a suit of armour to arm herself, which was delivered to her. Then, with her standard raised as has been said, she went to Blois where the muster was being made, and thence to Orléans with the others; and she was always armed, in complete armour, and in this same journey many men-at-arms placed themselves under her.

When the maid had come into the city of Orléans, they gave her a good reception, and some were greatly rejoiced at seeing her in their company.

And when the French troops who had brought the provisions into Orléans returned to the king, the maid remained there. And she was desired to go out to skirmish with the other by La Hire and some captains, but she made answer that she would not go unless the men-at-arms who had brought her were also with her: these were recalled from Blois and from the other places whither they had now withdrawn. And they returned to Orléans, where they were joyfully received by the maid. So she went out to welcome them, saying that she had well seen and considered the governance of the English, and that if they would believe in her she would make them all rich.

So she began that day to sally out of the town, and went with great alacrity to attack one of the English towers, which she took by force; and going on from that time she did some very marvellous things, whereof mention shall be made hereafter in their order.

Waurin, *Recueil des Chroniques*, Vol. III, translated by E. L. C. P. Hardy (1884)

1455–1485 Wars of the Roses

'As your father killed mine, I will kill you!' (John de Clifford, thirteenth Baron Clifford, as he stabbed Lord Rutland, the sixteen-year-old son of Richard, Duke of York, at the battle of Wakefield, 30 December 1460. Baron Clifford's father, Thomas de Clifford, was slain at the battle of St Albans, 22 May 1455.)

The Wars of the Roses, which form the basis of much of the action of Shakespeare's early cycle of history plays, are the civil/dynastic wars fought between the rival families of Lancaster and York. The rose was selected by each house as its badge, the House of Lancaster wearing the red rose and the House of York the white rose. The conflict erupted during the insanity of Henry VI (1453–4), when Richard of York, who claimed descent from John of Gaunt's family, was made Lord Protector. After Henry's recovery, Richard attempted to usurp power, and the dynastic wars lasted until 1485 when Henry Tudor united the white rose and the red by marrying Elizabeth of York, daughter of Edward IV, son of Richard of York.

This account of the beginnings of the wars is taken from *The Brut*, or *The Chronicles of Englande*:

1455

On 6 February, the duke of Somerset was released from the Tower of London on bail. Very shortly afterwards the duke of York resigned his office to the king at Greenwich, after he had governed England most excellently for a whole year, miraculously calming rebels and villains, according to the laws and without unnecessary violence; and he resigned his office much honoured and much loved.

Then the king, in response to the intercession of the archbishop of Canterbury and the duke of Buckingham, pardoned all those who had entered into recognizances for the duke of Somerset. Once more, the duke of Somerset became head of the government under the king, although in the past he had almost ruined the whole of England with his misrule.

On 13 October the duke of York fled to Wales, and the earl of Salisbury, the earl of Warwick and the earl of March fled to Calais. The king ransacked all their property between Worcester and Ludlow, and then made the duke of Somerset captain of Calais.

The king then held a parliament at Coventry, which began on 20 November. In this parliament, the duke of York, his son Edward, earl of March, the earl of Rutland, the earl of Warwick, the earl of Salisbury and many other knights and squires, were declared traitors throughout England.

1460

Around 8 September, the duke of York returned from Ireland to England. Then on 7 October, which was a Tuesday, the king opened parliament at Westminster.

On 10 October, Richard, duke of York, came to Westminster to the king's palace where he stayed for three weeks, without speaking with the king or even setting eyes on him. He then claimed in parliament that the king's title should be 'King of England and France and Lord of Ireland'. This title met with the approval of parliament. So on 31 October the king and Richard were reconciled. On the next day, in St Paul's church in London, the king wore his crown and led a procession of dukes, earls and lords, as a symbol of concord.

Thus it was resolved in parliament by the king and all the lords and commons that King Henry should enjoy the thrones of England and France and the dominion of Ireland, for as long as he should live.

The duke of York was made heir apparent to the kingdoms of England and France and to the dominion of Ireland, and the duke received from the king, as an annual pension, ten thousand marks. All the lords, spiritual and temporal, swore allegiance to Richard, duke of York, and the duke of York swore allegiance to the king and the lords, saying that for his part he would abide by all the conventions and compacts agreed.

On 5 December, the duke of York, the earl of Salisbury and the earl of Rutland left London and went to Sandal Castle with twelve thousand men. The duke of Somerset came against them on 30 December [at the battle of Wakefield], together with about twenty thousand men. About a thousand were killed, including the duke of York himself.

> *The Brut*, or *The Chronicles of Englande*, Part Two, adapted by William Caxton and
> incorporated in *Chronicles of England* (1480)

1460 Battle of Wakefield

In this engagement the Lancastrian forces under the Duke of Somerset met the Yorkists, commanded by Richard, Duke of York, on 30 December 1460. The Yorkist army was depleted as some units were off foraging when attacked, but Somerset had prepared an ambush into which the Yorkists fell as they left Wakefield.

In one of the most memorable scenes in Shakespeare's histories, Queen Margaret taunts the captured Duke of York, putting a paper crown on his head, before killing him. He goes to his end with stoic resolve:

DUKE OF YORK   She-wolf of France, but worse than wolves of France.
  Whose tongue more poisons than the adder's tooth!
  How ill-beseeming is it in thy sex
  To triumph like an Amazonian trull

Upon their woes whom fortune captivates!
But that thy face is visard-like, unchanging,
Made impudent with use of evil deeds,
I would assay, proud queen, to make thee blush.
To tell thee whence thou cam'st, of whom deriv'd,
Were shame enough to shame thee, wert thou not shameless.
Thy father bears the type of King of Naples,
Of both the Sicils and Jerusalem,
Yet not so wealthy as an English yeoman.
Hath that poor monarch taught thee to insult?
It needs not, nor it boots thee not, proud queen:
Unless the adage must be verified,
That beggars mounted run their horse to death.
'Tis beauty that doth oft make women proud;
But, God He knows, thy share thereof is small.
'Tis virtue that doth make them most admir'd;
The contrary doth make thee wond'red at.
'Tis government that makes them seem divine;
The want thereof makes thee abominable.
Thou art as opposite to every good
As the Antipodes are unto us.
Or as the south to the septentrion.
O tiger's heart wrapp'd in a woman's hide!
How couldst thou drain the life-blood of the child,
To bid the father wipe his eyes withal,
And yet be seen to bear a woman's face?
Women are soft, mild, pitiful, and flexible:
Thou stern, obdurate, flinty, rough, remorseless.
Bid'st thou me rage? Why, now thou hast thy wish;
Wouldst have me weep? Why, now thou hast thy will;
For raging wind blows up incessant showers,
And when the rage allays, the rain begins.
These tears are my sweet Rutland's obsequies;
And every drop cries vengeance for his death
'Gainst thee, fell Clifford, and thee, false Frenchwoman.
NORTHUMBERLAND Beshrew me, but his passions move me so.
    That hardly can I check my eyes from tears.
DUKE OF YORK That face of his the hungry cannibals
    Would not have touch'd, would not have stain'd with blood;
    But you are more inhuman, more inexorable –
    O, ten times more – than tigers of Hyrcania.
    See, ruthless queen, a hapless father's tears.

This cloth thou dipp'dst in blood of my sweet boy,
And I with tears do wash the blood away.
Keep thou the napkin, and go boast of this;
And if thou tell'st the heavy story right,
Upon my soul, the hearers will shed tears;
Yea, even my foes will shed fast-falling tears
And say 'Alas, it was a piteous deed!'
There, take the crown, and with the crown my curse;
And in thy need such comfort come to thee
As now I reap at thy too cruel hand!
Hard-hearted Clifford, take me from the world;
My soul to heaven, my blood upon your heads!

William Shakespeare, *Henry VI, Part Three*, Act I, Scene 4 (*c.*1590)

Later in the play, Shakespeare drives home the horrors of civil war in
a pathetic scene between a father who has killed his son, and a son who
has killed his father at the battle where the opposing factions have met:

Alarum. Enter a Son *that hath kill'd his Father, at one door; and a* Father
that hath kill'd his Son, at another door.

SON   Ill blows the wind that profits nobody.
This man whom hand to hand I slew in fight
May be possessed with some store of crowns;
And I, that haply take them from him now,
May yet ere night yield both my life and them
To some man else, as this dead man doth me.
Who's this? O God! It is my father's face,
Whom in this conflict I unwares have kill'd.
O heavy times, begetting such events!
From London by the King was I press'd forth;
My father, being the Earl of Warwick's man,
Came on the part of York, press'd by his master;
And I, who at his hands receiv'd my life,
Have by my hands of life bereaved him.
Pardon me, God, I knew not what I did.
And pardon, father, for I knew not thee.
My tears shall wipe away these bloody marks;
And no more words till they have flow'd their fill.
KING HENRY   O piteous spectacle! O bloody times!
Whiles lions war and battle for their dens,
Poor harmless lambs abide their enmity.
Weep, wretched man; I'll aid thee tear for tear;

And let our hearts and eyes, like civil war,
Be blind with tears and break o'ercharg'd with grief.

Enter Father, *bearing of his* Son.

FATHER   Thou that so stoutly hath resisted me,
Give me thy gold, if thou hast any gold;
For I have bought it with an hundred blows.
But let me see. Is this our foeman's face?
Ah, no, no, no, it is mine only son!
Ah, boy, if any life be left in thee,
Throw up thine eye! See, see what show'rs arise,
Blown with the windy tempest of my heart
Upon thy wounds, that kills mine eye and heart!
O, pity, God, this miserable age!
What stratagems, how fell, how butcherly,
Erroneous, mutinous, and unnatural,
This deadly quarrel daily doth beget!
O boy, thy father gave thee life too soon,
And hath bereft thee of thy life too late!

KING HENRY   Woe above woe! grief more than common grief!
O that my death would stay these ruthful deeds!
O pity, pity, gentle heaven, pity!
The red rose and the white are on his face,
The fatal colours of our striving houses:
The one his purple blood right well resembles;
The other his pale cheeks, methinks, presenteth.
Wither one rose, and let the other flourish!
If you contend, a thousand lives must perish.

SON   How will my mother for a father's death
Take on with me, and ne'er be satisfied!

FATHER   How will my wife for slaughter of my son
Shed seas of tears, and ne'er be satisfied!

KING HENRY   How will the country for these woeful chances
Misthink the King, and not be satisfied!

SON   Was ever son so rued a father's death?

FATHER   Was ever father so bemoan'd his son?

KING HENRY   Was ever king so griev'd for subjects' woe?
Much is your sorrow; mine ten times so much.

SON   I'll bear thee hence, where I may weep my fill.

[Exit with the body.]

FATHER   These arms of mine shall be thy winding-sheet;
My heart, sweet boy, shall be thy sepulchre,

For from my heart thine image ne'er shall go;
My sighing breast shall be thy funeral bell;
And so obsequious will thy father be,
Even for the loss of thee, having no more,
As Priam was for all his valiant sons.
I'll bear thee hence; and let them fight that will,
For I have murdered where I should not kill.

William Shakespeare, *Henry VI, Part Three*, Act II, Scene 5 (*c.*1590)

1485 Battle of Bosworth

With Richard III's popularity on the wane, Henry Tudor, Duke of Richmond, had received promise of support should he return from exile and claim the throne through his descent from Henry V's widow. Lord Stanley assured him that he would desert Richard's cause during the battle. King Richard believed he had guaranteed Stanley's loyalty by arresting his son, but at a crucial moment, on 21 August 1485, Stanley's troops came over to Richmond's side and carried the day; Richard was routed and killed. The Wars of the Roses were ended with the crowning of Richmond as Henry VII and his marriage to Elizabeth of York.

When king Richard was come to Bosworth, he sent a purseuant to the lord Stanleie, commanding him to aduance forward with his companie, and to come to his presence; which thing if he refused to doo, he sware, by Christes passion, that he would strike off his sonnes head before he dined. The lord Stanleie answered the purseuant that, if the king did so, he had more sonnes aliue; and, as to come to him, he was not then so determined. When king Richard heard this answer, he commanded the lord Strange incontinent to be beheaded: which was at that verie same season, when both the armies had sight ech of other. But the councellors of king Richard pondered the time and cause, (knowing also the lord Strange to be innocent of his fathers offence,) & persuaded the king that it was now time to fight, & no time to execute.

Besides that, they aduised him to keepe the lord Strange as prisoner till the battell were ended, and then at leisure his pleasure might be accomplished. So (as God would) king Richard brake his holie oth, and the lord was deliuered to the keepers of the kings tents, to be kept as prisoner.

Betweene both armies there was a great marish then (but at this present, by reason of diches cast, it is growne to be firme ground) which the earle of Richmond left on his right hand; for this intent, that it should be on that side a defense for his part, and in so dooing he had the sunne at his backe, and in the faces of his enimies. When king Richard saw the earles companie was passed the marish, he did command with all hast to set vpon them.

When the losse of the battell was imminent and apparant, they brought to [Richard] a swift and a light horsse, to conueie him awaie. He which was not ignorant of the grudge and ill will that the common people bare towards him, casting awaie all hope of fortunate successe and happie chance to come, answered (as men saie) that on that daie he would make an end of all battels, or else there finish his life.

King Richard was admonished by his explorators and espials, that the earle of Richmond (accompanied with a small number of men of armes) was not far off. And, as he approched and marched toward him, he perfectlie knew his personage by certeine demonstrations and tokens, which he had learned and knowen of others that were able to giue him full information. Now, being inflamed with ire, and vexed with outragious malice, he put his spurres to his horsse, and rode out of the side of the range of his battell, leauing the vant-gard fighting; and like a hungrie lion ran with speare in rest toward him. The earle of Richmond perceiued well the king furiouslie comming toward him, and, bicause the whole hope of his wealth and purpose was to be determined by battell, he gladlie proffered to incounter with him bodie to bodie, and man to man.

King Richard set on so sharplie at the first brunt, that he ouerthrew the earles standard, and slue sir William Brandon his standard-bearer, (which was father to sir Charles Brandon, by king Henrie the eight created duke of Suffolke,) and matched hand to hand with sir Iohn Cheinie, a man of great force and strength, which would haue resisted him: but the said Iohn was by him manfullie ouerthrowen. And so, he making open passage by dint of sword as he went forward, the earle of Richmond withstood his violence, and kept him at the swords point, without aduantage, longer than his companions either thought or iudged: which being almost in despaire of victorie, were suddenlie recomforted by sir William Stanleie, which came to his succors with three thousand tall men. At which verie instant, king Richards men were driuen backe and fled, & he himselfe, manfullie fighting in the middle of his enimies, was slaine; and (as he worthilie had deserued) came to a bloudie death, as he had lead a bloudie life.

Raphael Holinshed, *Chronicles of Englande, Scotlande and Irelande* (1577)

1513 Battle of Flodden

On 9 September 1513 an English army under the Earl of Surrey, assisted by the brilliant generalship of the Earl of Stanley on the left wing, totally defeated the Scots at Flodden Hill. King James IV and many of the leading nobility of Scotland were slain. This anonymous early sixteenth-century poem commemorates the English victory, seen south of the border as a punishment for James's support of the French against Henry VIII:

THE BATTLE OF FLODDEN

Then the sun full soone shott under the clouds,
And it darkened full dimlie and drew towards night.
Every ryncke to his rest full radlye him dressed;
Beeten fires full fast, and feteled them to sowpe
Besides Barwicke on a banke, within a broad woode.
Then dauned the day, soe deere God ordayned;
Clowdes cast up full cleerlye, like castles full hie.
Then Phebus full faire flourished out his beames
With leames full light all the land over.
All was damped with dew the daysies about;
Flowers flourished in the feild, faire to behold;
Birrds bradden to the boughes, and boldlye thé songen –
It was solace to heare for any seege living!
Then full boldlye on the broad hills we busked our standards,
And on a soughe us beside there seene we our enemies
Were moving over the mountaines – to macch us they thoughten –
As boldly as any bearnes that borne was of mothers.
And we egerlie with ire attilld them to meete.
Then trunmpetts full truly they tryden together,
Many shames in that shawe with theire shrill pipes –
Heavenly was theire melody, their mirth to heare,
How thé songen with a showte all the shawes over!
There was gurding forth of gunns with many great stones,
Archers uttered out their arrowes, and egerlie they shotten;
They proched us with speares, and put many over
That the blood out brast at there broken harnes.
There was swinging out of swords, and swapping of headds;
We blanked them with bills through all their bright armor,
That all the dale dunned of theire derfe strokes . . .

*   *   *

. . . Then the Scottish king carped these words,
'I will fight with yonder frekes that are soe feirce holden —
And I beate those bearnes the battle is ours!'
Then thé moved towards the mountaines, and manly came downwards.
Wee mett him in the midway, and mached him full even —
Then there was dealing of dints, that all the dales rangen;
Many helmes with heads were hewd all to peeces!
This layke lasted on the land the length of .iiii. houres.
Yorkshire like yearne men eagerlye they foughten;
Soe did Darbyshire that day — deered many Scotts;
Lancashire like lyons laid them about.
All had beene lost, by Our Lord, had not those leeds beene!
But the care of the Scotts increased full sore,
For their king was downe knocked, and killed in there sight,
Under the banner of a bishoppe, that was the bold Standlye.
Then they fettled them to flye as fast as they might,
But it serveth not, for sooth, whosoe truth telleth —
Our Englishmen full egerlye, after them followed,
And killed them like caitives, in clowes all about.
There were killed of the Scotts, that told were by tale,
That were found in the feild .xv. thousand.
Loe, what it is to be false, and the feende serve!
They have broken a book-othe to our blithe kinge,
And the truce that was taken the space of .ii. yeeres.
All the Scotts that were scaped were scattered all assunder,
They removed over the more upon the other morning,
And their stode like stakes, and stirr durst no further,
For all the lords of their lande were left them behind.
Besids Brinston in a brynke breathelesse thé lyen,
Gaping against the moone — theire ghostes were away!

IV

THE EXPANDING WORLD

1532 Spanish Conquest of Peru: Seizure of Atahualpa

Francisco Pizarro landed at Tumbes (San Miguel) with an expedition of 180 men, twenty-seven horses and two cannon. He awaited reinforcements and then advanced inland with one hundred and two infantrymen and sixty-two cavalrymen. Negotiations were undertaken with the Inca Atahualpa and it was explained that the Spanish had come to his empire to bring him and his people to the true faith. Pizarro and his followers realized they had proceeded inland too far and were too remote for help to reach them. The vast numbers of Inca forces placed them in a very dangerous position. Pizarro resolved to achieve power by a stratagem – to take possession of Atahualpa by a trick in the face of his whole army.

On 16 November 1532, Atahualpa and his vast retinue were invited to dine and spend the evening with the Spanish party. Pizarro secreted the main body of his infantry and cavalry on three sides of the plaza at the centre of Caxamalca (Cajamarca). They were instructed to remain hidden until they heard the signal – the discharge of a gun – then rush out and take the Indians by surprise.

Atahualpa, carried on a litter, seated on a gold throne, followed by hundreds of supporters, duly arrived and listened to a long explanation of the Christian revelation by a Dominican friar, Fray Vicente de Valverde. At the close of this address Atahualpa threw the proffered Bible to the ground.

The friar called to Pizarro: 'Set on at once! I absolve you!'
Pizarro gave the signal:

The fatal gun was fired from the fortress. Then springing into the square, the Spanish captain and his followers shouted the old war-cry of 'St. Jago and at them!' It was answered by the battle-cry of every

Spaniard in the city, as, rushing from the avenues of the great halls where they had been concealed, they poured into the plaza, horse and foot, each in his own dark column, and threw themselves into the midst of the Indian crowd. The latter, taken by surprise, stunned by the report of artillery and muskets, the echoes of which reverberated like thunder from the surrounding buildings, and, blinded by the smoke which rolled in sulphurous volumes along the square, were seized with a panic. They knew not whither to fly from the coming ruin. Nobles and commoners – all were trampled down under the fierce charge of the cavalry, who dealt blows right and left, without sparing; while their swords, flashing through the thick gloom, carried dismay into the hearts of the wretched natives, who now for the first time saw the horse and rider in all their terrors. They made no resistance – as, indeed, they had no weapons with which to make it. Every avenue of escape was closed, for the entrance of the square was choked up with the dead bodies who had perished in vain efforts to fly; and such was the agony of the survivors under the terrible pressure of their assailants that a large body of Indians . . . burst through the wall of stone and dried clay . . . It fell, leaving an opening of more than a hundred paces, through which the multitudes now found their way into the country, still hotly pursued by the cavalry . . .

Meanwhile the fight, or rather massacre, continued hot around the Inca . . . His faithful nobles . . . threw themselves in the way of the assailants . . . The Indian monarch, stunned and bewildered, saw his faithful servants falling around him without fully comprehending his situation. The litter on which he rode heaved to and fro, as the mighty press swayed backward and foward . . . At length . . . the Spaniards felt afraid that the royal prize might, after all, elude them; and some of the cavaliers made a desperate attempt to end the affray by taking Atahualpa's life. But Pizarro . . . called out: 'Let no one who values his life strike at the Inca,' and stretching out his arm to shield him, received a wound on the hand from one of his own men – the only wound received by a Spaniard in the action.

The struggle now became fiercer than ever round the royal litter. It reeled more and more, and at length, several of the nobles who supported it having been slain, it was overturned, and the Indian prince would have come with violence to the ground, had not his fall been broken by the efforts of Pizarro and some other cavaliers, who caught him in their arms . . .

All attempts at resistance now ceased. The fate of the Inca soon spread over town and country. The charm which might have held the

Peruvians together was dissolved. Every man thought only of his own safety. Even the soldiery encamped on the adjacent fields took the alarm, and learning the fatal tidings, were seen flying in every direction before their pursuers, who in the heat of triumph showed no touch of mercy. At length night, more pitiful than man, threw her friendly mantle over the fugitives, and the scattered troops of Pizarro rallied once more at the sound of the trumpet in the bloody square of Caxamalca.

William H. Prescott, *History of the Conquest of Peru* (1847)

1571 Battle of Lepanto

This was the last battle fought with oar-powered galleys. The Turkish fleet was resoundingly defeated by a fleet of 300 Christian vessels, Spanish, Venetian and Papal, commanded by Don Juan of Austria. Among the wounded was Miguel Cervantes, who lost his left hand. This was the end of Ottoman domination of the Mediterranean.

This is how news of the victory was published in Venice:

This morning the galley of the magnificent Onfre Giustiniano arrived with much firing of cannon, dragging the Turkish ensigns through the water and bringing the best possible news that this most serene republic of Venice, and indeed the whole of Christianity, could receive: the total rout and ruin of the whole Turkish fleet, which had taken place on Sunday 7 October, at about the third hour of the day.

The two fleets met near the place called Curzolari in the Gulf of Lepanto. The Turk was the first into the attack, to be met by the galleys of the noble captain Augustin Barbarigo, in a dead calm which lasted the whole day.

So it was that one hundred and eighty Turkish galleys were captured and towed by our fleet to Corfu. Of the rest of the Turkish force, some were sunk and some were burned, upward of fifteen thousand Turks were cut to pieces, seven thousand were taken prisoner, and twenty thousand slaves were freed; and of the forty flagships in the Turkish fleet thirty-nine were captured. The survivor, that of Uluch Ali, had fled with five galleys but was followed by the same number of our ships. Of our fleet some ten galleys were destroyed with their men, the noble Signor Augustin Barbarigo was killed by an arrow in the face and also, it is said, about eighteen galley commanders, but that is not certain, and the magnificent Mark Querini was wounded.

There was much booty, and it is thought that every soldier has profited considerably. The city of Venice is rejoicing at this most glorious victory that God has given us, the like of which has perhaps never been seen in Christian times, and all is festivity and elation. His Serene Highness, the Doge, with the signoria and the foreign ambassadors, went at once to Saint Mark's, where Mass was sung with the 'Te Deum Laudamus'.

All the people of the city are wild with delight, shutting up their shops, abandoning business and spending all their time with joy and celebration, and thanking God who has given us such consolation. Those imprisoned for civil debts have been released and other celebratory measures will follow. May it please the Divine Majesty to grant that our captains who have won this victory may chase the dog from his throne in Constantinople itself, as there is reason to hope they may.

J. R. Hale, *Famous Sea Fights* (1919)

This battle is celebrated in the well-known poem by G. K. Chesterton

LEPANTO

White founts falling in the courts of the sun,
And the Soldan of Byzantium is smiling as they run;
There is laughter like the fountains in that face of all men feared,
It stirs the forest darkness, the darkness of his beard,
It curls the blood-red crescent, the crescent of his lips,
For the inmost sea of all the earth is shaken with his ships.
They have dared the white republics up the capes of Italy,
They have dashed the Adriatic round the Lion of the Sea,
And the Pope has cast his arms abroad for agony and loss,
And called the kings of Christendom for swords about the Cross,
The cold queen of England is looking in the glass;
The shadow of the Valois is yawning at the Mass;
From evening isles fantastical rings faint the Spanish gun,
And the Lord upon the Golden Horn is laughing in the sun.
Dim drums throbbing, in the hills half heard,
Where only on a nameless throne a crownless prince has stirred,
Where, risen from a doubtful seat and half-attainted stall,
The last knight of Europe takes weapons from the wall,
The last and lingering troubadour to whom the bird has sung,
That once went singing southward when all the world was young,
In that enormous silence, tiny and unafraid,
Comes up along a winding road the noise of the Crusade.

Strong gongs groaning as the guns boom far,
Don John of Austria is going to the war,
Stiff flags straining in the night-blasts cold
In the gloom black-purple, in the glint old-gold,
Torchlight crimson on the copper kettle-drums,
Then the tuckets, then the trumpets, then the cannon, and he comes.
Don John laughing in the brave beard curled,
Spurning of his stirrups like the thrones of all the world,
Holding his head up for a flag of all the free.
Love-light of Spain — hurrah!
Death-light of Africa!
Don John of Austria
Is riding to the sea.

Mahound is in his paradise above the evening star,
(*Don John of Austria is going to the war.*)
He moves a mighty turban on the timeless houri's knees,
His turban that is woven of the sunsets and the seas.
He shakes the peacock gardens as he rises from his ease,
And he strides among the tree-tops and is taller than the trees,
And his voice through all the garden is a thunder sent to bring
Black Azrael and Ariel and Ammon on the wing.
Giants and the Genii,
Multiplex of wing and eye,
Whose strong obedience broke the sky
When Solomon was king.

They rush in red and purple from the red clouds of the morn,
From temples where the yellow gods shut up their eyes in scorn;
They rise in green robes roaring from the green hells of the sea
Where fallen skies and evil hues and eyeless creatures be;
On them the sea-valves cluster and the grey sea-forests curl,
Splashed with a splendid sickness, the sickness of the pearl;
They swell in sapphire smoke out of the blue cracks of the ground, —
They gather and they wonder and give worship to Mahound.
And he saith, 'Break up the mountains where the hermit-folk may
      hide,
And sift the red and silver sands lest bone of saint abide,
And chase the Giaours flying night and day, not giving rest,
For that which was our trouble comes again out of the west.
We have set the seal of Solomon on all things under sun,
Of knowledge and of sorrow and endurance of things done,
But a noise is in the mountains, in the mountains, and I know
The voice that shook our palaces — four hundred years ago:

It is he that saith not 'Kismet': it is he that knows not Fate;
It is Richard, it is Raymond, it is Godfrey in the gate!
It is he whose loss is laughter when he counts the wager worth,
Put down your feet upon him, that our peace be on the earth.'
For he heard drums groaning and he heard guns jar,
(*Don John of Austria is going to the war.*)
Sudden and still — hurrah!
Bolt from Iberia!
Don John of Austria
Is gone by Alcalar.

St. Michael's on his Mountain in the sea-roads of the north
(*Don John of Austria is girt and going forth.*)
Where the grey seas glitter and the sharp tides shift
And the sea folk labour and the red sails lift.
He shakes his lance of iron and he claps his wings of stone;
The noise is gone through Normandy; the noise is gone alone;
The North is full of tangled things and texts and aching eyes
And dead is all the innocence of anger and surprise,
And Christian killeth Christian in a narrow dusty room,
And Christian dreadeth Christ that hath a newer face of doom,
And Christian hateth Mary that God kissed in Galilee,
But Don John of Austria is riding to the sea.
Don John calling through the blast and the eclipse,
Crying with the trumpet, with the trumpet of his lips,
Trumpet that sayeth ha!
        Domino Gloria!
Don John of Austria
Is shouting to the ships.

King Philip's in his closet with the Fleece about his neck,
(*Don John of Austria is armed upon the deck.*)

The walls are hung with velvet that is black and soft as sin,
And little dwarfs creep out of it and little dwarfs creep in.
He holds a crystal phial, that has colours like the moon,
He touches, and it tingles, and he trembles very soon,
And his face is as a fungus of a leprous white and grey
Like plants in the high houses that are shuttered from the day,
And death is in the phial, and the end of noble work,
But Don John of Austria has fired upon the Turk.
Don John's hunting, and his hounds have brayed —
Booms away past Italy the rumour of his raid.

Gun upon gun, ha! ha!
Gun upon gun, hurrah!
Don John of Austria
Has loosed the cannonade.

The Pope was in his chapel before day or battle broke,
(*Don John of Austria is hidden in the smoke.*)
The hidden room in a man's house where God sits all the year,
The secret window whence the world looks small and very dear.
He sees as in a mirror on the monstrous twilight sea
The crescent of his cruel ships whose name is mystery;
They fling great shadows foe-wards, making Cross and Castle dark,
They veil the plumèd lions on the galleys of St. Mark;
And above the ships are palaces of brown, black-bearded chiefs,
And below the ships are prisons, where with multitudinous griefs,
Christian captives sick and sunless, all a labouring race repines
Like a race in sunken cities, like a nation in the mines.
They are lost like slaves that swat, and in the skies of morning hung
The stairways of the tallest gods when tyranny was young.
They are countless, voiceless, hopeless as those fallen or fleeing on
Before the high Kings' horses in the granite of Babylon.
And many a one grows witless in his quiet room in hell
Where a yellow face looks inward through the lattice of his cell,
And he finds his God forgotten, and he seeks no more a sign —
(*But Don John of Austria has burst the battle-line!*)
Don John pounding from the slaughter-painted poop,
Purpling all the ocean like a bloody pirate's sloop,
Scarlet running over on the silvers and the golds,
Breaking of the hatches up and bursting of the holds,
Thronging of the thousands up that labour under sea,
White for bliss and blind for sun and stunned for liberty.
Viva Hispania!
Domino Gloria!
Don John of Austria
Has set his people free!

Cervantes on his galley sets the sword back in the sheath
(*Don John of Austria rides homeward with a wreath.*)
And he sees across a weary land a straggling road in Spain,
Up which a lean and foolish knight forever rides in vain,
And he smiles, but not as Sultans smile, and settles back the blade . . .
(*But Don John of Austria rides home from the Crusade.*)

G. K. Chesterton (1911)

1586 Battle of Zutphen

The battle of Zutphen was fought on 22 September 1586. The Spanish were commanded by the Duke of Parma and the British, who were besieging Zutphen, by the Earl of Leicester. The Spanish endeavoured to get supplies in Zutphen and beat back British assaults. The most celebrated casualty on the British side was Sir Philip Sidney.

Thus they go on, every man in the head of his own troop, and the weather being misty, they fell unawares upon the enemy, who had made a very strong stand to receive them, near to the very walls of Zutphen; by reason of which accident their troops fell not only unexpectedly to be engaged within the level of the great shot that played from the ramparts, but more fatally within shot of their muskets, which were laid within ambush within their own trenches . . . Howsoever by this stand, an unfortunate hand out of those fore-spoken trenches brake the bone of Sir Philip's thigh with a musket shot. The horse he rode upon was rather furiously choleric, than bravely proud, and so forced him to forsake the field, but not his back, as the noblest and fittest bier to carry a martial commander to his grave. In this sad progess, passing along by the rest of the army, where his uncle the General was, and being thirsty with excess of bleeding he called for drink, which was presently brought him; but as he was putting the bottle to his mouth, he saw a poor soldier carried along, who had eaten his last at the same feast, ghastly casting up his eyes at the bottle; which Sir Philip Sidney perceiving, took it from his head before he drank, and delivered it to the poor man with these words: 'Thy necessity is yet greater than mine!' And when he had pledged this poor soldier, he was presently carried to Arnhem . . .

The last scene of this tragedy, was the parting between these two brothers; the weaker showing infinite strength in suppressing sorrow and the stronger infinite weakness in expressing of it. So far did invaluable worthiness in the dying brother enforce the living to descend beneath his own worth, and by the soundance of childish tears, bewail the public, in his particular loss . . . And to stop his natural torrent of affection in both [Sir Philip] took his leave with these admonishing words: 'Love my memory; cherish my friends; their faith to me may assure you they are honest. But above all govern your will and affections by the will and word of your Creator; in me beholding the end of this world, with all her vanities.' And with this farewell desired the company to lead him away. Here this noble gentleman ended the too short scene of his life; in which path whosoever is not confident that he walked the next way to eternal rest, will be found to judge uncharitably . . . For my own part, I confess, in all I have here set down of his worth and goodness, I find myself still short of that honour he deserved, and I desired to do him.

Fulke Greville, *Life of Sir Philip Sidney* (1652)

1588 Defeat of the Spanish Armada

Philip II of Spain had planned to take his army to England under convoy of a huge Armada for several years. Drake had learned of this and undertook raids to harass the Spanish preparations. In April 1587 he sailed into Cadiz with twenty-three ships and destroyed over thirty Spanish vessels – this he called 'singeing the King of Spain's beard'.

The Spanish Armada – twenty great galleons, forty-four armed ships, twenty-three transports, four galleys and forty miscellaneous vessels, between them carrying 3,431 guns and 19,000 soldiers – was sighted off Lizard Head by English scout vessels on 20 July 1588.

The engagement lasted until the first days of August and was fought off the coasts of Devon, Dorset, Calais, and Flanders. The Spanish sailed up through the Bay of Biscay, round the English counties of the south east, up and round Scotland and down past Donegal, north-west Ireland and – what was left of them – sailed back to the continent. The Spanish suffered a crippling defeat, from terrible weather, merciless English gunnery, starvation and thirst. Of the 130 ships that started, nineteen were wrecked, sixty-three were lost, the English sank or captured fifteen, and thirty-three were unaccounted for.

This account is by Richard Hakluyt:

Upon the 29th of July in the morning, the Spanish fleet after the forsayd tumult, having arranged themselues againe into order, were, within sight of Greveling, most bravely and furiously encountered by the English; where they once again got the wind of the Spaniards; who suffered themselues to be deprived of the commodity of the place in Caleis road, and of the advantage of the wind neer unto Dunkerk, rather than they would change their array or separate their forces now conjoyned and united together, standing only upon their defence.

And howbeit there were many excellent and warlike ships in the English fleet, yet scarce were there 22 or 23 among them all, which matched 90 of the Spanish ships in the bigness, or could conveniently assault them. Wherefore the English ships using their prerogative of nimble steerage, whereby they could turn and wield themselves with the wind which way they listed, came often times very near upon the Spaniards, and charged them so sore, that now and then they were but a pike's length asunder: and so continually giving them one broadside after another, they discharged all their shot both great and small upon them, spending one whole day from morning till night in that violent kind of conflict, until such time as powder and bullets failed them. In regard of which want they thought it convenient not to pursue the Spaniards any longer, because they had many great vantages of the English, namely, for the extraordinary bigness of their ships, and also for that they were so neerly conjoyned, and kept together in so good array, that they could by no meanes be fought withall one to one. The English thought, therefore, that they had right well acquitted themselues, in chasing the Spaniards first from Caleis, and then from Dunkerk, and by that meanes to have hindered them from joyning with the Duke of Parma his forces, and getting the wind of them, to have driven them from their own coasts.

The Spaniards that day sustained great loss and damage, having many of their shippes shot thorow and thorow, and they discharged likewise great store of ordinance against the English; who, indeed, sustained some hindrance, but not comparable to the Spaniard's loss: for they lost not any one ship or person of account, for very diligent inquisition being made, the English men all that time wherein the Spanish navy sayled upon their seas, are not found to haue wanted aboue one hundred of their people: albeit Sir Francis Drake's ship was pierced with shot aboue forty times, and his very cabben was twice shot thorow, and about the conclusion of the fight, the bed of a certaine gentleman lying weary thereupon, was taken quite from under him with the force of a bullet. Likewise, as the Earle of Northumberland and Sir Charles Blunt were at dinner upon a time, the bullet of a demy-culverin brake thorow the middest of their cabben, touched their feet, and strooke downe two of the standers by, with many such accidents befalling the English shippes, which it were tedious to rehearse.

Richard Hakluyt, *Principall Navigations, Voyages and Discoveries of the English Nation* (1600)

The very vastness, heavy construction and armament of many of the Spanish vessels contributed to their undoing:

Being always to leeward and the wind blowing hard, the hulls of the galleons as they heeled over were exposed below the water line. The massive timbers which were to have furnished so secure a shelter added only to the effect of the shot. The middle decks were turned into slaughter houses, and in one ship blood was seen streaming from the lee scuppers. Their guns were most of them dismounted or knocked in pieces, and their chief work was to save themselves from sinking by nailing sheets of lead over the shot-holes. The action was on so large a scale, and there was so much smoke and confusion, that individuals could only see what was immediately near them.

Don Pedro Coco Caldèron, purser of the fleet, lay most of the day at the side of Medina Sidonia, himself exposed to the tempest of balls. Alonso da Leyva with the Rata was next to him, and close by were the San Matteo and the San Felipe, commanded by Don Diego de Pimentel and Don Francesco de Toledo. They were opposed to Drake in person and frightful as was their disadvantage, they fought with conspicuous courage. With men falling in all directions, and heads and arms flying in the smoke, they still manned their maintops, keeping up a fire of musket balls. Don Francesco finding . . . that the San Felipe was sinking, attempted to grapple with the English ship that was nearest to him. He had fought so well, that one of the English officers seeing his apparently desperate condition, sprung upon his forecastle and called to him in Spanish complimenting his valour, and bidding him save the lives of his brave crew by an honourable surrender. One of the Spaniards replied with a shot from a musket. The officer fell: the English ship filled her sails and backed away, leaving the San Felipe to her fate . . .

James Anthony Froude, *History of England from the Fall of Wolsey to the Defeat of the Spanish Armada* (1870)

1591 Loss of the Revenge

In July 1591 Hawkyns and Frobisher were sent to intercept a Spanish fleet off the Azores. On 19 August fifteen Spanish warships drove seven English ships to Flores. During this engagement the gallant fight – which lasted fifteen hours – was made by the *Revenge* under Sir Richard Grenville. His ship, badly crippled, was surrounded and Grenville was eventually mortally wounded before they surrendered at daybreak.

THE *REVENGE*

A BALLAD OF THE FLEET

I

At Flores in the Azores Sir Richard Grenville lay,
And a pinnace, like a fluttered bird, came flying from far away:

'Spanish ships of war at sea! we have sighted fifty-three!'
Then sware Lord Thomas Howard: ''Fore God I am no coward;
But I cannot meet them here, for my ships are out of gear,
And the half my men are sick. I must fly, but follow quick.
We are six ships of the line; can we fight with fifty-three?'

II

Then spake Sir Richard Grenville: 'I know you are no coward;
You fly them for a moment to fight with them again.
But I've ninety men and more that are lying sick ashore.
I should count myself the coward if I left them, my Lord Howard,
To these Inquisition dogs and the devildoms of Spain.'

III

So Lord Howard past away with five ships of war that day,
Till he melted like a cloud in the silent summer heaven;
But Sir Richard bore in hand all his sick men from the land
Very carefully and slow,
Men of Bideford in Devon,
And we laid them on the ballast down below;
For we brought them all aboard,
And they blest him in their pain, that they were not left to Spain,
To the thumbscrew and the stake, for the glory of the Lord.

IV

He had only a hundred seamen to work the ship and to fight,
And he sailed away from Flores till the Spaniard came in sight,
With his huge sea-castles heaving upon the weather bow.
'Shall we fight or shall we fly?
Good Sir Richard, tell us now,
For to fight is but to die!
There'll be little of us left by the time this sun be set.'
And Sir Richard said again: 'We be all good English men.
Let us bang these dogs of Seville, the children of the devil,
For I never turned my back upon Don or devil yet.'

V

Sir Richard spoke and he laughed, and we roared a hurrah, and so
The little *Revenge* ran on sheer into the heart of the foe,
With her hundred fighters on deck, and her ninety sick below;
For half of their fleet to the right and half to the left were seen,
And the little *Revenge* ran on through the long sea-lane between.

VI

Thousands of their soldiers looked down from their decks and laughed,
Thousands of their seamen made mock at the mad little craft
Running on and on, till delayed
By their mountain-like San Philip that, of fifteen hundred tons,
And up-shadowing high above us with her yawning tiers of guns,
Took the breath from our sails, and we stayed.

VII

And while now the great San Philip hung above us like a cloud
Whence the thunderbolt will fall
Long and loud,
Four galleons drew away
From the Spanish fleet that day,
And two upon the larboard and two upon the starboard lay,
And the battle-thunder broke from them all.

VIII

But anon the great San Philip, she bethought herself and went
Having that within her womb that had left her ill content;
And the rest they came aboard us, and they fought us hand to hand,
For a dozen times they came with their pikes and musqueteers,
And a dozen times we shook 'em off as a dog that shakes his ears
When he leaps from the water to the land.

IX

And the sun went down, and the stars came out far over the summer
    sea,
But never a moment ceased the fight of the one and the fifty-three.
Ship after ship, the whole night long, their high-built galleons came,
Ship after ship, the whole night long, with her battle-thunder and flame;
Ship after ship, the whole night long, drew back with her dead and her
    shame.
For some were sunk and many were shattered, and so could fight us
    no more —
God of battles, was ever a battle like this in the world before?

X

For he said 'Fight on! fight on!'
Though his vessel was all but a wreck;
And it chanced that, when half of the short summer night was gone,
With a grisly wound to be dressed he had left the deck,
But a bullet struck him that was dressing it suddenly dead,
And himself he was wounded again in the side and the head,
And he said 'Fight on! fight on!'

XI

And the night went down, and the sun smiled out far over the summer
    sea,
And the Spanish fleet with broken sides lay round us all in a ring;
But they dared not touch us again, for they feared that we still could
    sting,
So they watched what the end would be.
And we had not fought them in vain,
But in perilous plight were we,
Seeing forty of our poor hundred were slain,
And half of the rest of us maimed for life
In the crash of the cannonades and the desperate strife;
And the sick men down in the hold were most of them stark and cold,
And the pikes were all broken or bent, and the powder was all of it
    spent;
And the masts and the rigging were lying over the side;
But Sir Richard cried in his English pride,
'We have fought such a fight for a day and a night
As may never be fought again!
We have won great glory, my men!
And a day less or more
At sea or ashore,
We die — does it matter when?
Sink me the ship, Master Gunner — sink her, split her in twain!
Fall into the hands of God, not into the hands of Spain!'

XII

And the gunner said 'Ay, ay,' but the seamen made reply:
'We have children, we have wives,
And the Lord hath spared our lives.
We will make the Spaniard promise, if we yield, to let us go;
We shall live to fight again and to strike another blow.'
And the lion there lay dying, and they yielded to the foe.

XIII

And the stately Spanish men to their flagship bore him then,
Where they laid him by the mast, old Sir Richard caught at last,
And they praised him to his face with their courtly foreign grace;
But he rose upon their decks, and he cried:
'I have fought for Queen and Faith like a valiant man and true;
I have only done my duty as a man is bound to do:
With a joyful spirit I Sir Richard Grenville die!'
And he fell upon their decks, and he died.

XIV

And they stared at the dead that had been so valiant and true,
And had holden the power and glory of Spain so cheap
That he dared her with one little ship and his English few;
Was he devil or man? He was devil for aught they knew,
But they sank his body with honour down into the deep,
And they manned the *Revenge* with a swarthier alien crew,
And away she sailed with her loss and longed for her own;
When a wind from the lands they had ruined awoke from sleep,
And the water began to heave and the weather to moan,
And or ever that evening ended a great gale blew,
And a wave like the wave that is raised by an earthquake grew,
Till it smote on their hulls and their sails and their masts and their
    flags,
And the whole sea plunged and fell on the shot-shattered navy of
    Spain,
And the little *Revenge* herself went down by the island crags
To be lost evermore in the main.

Alfred, Lord Tennyson

1596 *The Sack of Cadiz*

Lord Howard of Effingham and the Earl of Essex led an expedition to
sack the Spanish port of Cadiz, ravaging the coast and bringing back
considerable booty. King Philip II was thus prevented from sending an
Armada against England.

Sir Walter Raleigh took part in this brilliantly executed expedition
and has left this account in a letter:

. . . the charge for the performance . . . was upon my humble suit
granted and assigned unto me.

The Lord Thomas Howard – because the *Meere-Honour*, which he
commanded, was one of the greatest ships – was also left behind with
the Generals to have the service committed unto him, and left the
Meere-Honour to Mr. Dudley, putting himself into the *Nonpareill*, for
mine own part, as I was willing to give honour to my Lord Thomas,
having both precedency in the army, and being a nobleman whom I
much honoured, so yet I was resolved to give and not take example
for his service, holding mine own reputation dearest, and remembering my great duty to Her Majesty. With the first peep of day,
therefore, I weighed anchor, and bare with the Spanish fleet, taking
the start of all ours a good distance . . .

Having, as aforesaid, taken the leading, I was first saluted by the fort called *Philip*, afterwards by the ordnance on the curtain, and lastly by all the galleys, in good order. To show scorn to all which, I only answered first the fort, and thereafter the galleys, to each piece a burr with a trumpet: disdaining to shoot one piece at any one or all of those esteemed dreadful monsters. The ships that followed beat upon the galleys so thick that they soon betook them to their oars, and got up to join with the galleons in the strait, as aforesaid; and then, as they were driven to come near me, and enforced to range their sides towards me, I bestowed a benediction amongst them.

But the *St Philip*, the great and famous Admiral of Spain, was the mark I shot at; esteeming those galleys but as wasps in respect of the powerfulness of the other; and being resolved to be avenged for the *Revenge*, or to second her with mine own life, I came to anchor by the galleons; of which the *Philip* and *Andrew* were two that boarded the *Revenge*. I was formerly commanded not to board, but was promised fly-boats, in which, after I had battered a while, I resolved to join unto them.

My Lord Thomas came to anchor by me, on the one hand, with the *Lyon*; the *Mary Rose*, on the other, with the *Dreadnaught*; the Marshall [Sir Francis Vere] towards the side of Puntall; and towards ten of the clock, my Lord General Essex, being impatient to abide far off, hearing so great athunder of ordnance, thrust up through the fleet, and headed all those on the left hand, coming to anchor next unto me on that side; and afterward came in the *Swiftsure*, as near as she could. Always I must, without glory, say for myself, that I held single in the head of all.

Now, after we had beat, as two butts, one upon another almost three hours (assuring your Honour that the volleys of cannon and culverin came as thick as if it had been a skirmish of musketeers), and finding myself in danger to be sunk in the place, I went to my Lord General in my skiff, to desire him that he would enforce the promised fly-boats to come up, that I might board; for as I rid, I could not endure so great battery any long time. My Lord General was then coming up himself; to whom I declared that if the fly-boats came not, I would board with the Queen's ship, for it was the same loss to burn, or sink, for I must endure the one. The Earl finding that it was not in his power to command fear, told me that, whatsoever I did, he would second me in person, upon his honour. My Lord Admiral, having also a disposition to come up at first, but the river was so choked as he could not pass with the *Ark*, came up in person into the *Nonpareill*, with my Lord Thomas.

While I was thus speaking with the Earl, the Marshall who thought it some touch to his great esteemed valour to ride behind me so many hours, got up ahead my ship; which my Lord Thomas perceiving headed him again; – myself being but a quarter of an hour absent. At my return, finding myself from being the first to being but the third, I presently let slip anchor, and thrust in between my Lord Thomas and the Marshall, and went up further ahead than all them before, and thrust my self athwart the channel; so as I was sure none should outstart me again, for that day. My Lord General Essex, thinking his ship's side stronger than the rest thrust the *Dreadnaught* aside, and came next the *Warspight* on the left hand; ahead all that rank, but my Lord Thomas. The Marshall, while we had no leisure to look behind us, secretly fastened a rope on my ship's side towards him, to draw himself up equally with me; but some of my company advertising me thereof, I caused it to be cut off, and so he fell back into his place, whom I guarded, all but his very prow, from the sight of the enemy.

Now, if it please you to remember, that having no hope of my fly-boats to board, and that the Earl and my Lord Thomas both promised to second me, I laid out a warp by the side of the *Philip* to shake hands with her (for with the wind we could not get aboard): which when she and the rest perceived, finding also that the *Repulse* (seeing mine) began to do the like, and the Rear-Admiral my Lord Thomas, they all let slip, and ran aground, tumbling into the sea heaps of soldiers, so thick as if coals had been poured out of a sack in many ports at once; some drowned and some sticking in the mud. The *Philip* and the *St Thomas* burnt themselves: the *St Matthew* and the *St Andrew* were recovered with our boats ere they could get out to fire them. The spectacle was very lamentable on their side, for many drowned themselves; many, half burnt, leapt into the water; very many hanging by the ropes' ends by the ships' side, under the water even to the lips; many swimming with grievous wounds, strucken under water, and put out of their pain: and withal so huge a fire, and such tearing of the ordnance in the great *Philip*, and the rest, when the fire came to them, as, if any man had a desire to see Hell itself, it was there most lively figured. Ourselves spared the lives of all, after the victory; but the Flemings, who did little or nothing in the fight, used merciless slaughter, till they were by myself, and afterwards by my Lord Admiral, beaten off . . . this being happily finished, we prepared to land the army . . .

The town . . . was very rich in merchandize, in plate, and money; many rich prisoners given to the land commanders; so as that sort are very rich. Some had prisoners for sixteen thousand ducats; some for twenty thousand; some for ten thousand; and besides, great houses of merchandize. What the Generals have gotten, I know least; they protest it is little. For my part, I have gotten a lame leg, and a deformed.

Sir Walter Raleigh, Letter to an unknown friend (June 1596), quoted in Edward
Edwards, The Life of Sir Walter Raleigh, Together with his Letters (1868)

1618–1648 Thirty Years War

Der Abenteurliche Simplicissimus Teutsch, one of the most impressive works about war, was written by Johann Jakob Christoffel von Grimmelshausen (1622–1676) who was abducted by Hessian soldiers in 1635 when he was a boy, and served in various regiments during the Thirty Years War.

These experiences obviously serve as the basis for many of the adventures of the hero of his fiction, which eventually appeared as six volumes. The use of a simple, well-meaning but rather innocent and blundering person portrayed in collision with the harsh and cruel realities of the world is echoed in Hasek's Great War satire, *The Good Soldier Švejk*. In this excerpt, Grimmelshausen comments on the familiar theme of social rank and military promotion:

So must the roots of these trees suffer and endure toil and misery in the midst of trouble and complaint, and those upon the lower boughs in yet greater hardship: yet were these last mostly merrier than the first named, yea and moreover, insolent and swaggering, and for the most part godless folk, and for the roots a heavy unbearable burden at all times. And this was the rhyme upon them:

  'Hunger and thirst, and cold and heat, and work and woe, and all we meet;

  And deeds of blood and deeds of shame, all may ye put to the landsknecht's name.'

Which rhymes were the less like to be lyingly invented in that they answered to the facts. For gluttony and drunkenness, hunger and thirst, wenching and dicing and playing, riot and roaring, murdering and being murdered, slaying and being slain, torturing and being tortured, hunting and being hunted, harrying and being harried, robbing and being robbed, frighting and being frighted, causing trouble and suffering trouble, beating and being beaten: in a word, hurting and harming, and in turn being hurt and harmed – this was their whole life. And in this career they let nothing hinder them:

92

neither winter nor summer, snow nor ice, heat nor cold, rain nor wind, hill nor dale, wet nor dry; ditches, mountain-passes, ramparts and walls, fire and water, were all the same to them. Father nor mother, sister nor brother, no, nor the danger to their own bodies, souls, and consciences, nor even loss of life and of heaven itself, or aught else that can be named, will ever stand in their way, for ever they toil and moil at their own strange work, till at last, little by little, in battles, sieges, attacks, campaigns, yea, and in their winter quarters too (which are the soldiers' earthly paradise, if they can but happen upon fat peasants) they perish, they die, they rot and consume away, save but a few, who in their old age, unless they have been right thrifty reivers and robbers, do furnish us with the best of all beggars and vagabonds.

Next above these hard-worked folk sat old henroost-robbers, who, after some years and much peril of their lives, had climbed up the lowest branches and clung to them, and so far had had the luck to escape death. Now these looked more serious, and somewhat more dignified than the lowest, in that they were a degree higher ascended: yet above them were some yet higher, who had yet loftier imaginings because they had to command the very lowest. And these people did call coat-beaters, because they were wont to dust the jackets of the poor pikemen, and to give the musqueteers oil enough to grease their barrels with.

Just above these the trunk of the tree had an interval or stop, which was a smooth place without branches, greased with all manner of ointments and curious soap of disfavour, so that no man save of noble birth could scale it, in spite of courage and skill and knowledge, God knows how clever he might be. For 'twas polished as smooth as a marble pillar or a steel mirror. Just over that smooth spot sat they with the flags: and of these some were young, some pretty well in years: the young folk their kinsmen had raised so far: the older people had either mounted on a silver ladder which is called the Bribery Backstairs or else on a step which Fortune, for want of a better client, had left for them. A little further up sat higher folk, and these had also their toil and care and annoyance: yet had they this advantage, that they could fill their pokes with the fattest slices which they could cut out of the roots, and that with a knife which they called 'War-contribution'. And these were at their best and happiest when there came a commissary-bird flying overhead, and shook out a whole panfull of gold over the tree to cheer them: for of that they caught as much as they could, and let but little or nothing at all fall to the lowest branches: and so of these last more died of hunger than of the enemy's attacks, from which danger those placed above seemed to be free.

Therefore was there a perpetual climbing and swarming going on on those trees; for each would needs sit in those highest and happiest places: yet were there some idle, worthless rascals, not worth their commissariat-bread, who troubled themselves little about higher places, and only did their duty. So the lowest, being ambitious, hoped for the fall of the highest, that they might sit in their place, and if it happened to one among ten thousand of them that he got so far, yet would such good luck come to him only in his miserable old age when he was more fit to sit in the chimney-corner and roast apples than to meet the foe in the field. And if any man dealt honestly and carried himself well, yet was he ever envied by others, and perchance by reason of some unlucky chance of war deprived both of office and of life. And nowhere was this more grievous than at the before-mentioned smooth place on the tree: for there an officer who had had a good sergeant or corporal under him must lose him, however unwillingly, because he was now made an ensign. And for that reason they would take, in place of old soldiers, ink-slingers, footmen, overgrown pages, poor noblemen, and at times poor relations, tramps and vagabonds. And these took the very bread out of the mouths of those that had deserved it, and forthwith were made Ensigns.

Johann Jakob von Grimmelshausen, *Der Abenteurliche Simplicissimus Teutsch* (1688), translated by A. T. S. Goodrick (1924)

Mother Courage

Bertolt Brecht wrote *Mutter Courage und ihre Kinder* in 1938–9. It was first produced in Zürich in 1941.

The twelve scenes of the play cover twelve years (1624–36) of the Thirty Years War in various locations – Sweden, Poland, Germany – and depict Mother Courage's ability to strive and survive. She follows the Protestant forces wherever they go with her supply-wagon, which is her family home. All three of her children (by different fathers) die during the course of the play. At the end of the play she is still pulling her wagon, determined to go on.

Brecht's theme is the horror of war, especially as experienced by society's victims – the ordinary people of the world – and the terrible order which war temporarily brings to what is otherwise the social chaos of class war.

Spring 1624. In Dararna, the Swedish Commander Oxenstrierna is recruiting for the campaign in Poland. The canteen woman Anna Fierling, commonly known as Mother Courage, loses a son.

94

Highway Outside a Town
A Sergeant and a Recruiting Officer stand shivering.

THE RECRUITING OFFICER   How the hell can you line up a company in a place like this? You know what I keep thinking about, Sergeant? Suicide. I'm supposed to knock four platoons together by the twelfth — four platoons the Chief's asking for! And they're so friendly round here, I'm scared to go to sleep at night. Suppose I do get my hand on some character and squint at him so I don't notice he's pigeon-chested and has varicose veins. I get him drunk and relaxed, he signs on the dotted line. I pay for the drinks, he steps outside for a minute. I have a hunch I should follow him to the door, and am I right? Away he's gone like a louse from a scratch. You can't take a man's word any more, Sergeant. There's no loyalty left in the world, no trust, no faith, no sense of honour. I'm losing my confidence in mankind, Sergeant.

THE SERGEANT   What they could do with round here is a good war. What else can you expect with peace running wild all over the place? You know what the trouble with peace is? No organisation. And when do you get organisation? In a war. Peace is one big waste of equipment. Anything goes, no one gives a damn. See the way they eat? Cheese on pumpernickel, bacon on the cheese? Disgusting! How many horses have they got in this town? How many young men? Nobody knows! They haven't bothered to count 'em! That's peace for you! I've been in places where they haven't had a war for seventy years and you know what? The people haven't even been given names! They don't know who they are! It takes a war to fix that. In a war, everybody registers, everyone's name's on a list. Their shoes are stacked, their corn's in the bag, you count it all up — cattle, men, *Et cetera* — and you take it away! That's the story: no organisation, no war!

THE RECRUITING OFFICER   In God's truth, you know!

THE SERGEANT   Of course, a war's like any good deal: hard to get going. But when it does get moving, it's a real winner, and they're all scared of peace, like a dice-player who daren't stop — 'cause when peace comes they have to pay up. Of course, *until* it gets going, they're just as scared of war, it's such a novelty!

THE RECRUITING OFFICER   Hey, look, here's a canteen wagon. Two women and a couple of young lads. Stop the old lady, Sergeant. And if there's nothing doing this time, you won't catch me freezing my arse in the April wind a minute longer.

A harmonica is heard. A canteen wagon rolls on, drawn by two young fellows. Mother Courage is sitting on it with her dumb daughter, Kattrin.

MOTHER COURAGE   A good day to you, Sergeant!

THE SERGEANT (*barring the way*)   Good day to *you*! Who d'you think *you* are?

MOTHER COURAGE   Trade people.

She sings:

Here's Mother Courage and her wagon!
Hey, Captain, let them come and buy!
Beer by the keg! Wine by the flagon!
Let your men drink before they die!
Sabres and swords are hard to swallow:
First you must give them beer to drink.
Then they can face what is to follow –
But let 'em swim before they sink!
    Christians awake! The winter's gone!
    The snow's depart, the dead sleep on.
    And though you may not long survive
    Get out of bed and look alive!
Your men will march till they are dead, sir.
But cannot fight unless they eat.
The blood they spill for you is red, sir.
What fires that blood is my red meat.
For meat and soup and jam and jelly
In this old cart of mine are found:
So fill the hole up in your belly
Before you fill one underground.
    Christians, awake! the winter's gone!
    The snows depart, the dead sleep on.
    And though you may not long survive
    Get out of bed and look alive!

THE SERGEANT   Halt! where are you from, riff-raff?

EILIF   Second Finnish regiment!

THE SERGEANT   Where are your papers?

MOTHER COURAGE   Papers?

SWISS CHEESE   But this is Mother Courage!

THE SERGEANT   Never heard of her. Where'd she get a name like that?

MOTHER COURAGE   They call me Mother Courage 'cause I was afraid I'd be ruined. So I drove through the bombardment of Riga like a madwoman, with fifty loaves of bread in my cart. They were going mouldy, I couldn't please myself.

THE SERGEANT   No funny business! Where are your papers?

MOTHER COURAGE   (*rummages among papers in a tin box and clambers down from her wagon*)   Here, Sergeant! Here's a Bible – I got it in

Altoetting to wrap my cucumbers in. Here's a map of Moravia — God knows if I'll ever get there — the birds can have it if I don't. And here's a document saying my horse hasn't got foot and mouth disease — pity he died on us, he cost fifteen gilders, thank God I didn't pay it. Is that enough paper?

THE SERGEANT   Are you pulling my leg? Well, you've got another guess coming. You need a licence and you know it.

MOTHER COURAGE   Show a little respect for a lady and don't go telling these grown-up children of mine I'm pulling anything of yours. What would I want with you? My licence in the Second Protestant Regiment is an honest face. If *you* wouldn't know how to read it, that's not my fault, I want no rubber stamp on it anyhow.

THE RECRUITING OFFICER   Sergeant, we have a case of insubordination on our hands. You know what we need in the army? Discipline!

MOTHER COURAGE   I was going to say sausages.

Bertolt Brecht, *Mother Courage and her children — A Chronicle of the Thirty Years War*, translated by Eric Bentley (1962).

Wallenstein

The commander of the Austrian armies during the Thirty Years War, Albrecht Eusebius Wenzel von Wallenstein, Herzog von Friedland und Mecklenberg (1583–1634), was the subject of the dramatic trilogy *Wallenstein* (1797–1799) by Schiller. Wallenstein was seen as a danger to his allies during the dynastic struggles which surfaced during the war. He considered deserting to the Protestant cause but was assassinated in a conspiracy among his officer corps, led by Octavio, Duke of Amalfi. Schiller increases the pathos of the drama by developing a Romeo and Juliet love relationship between the Duke's son, Max, and Thekla, Wallenstein's daughter. In this scene Max and Octavio talk of war and peace:

OCTAVIO   My son, the nursling of the camp spoke in thee!
A war of fifteen years
Hath been thy education and thy school.
Peace hast thou never witness'd! There exists
An higher than a warrior's excellence.
In war itself is no ultimate purpose.
The vast and sudden deeds of violence,
Adventures wild, and wonders of the moment,

These are not they, my son, that generate
The Calm, the Blissful, and the enduring Mighty!
Lo there! the soldier, rapid architect!
Builds his light town of canvas, and at once
The whole scene moves and bustles momently,
With arms, and neighing steeds, and mirth and quarrel
The motley market fills; the roads, the streams
Are crowded with new freights; trade stirs and hurries!
But on some morrow morn, all suddenly,
The tents drop down, the horde renews its march.
Dreary, and solitary as a church-yard
The meadow and down-trodden seed-plot lie,
And the year's harvest is gone utterly.
MAX   O let the Emperor make peace, my father!
Most gladly would I give the blood-stained laurel
For the first violet of the leafless spring,
Pluck'd in those quiet fields where I have journey'd!
OCTAVIO   What ails thee? What so moves thee all at once?
MAX   Peace have I ne'er beheld? I *have* beheld it.
From thence am I come hither: O! that sight,
It glimmers still before me, like some landscape
Left in the distance, – some delicious landscape!
My road conducted me through countries where
The war has not yet reach'd. Life, life, my father –
My venerable father, life has charms
Which *we* have ne'er experienced. We have seen
But voyaging along its barren coasts,
Like some poor ever-roaming horde of pirates,
That, crowded in the rank and narrow ship,
House on the wild sea with wild usages,
Now know aught of the mainland, but the bays
Half where safeliest they may venture a thieves' landing.
Whate'er in the inland dales the land conceals
Of fair and exquisite, O! nothing, nothing
Do we behold of that in our rude voyage.
OCTAVIO   And so your journey has revealed this to you?
MAX   'Twas the first leisure of my life. O tell me,
What is the need and purpose of the toil
The painful toil which robbed me of my youth,
Left me a heart unsoul'd and solitary,
A spirit uninform'd, unornamented!
For the camp's stir, and crowd, and ceaseless larum,

The neighing war-horse, the air-shattering trumpet,
The unvaried, still returning hour of duty,
Word of command, and exercise of arms —
There's nothing here, there's nothing in all this,
To satisfy the heart, the gasping heart!
Mere bustling nothingness, where the soul is not —
This cannot be the sole felicity,
These cannot be man's best and only pleasures!
OCTAVIO   Much hast thou learnt, my son, in this short journey.
MAX   O! day thrice lovely! when at length the soldier
Returns home into life; when he becomes
A fellow-man among his fellow-men.
The colours are unfurl'd, the cavalcade
Marshals, and now the buzz is hush'd, and hark!
Now the soft peace-march beats, home, brothers, home!
The caps and helmets are all garlanded
With green boughs, the last plundering of the fields.
The city gates fly open of themselves,
They need no longer the petard to tear them.
The ramparts are all filled with men and women,
With peaceful men and women, that send onwards
Kisses and welcomings upon the air,
Which they make breezy with affectionate gestures . . .

Schiller, *The Piccolomini*, Act I, Scene iv, translated by Samuel Taylor
Coleridge (1800)

V

COMMONWEALTH AND RESTORATION

1642–1649 English Civil War

Quarrels between Charles I and Parliament led to the English Civil Wars. Oliver Cromwell's commanding successes at Marston Moor and Naseby led to the King's surrender in 1645. Charles then escaped to the Isle of Wight and war recommenced, lasting until 1647. Charles I was finally tried and executed in 1649, and Britain was ruled as a republic until 1660.

1642 Battle of Edge Hill

Fought on 24 October 1642, Edge Hill was the first pitched engagement of the Civil War. The Royalist army was commanded by Charles I himself, the Parliamentarian forces by the Earl of Essex. The outcome was inconclusive, but was probably to the advantage of the Royalists.

This eye-witness account – from a Royalist point of view – is from a letter by Sir Edward Sydenham to Ralph Verney:

27 October 1642. For all our great victory I have had the greatest loss by the death of your noble father that any friend did, which next to my wife and master was the greatest misfortune that by death could have fallen to me. He himself killed two with his own hands, whereof one of them had killed poor Jason, and broke the point of his standard at push of pike before he fell, which was the last account I could receive of any of our own side of him. The next day the king sent a herald to offer mercy to all that would lay down arms, and to enquire for my Lord of Linsey, my Lord Willoughby and him. He brought word that my Lord Linsey was hurt, your father dead, and my Lord Willoughby only prisoner. He would neither put on arms or buff coat the day of battle, the reason I know not. The battle was bloody on your side, for your horses ran away at the first charge, and our men

had the execution of them for three miles; it began at three a clock and ended at six. The king is a man of the least fear and the greatest mercy and resolution that ever I saw, and had not been in the field, we might have suffered. My Lord of Essex is retired in great disorder to Warwick, for the next morning he suffered his cannon to be taken away within musket shot of his army, and never offered to hinder them; it is said there was killed and run away since eight thousand of his army. This day the king took in bamberie our army daily increases. God in mercy send us peace, and although your loss be as great as a son can lose in a father, yet God's children must bear with patience what affliction soever he shall please to lay upon them.

As the fortunes of the Civil War turned this way and then that way, the social and economic life of the nation was subject to severe disruption. Those who enjoyed plenty and luxury found themselves in desperate straits. Lady Anne Fanshawe (*née* Harrison), wife of the Royalist diplomat Sir Richard Fanshawe (who was taken prisoner at the Battle of Worcester), recorded:

We that had till that hour lived in great plenty and great order, found ourselves like fishes out of the water, and the scene so changed that we knew not at all how to act any part but obedience, for from as good a house as any gentleman in England had, we came to a baker's house in an obscure street, and from rooms well furnished, to be in a very bad bed in a garret, to one dish of meat, and that not the best ordered, no money, for we were as poor as Job, nor clothes more than a man or two brought in their cloak bags: we had the perpetual discourse of losing or gaining towns and men; at the windows the sad spectacle of war, sometimes plague, sometimes sickness of other kinds, by reason of so many people being packed together, as I believe, there never was before of that quality; always in want, yet I must needs say that most bore it with a martyr-like cheerfulness. For my own part, I began to think we should all, like Abraham, live in tents all the days of our lives.

Memoirs of Lady Anne Fanshawe (1676)

1642 Parliamentary Army in Warwickshire

This letter was written by Nehemiah Wharton, a subaltern in the Parliamentary Army commanded by Robert Devereux, third Earl of Essex. Wharton is writing to his former employer, George Willingham, a merchant in Coventry:

Coventry,
Aug. 26, 1642.

Worthy Sir,

August 17, our companies, after they had taken sixe delinquents and sent them to London, returned to Alesbury this day; we retained two feild pieces and two troopes of horse, with other necessaries for warre. Wensday morning, a Warwickshire minister, which the Calualleres[1] had pillaged to the skin, gave us a sermon. After noone our regiment marched into the field and skirmished. Thursday morning another sermon was given us. After noone our regiment marched into the feild, but by reason of foule weather were immediately definished.[2] This night our regiment was commanded to march the next morninge by four of the clock under our Lieftenant Colonell, but our sargeants refused to surrender their halberts, and the souldiers their armes, and not to march.[3] Friday, very early in the morninge, our Lieftenant Colonell was cashiered, for which I give you hearty thanks, and Sergeant-Major[4] Quarles imployed in his roome, whereat both commaunders, officers, and souldiers exceedingly rejoysed. This morninge wee cherfully marched towards Buckingham in the rear of Colonell Chomley's regiment, by reason whereof we could get no quarter there, but were constrained to quarter ourselves about the countrey, whereupon I and three gentlemen of my company visited that thrice noble gentleman Sr Richard Inglisby, where his owne table was our quarter, and Sergeant-Major Burrif, and his sonne Captaine Inglisby, and several other noble gentlemen were our comrades.

Saturday, early in the morning, I departed hence and gathered a compliete file of my owne men about the countrey, and marched to Sir Alexander Denton's parke, who is a malignant fellow, and killed a fat buck, fastened his head upon my halbert, and commanded two of my pickes[5] to bring the body after me to Buckingham, with a guard of musquetteers comminge theither. With part of it I feasted my captaine, Captaine Parker, Captaine Beacon, and Colonell Hamden's sonne, and with the rest severall leiftenants, enseignes, and serjeants, and had much thankes for my paines. This day Sergeant Major our Generall came unto us, and declared the commaund given him over our regiments. Sunday morninge wee marched from Buckingham into Northamptonshire, a longe and tedious jorney, wantinge both bread and water, and about ten at night came unto Byfeild in dispight of our enemies, at which towne we could get no quarter, neither meate, drinke, nor lodginge, and had we not bin suplyed with ten cart loade of provision and beare from Banbury, many of us had perished. This

103

night our company was commanded to guard the towne all night, whiche after a longe and tedious marche, was very grevious unto me. Monday morninge wee marched into Warwick-shere with about three thousand foote and four hundred horse, until we came to Southam. In the way we tooke two Calvalleres spies. This is a very malignant towne, both minister and people. We pillaged the minister, and tooke from him a drum and severall armes. This night our soildiers, wearied out, quartered themselves about the towne for foode and lodginge, but before we could eat or drinke an alarum cryed 'arme, arme, for the enemy is commenge,' and in halfe an hower all our soildiers, though dispersed, were cannybals in armes, ready to encounter enemy, cryinge out for a dish of Calvellaers to supper. Our horse were quartered about the countrey, but the enemy came not, whereupon our soildiers cryed out to have a breakefast of Cauallers. We barecaded the towne, and at every passage placed our ordinance and watched it all night, our soildiers contented to lye upon hard stones. In the morning early our enemise, consisting of about eight hundred horse and three hundred foote, with ordinance, led by the Earl of Northampton, the Lord of Carnarvan, and the Lord Compton and Captn Legge, and other, intended to set upon us before we could gather our companies together, but beinge ready all night, early in the morninge wee went to meet them with a few troopes of horse and sixe feild pieces, and beinge on fier to be at them wee marched thorow the coarn and got the hill of them, wherupon they played upon us with their ordinances, but they came short. Our gunner tooke theire owne bullet, sent it to them againe, and killed a horse and a man. After we gave them eight shot more, whereupon all their foote companies fled and offered their armes in the townes adjacent for twelve pence a peece.

Ther troopse, whelinge about, toke up their dead bodies and fled; but the horse they left behind, some of them having ther guts beaten out on both sides. One drummer, being dead at the bottom of the hill, our knapsack boyes rifled to the shirt, which was very louzy. Another drummer wee found two miles of, with his arme shot of, and lay a dieinge. Severall dead corps wee found in corne feilds, and amongst them a trumpeter, whose trumpet our horsemen sounded into Coventry. Wee tooke severall prisoners, and amongst them Capt. Legge and Captaine Clarke. From thence wee marched valiantly after them toward Coventry, and at Dunsmore Heath they threatned to give us battaile, but we got the hill of them, ordered our men, and cryed for a messe of Calualleres to supper, as we had to breakefast; but they all fled, and we immediately marched into Coventry, where the countrey met us in armes and welcomed us, and gave us good quarter both for horse and foote. In this battell I met with your horseman Davy, and he and I present you and my Mistris with our most humble service, desiringe you to pray for us, and doubt not that both of (us) will valiantly fight the Lord's battaile. Thus, with my service to Mrs. Elizabeth, Anne, John, and Samuell, and my love to all my fellow servants, I rest,

Yours, in all good services,

NEHEMIAH WHARTON.

Archaeologia, Volume XXXV (1853)

1 Cavaliers.
2 Dismissed.
3 This mutiny was the result of the unpopularity of the commanding officer, Lieutenant Colonel Biddenman, who was eventually removed from his office.
4 This rank would be equivalent to Major today.
5 Pikemen.

1645 Battle of Naseby

Oliver Cromwell writes to William Lenthall, Speaker of the House of Commons, after the Parliamentary victory at Naseby, on the north-western border of Northamptonshire:

Harborough, 14th June 1645.

Sir, – Being commanded by you to this service, I think myself bound to acquaint you with the good hand of God towards you and us.

We marched yesterday after the King, who went before us from Daventry to Harborough; and quartered about six miles from him. This day we marched towards him. He drew-out to meet us; both Armies engaged. We, after three-hours fight very doubtful, at last routed his Army; killed and took about 5,000, – very many officers, but of what quality we yet know not. We took also about 200 carriages, all he had; and all his guns, being 12 in number, whereof two were demi-cannon, two demi-culverins, and I think the rest sackers. We pursued the Enemy from three miles short of Harborough to nine beyond, even to the sight of Leicester, whither the King fled.

Sir, this is none other but the hand of God; and to Him alone belongs the glory, wherein none are to share with Him. The General served you with all faithfulness and honour: and the best commendation I can give him is, That I daresay he attributes all to God, and would rather perish than assume to himself. Which is an honest and a thriving way: – and yet as much for bravery may be given to him, in this action, as to a man. Honest men served you faithfully in this action. Sir, they are trusty; I beseech you, in the name of God, not to discourage them. I wish this action may beget thankfulness and humility in all that are concerned in it. He that ventures his life for the liberty of his country, I wish he trust God for the liberty of his conscience, and you for the liberty he fights for. In this he rests, who is your most humble servant,   OLIVER CROMWELL.

Oliver Cromwell's Letters and Speeches, edited by Thomas Carlyle (1845)

1649 Massacre of Drogheda

During his campaign in Ireland, Cromwell besieged the town of Drogheda, a seaport on the Boyne, thirty miles from Dublin. It was defended by James Butler, Marquis of Ormonde, with a force of 3,000. On 13 September 1649 Drogheda was stormed and taken and the garrison put to the sword — 4,000, including women and children, were slaughtered.

On 17 September 1649 Cromwell wrote to William Lenthall, Speaker of the House of Commons:

And indeed, being in the heat of action, I forbade them to spare any that were in arms in the town, and, I think, that night they put to the sword about 2,000 men, divers of the officers and soldiers being fled over the bridge into the other part of the town, where about one hundred of them possessed St Peter's church-steeple. . . . These being summoned to yield to mercy, refused, whereupon I ordered the steeple of St Peter's church to be fired, where one of them was heard to say in the midst of the flames: 'God damn me, God confound me: I burn, I burn.'

The next day, the other two towers were summoned, in one of which was about six or seven score; but they refused to yield themselves, and we knowing that hunger must compel them, set only good guards to secure them from running away until their stomachs were come down. . . . When they submitted, their officers were knocked on the head, and every tenth man of the soldiers killed, and the rest shipped for the Barbadoes . . . .

I am persuaded that this is a righteous judgment of God upon these barbarous wretches, who have imbrued their hands in so much innocent blood; and that it will tend to prevent the effusion of blood for the future, which are satisfactory grounds to such actions, which otherwise cannot but work remorse and regret. The officers of this garrison were the flower of all their army, and their great expectation was, that our attempting this place would put fair to ruin us . . . .

And now give me leave to say how it comes to pass that this work is wrought. It was set upon some of our hearts, that a great thing should be done, not by power or might but by the spirit of God. And is it not so clear? That which caused your men to storm so courageously, it was the spirit of God, who gave your men courage, and took it away again; and gave the enemy courage, and took it away again; and gave your men courage again, and therewith this happy success. And therefore it is good that God alone have all the glory.

Oliver Cromwell's Letters and Speeches, edited by Thomas Carlyle (1845).

Edmund Verney, a Royalist officer, served in Scotland, France and Ireland. An eye witness wrote this account of his death at the siege of Drogheda:

Your brother and my dear friend, Sir Edmund Verney, who behaved himself with the greatest gallantry that could be – he was slain at Drogheda three days after quarter was given him as he was walking with Cromwell by way of protection. One Ropier, who is brother to the Lord Ropier, called him aside in a pretence to speak with him, being formerly an acquaintance, and instead of some friendly office which Sir Edmund might expect from him, he barbarously ran him through with a tuck [sword], but I am confident to see this act once highly revenged. The next day after, one Lieutenant Colonel Boyle, who had quarter likewise given him, as he was at dinner with my Lady More, sister to the Earl of Sunderland, in the same town, one of Cromwell's soldiers came and whispered him in the ear to tell him must presently be put to death, who rising from the table, the lady asked him whither he was going, he answered, Madam to die, who no sooner stepped out of the room but he was shot to death. These are cruelties of those traitors, who no doubt will find the like mercy when they stand in need of it.

Memoirs of the Verney Family (1845)

1652–1674 Dutch Wars

Three wars of colonial rivalry – especially over the West African slave trade and the West Indies – were fought in the English Channel, along the Dutch coast and North America.

1665 Battle of Lowestoft

On 3 June 1665, a Dutch fleet of a hundred vessels raided English supply craft returning from Hamburg. The Dutch were then attacked by an English fleet of a hundred and fifty ships. Over thirty Dutch ships were sunk and among the dead were Cornelis Van Tromp and Admiral Koestenaar.

This account is from a letter by Sir Allen Apseley, an officer on the staff of James, Duke of York (later James II) who was Lord High Admiral:

Mr Boyle was shot with a cannon-ball that took off his head from his body and struck down another man with part of the skull; part of his brains were beaten into my hair and upon my shoulder and left arm. The same unlucky shot that took away that virtuous good youth killed my Lord of Muscary and the Earl of Falmouthe.

Mr Belcher, the yeoman of the cellar, had his head shot off, and the same shot killed a gentleman that waited on the Duke of Monmouthe.

We lost and had hurt about forty men in our ship. The poor Earl of Marlborough is killed and the Earl of Portlande, who was with him. Mr. Witherington had both his eyes shot out. Sir John Lawson is hurt upon the knee. What harm is done in Prince Robarte's [Rupert's] squadron I cannot tell, who (except the Duke of Yorke than whom nothing in nature can be braver) is without doubt the most valiant man alive. And so he shewed himself in this fight.

The battle began about half an hour past 3 in the morning on Saturday. They continued a fierce fight from that time till about 4 of the clock in the afternoon, at which time Updam's ship blew up with all her men. Not long after they began to fly towards their own coasts, but still fighting; which continued as long as we could see. Four of their great ships being foul of one another, a fireship of ours ran in amongst them and in a moment set them all on fire. And to see so many poor souls leaping from the fire to the sea, and swimming there as thick as ears of corn together, was the saddest sight I ever beheld. I think our catches saved about 120 of them.

Not long after, another fireship did the bravest action that ever man did, the gallantry of which is too long to describe; he was the occasion of the taking of a great ship of theirs. Another rascal that commanded a fireship did the most barbarous villany in the world. There being three or four great ships of theirs foul of one another, the poor men seeing the fireship come up sent out their boat and begged for quarter. This inhuman rogue runs in amongst them and sets them all on fire, and burned and drowned 500 men.

We have taken divers of their great ships, burned some more than those I have mentioned, and chased them all this morning as soon as it was light till 12 of the clock at noon, about which time those that escaped got into the Texel, which were about 48. The rest of them were either burned or taken or dispersed about the sea out of our sight.

This is the greatest victory that ever the English won, and our seamen say it is the most dreadful battle that ever was fought. Their Admiral blown up with all his men. Trump killed. The great braggadocio that swore he would board the Duke-Courtnape – killed. Another of their great commanders had his leg shot off, and many of them we have taken prisoners.

Letter quoted in Geoffrey Callender, Sea Kings of Britain (1909)

1667

Samuel Pepys, at this time an official in the Navy Office, gives a detailed account of reaction as news spread of Dutch successes at Harwich, the Nore, and Gravesend, burning English shipping and breaking the boom and chain across the channel of the Medway. At Chatham, English seamen – badly paid by their government – deserted to the Dutch. By 13 June Pepys had learned that the *Royal Charles* had been burned and an invasion was imminent:

13 JUNE 1667

No sooner up but hear the sad news confirmed, of the *Royall Charles* being taken by them and now in fitting by them . . . and burning several others, and that another fleet is come up into the Hope; upon which news the King and Duke of York have been below since 4 a-clock in the morning, to command the sinking of ships at Barking Creeke and other places, to stop their coming up higher; which put me into such fear that I presently resolved of my father's and wife's going into the country; and at two hours' warning they did go by the coach this day – with about 1300*l* in gold in their night-bag; pray God give them good passage and good care to hide it when they come home, but my heart is full of fear. They gone, I continued in frights and fear what to do with the rest. W. Hewer hath been at the banquiers and hath got 500*l* out of Backewell's hands of his own money; but they are so called upon that they will be all broke, hundreds coming to them for money – and their answer is 'It is payable at twenty days; when the days are out, we will pay you;' and those that are not so, they make tell over their money, and make their bags false on purpose to give cause to retell it and so spend time; I cannot have my 200 pieces of gold again for silver, all being bought up last night that were to be had – and sold for 24 and 25s. a-piece. So I must keep the silver by me, which sometimes I think to fling into the house of office – and then again, know not how I shall come by it if we be made to leave the office. Every minute some[one] or other calls for this order or that order; and so I forced to be at the office most of the day about the fireships which are to be suddenly fitted out . . .

My business the most of the afternoon is listening to everybody that comes to the office, what news, which is variously related, some better, some worse, but nothing certain. The King and Duke of York up and down all the day here and there; some time on Tower hill, where the City Militia was; where the King did make a speech to them that they should venture themselfs no further then he would himself. I also sent (my mind being in pain) Saunders after my wife and father, to overtake them at their night's lodging to see how matters go with them. In the evening I sent for my cousin Sarah and her husband; who came and I did deliver them my chest of writings about Brampton, and my brother Tom's papers and my Journalls, which I value much – and did send my two silver flagons to Kate Joyce's: that so, being scattered what I have, something might be saved. I have also made a girdle, by which with some trouble I do carry about me 300l in gold about my body, that I may not be without something in case I should be surprized; for I think, in any nation but ours, people that appear (for we are not endeed so) so faulty as we would have their throats cut. In the evening comes Mr. Pelling and several others to the office, and tell me that never were people so dejected as they are in the City all over at this day, and do talk most loudly, even treason; as, that we are bought and sold, that we are betrayed by the papists and others about the King – cry out that the Office of the Ordinance hath been so backward as no powder to have been at Chatham nor Upner Castle till such a time, and the carriages all broken . . .

They look upon us as lost; and remove their families and rich goods in the City and do think verily that the French, being come down with his army to Dunkirke, it is to invade us – and that we shall be invaded.

. . . Late at night comes Mr. Hudson the cooper, my neighbour, and tells me that he came from Chatham this evening at 5 a-clock and saw this afternoon the *Royall James, Oake,* and *London* burnt by the enemy with their fireships; that two or three men-of-war came up with them, and made no more of Upner castle's shooting then of a fly – that these ships lay below Upner Castle (but therein I conceive he is in an error) – that the Dutch are fitting out the *Royall Charles* – that we shot so far as from the yard thither, so that the shot did no good, for the bullets grazed on the water – that Upner played hard with their guns at first, but slowly afterward, either from the men being beat off or their powder spent. But we hear that the fleet in the Hope is not come up any higher the last flood. And Sir W. Batten tells me that ships are provided to sink in the River about Woolwich, that will prevent their coming up higher if they should attempt it. I made my will also this day, and did give all I had equally between my father and wife.

14 JUNE 1667

A man of Mr. Gawden's came from Chatham last night and saw the three ships burnt, they lying all dry, and boats going from the men-of-war and fire them. But that that he tells me of worst consequence is that he himself (I think he said) did hear many Englishmen on board the Dutch ships, speaking to one another in English, and that they did cry and say 'We did heretofore fight for tickets; now we fight for Dollers!' and did ask how such and such a one did, and would commend themself to them – which is a sad consideration. And several seamen came this morning to me to tell me that if I would get their tickets paid, they would go and do all they could against the Dutch; but otherwise they would not venture being killed and lose all they have already fought for – so that I was forced to try what I could do to get them paid.

The Diary of Samuel Pepys, A New and Complete Transcription, edited by
Robert Latham and William Matthews (1985)

STUART AND HANOVERIAN WARS

1685 Monmouth Rebellion: Battle of Sedgemoor

James, Duke of Monmouth, was the illegitimate son of Charles II and Lucy Walters. He was made the central figure in the movement to exclude Charles II's brother, James, Duke of York, from the succession. When Charles died, Monmouth returned from exile in the Low Countries and the tragic adventure known to history as the Monmouth Rebellion began after his landing at Lyme Regis, 11 June 1685. He raised a band of followers and was proclaimed king at Taunton. The rebellion was ended in the catastrophic engagement of 6 July 1685. The rebel plan was to surprise James's army, encamped at Sedgemoor near Bridgewater, during the night. James II's troops were commanded by Louis Duras, the Earl of Feversham, who was a French officer. The rebels' advance was betrayed by a chance musket shot. This account is from Macaulay's *History of England*.

That an attack was to be made under cover of the night was no secret in Bridgewater. The town was full of women, who had repaired thither by hundreds from the surrounding region, to see their husbands, sons, lovers, and brothers once more. There were many sad partings that day; and many parted never to meet again. The report of the intended attack came to the ears of a young girl who was zealous for the King. Though of modest character she had the courage to resolve that she would herself bear the intelligence to Feversham. She stole out of Bridgewater, and made her way to the royal camp. But that camp was not a place where female innocence could be safe. Even the officers, despising alike the irregular force to which they were opposed, and the negligent general who commanded them, had indulged largely in wine, and were ready for any excess of licentiousness and cruelty. One of them seized the unhappy maiden, refused to listen to her errand, and brutally outraged her. She fled in agonies of rage and shame, leaving the wicked army to its doom.

And now the time for the great hazard drew near. The night was not ill suited for such an enterprise. The moon was indeed at the full, and the northern streamers were shining brilliantly. But the marsh fog lay so thick on Sedgemoor that no object could be discerned there at the distance of fifty paces.

The clock struck eleven; and the Duke with his body guard rode out of the Castle. He was not in the frame of mind which befits one who is about to strike a decisive blow. The very children who pressed to see him pass observed, and long remembered, that his look was sad and full of evil augury. His army marched by a circuitous path, near six miles in length, towards the royal encampment on Sedgemoor. Part of the route is to this day called War Lane. The foot were led by Monmouth himself. The horse were confided to Grey, in spite of the remonstrances of some who remembered the mishap at Bridport. Orders were given that strict silence should be preserved, that no drum should be beaten, and no shot fired. The word by which the insurgents were to recognise one another in the darkness was Soho. It had doubtless been selected in allusion to Soho Fields in London, where their leader's palace stood.

At about one in the morning of Monday the sixth of July, the rebels were on the open moor. But between them and the enemy lay three broad rhines filled with water and soft mud. Two of these, called the Black Ditch and the Langmoor Rhine, Monmouth knew that he must pass. But, strange to say, the existence of a trench, called the Bussex Rhine, which immediately covered the royal encampment, had not been mentioned to him by any of his scouts.

The wains which carried the ammunition remained at the entrance of the moor. The horse and foot, in a long narrow column, passed the Black Ditch by a causeway. There was a similar causeway across the Langmoor Rhine: but the guide, in the fog, missed his way. There was some delay and some tumult before the error could be rectified. At length the passage was effected: but, in the confusion, a pistol went off. Some men of the Horse Guards, who were on watch, heard the report, and perceived that a great multitude was advancing through the mist. They fired their carbines, and galloped off in different directions to give the alarm. Some hastened to Weston Zoyland, where the cavalry lay. One trooper spurred to the encampment of the infantry, and cried out vehemently that the enemy was at hand. The drums of Dumbarton's regiment beat to arms; and the men got fast into their ranks. It was time; for Monmouth was already drawing up his army for action. He ordered Grey to lead the way with the cavalry, and followed himself at the head of the infantry. Grey pushed on till his progress was unexpectedly arrested by the Bussex Rhine. On the opposite side of the ditch the King's foot were hastily forming in order of battle.

'For whom are you?' called out an officer of the Foot Guards. 'For the King,' replied a voice from the ranks of the rebel cavalry. 'For which King?' was then demanded. The answer was a shout of 'King Monmouth,' mingled with the war cry, which forty years before had been inscribed on the colours of the parliamentary regiments, 'God with us.' The royal troops instantly fired such a volley of musketry as sent the rebel horse flying in all directions. The world agreed to ascribe this ignominious route to Grey's pusillanimity. Yet it is by no means clear that Churchill would have succeeded better at the head of men who had never before handled arms on horseback, and whose horses were unused, not only to stand fire, but to obey the rein.

A few minutes after the Duke's horse had dispersed themselves over the moor, his infantry came up running fast, and guided through the gloom by the lighted matches of Dumbarton's regiment.

Monmouth was startled by finding that a broad and profound trench lay between him and the camp which he had hoped to surprise. The insurgents halted on the edge of the rhine, and fired. Part of the royal infantry on the opposite bank returned the fire. During three quarters of an hour the roar of the musketry was incessant. The Somersetshire peasants behaved themselves as if they had been veteran soldiers, save only that they levelled their pieces too high.

But now the other divisions of the royal army were in motion. The Life Guards and Blues came pricking fast from Weston Zoyland, and scattered in an instant some of Grey's horse, who had attempted to rally. The fugitives spread a panic among their comrades in the rear, who had charge of the ammunition. The waggoners drove off at full speed, and never stopped till they were many miles from the field of battle. Monmouth had hitherto done his part like a stout and able warrior. He had been seen on foot, pike in hand, encouraging his infantry by voice and by example. But he was too well acquainted with military affairs not to know that all was over. His men had lost the advantage which surprise and darkness had given them. They were deserted by the horse and by the ammunition waggons. The King's forces were now united and in good order. Feversham had been awakened by the firing, had got out of bed, had adjusted his cravat, had looked at himself well in the glass, and had come to see what his men were doing. Meanwhile, what was of much more importance, Churchill had rapidly made an entirely new disposition of the royal infantry. The day was about to break. The event of a conflict on an open plain, by broad sunlight, could not be doubtful. Yet Monmouth should have felt that it was not for him to fly, while thousands whom affection for him had hurried to destruction were still fighting manfully in his cause. But vain hopes and the intense love of life prevailed. He saw that if he tarried the royal cavalry would soon intercept his retreat. He mounted and rode from the field.

Yet his foot, though deserted, made a gallant stand. The Life Guards attacked them on the right, the Blues on the left: but the Somersetshire clowns, with their scythes and the but ends of their muskets, faced the royal horse like old soldiers. Oglethorpe made a vigorous attempt to break them and was manfully repulsed. Sarsfield, a brave Irish officer, whose name afterwards obtained a melancholy celebrity, charged on the other flank. His men were beaten back. He was himself struck to the ground, and lay for a time as one dead. But the struggle of the hardy rustics could not last. Their powder and ball were spent. Cries were heard of 'Ammunition! for God's sake ammunition!' But no ammunition was at hand. And now the King's artillery came up. It had been posted half a mile off, on the high road from Weston Zoyland to Bridgewater. So defective were then the appointments of an English army that there would have been much difficulty in dragging the great guns to the place where the battle was raging, had not the Bishop of Winchester offered his coach horses and traces for the purpose. This interference of a Christian prelate in a matter of blood has, with strange inconsistency, been condemned by some Whig writers who can see nothing criminal in the conduct of the numerous Puritan ministers then in arms against the government. Even when the guns had arrived, there was such a want of gunners that a sergeant of Dumbarton's regiment was forced to take on himself the management of several pieces. The cannon, however, though ill served, brought the engagement to a speedy close. The pikes of the rebel battalions began to shake: the ranks broke; the King's cavalry charged again, and bore down everything before them; the King's infantry came pouring across the ditch. Even in that extremity the Mendip miners stood bravely to their arms and sold their lives dearly. But the rout was in a few minutes complete. Three hundred of the soldiers had been killed or wounded. Of the rebels more than a thousand lay dead on the moor.

So ended the last fight, deserving the name of battle, that has been fought on English ground. The impression left on the simple inhabitants of the neighbourhood was deep and lasting. That impression, indeed, has been frequently renewed. For even in our own time the plough and the spade have not seldom turned up ghastly memorials of the slaughter, skulls, and thighbones, and strange weapons made out of implements of husbandry. Old peasants related very recently that, in their childhood, they were accustomed to play on the moor at the fight between King James's men and King Monmouth's men.

It was four o'clock: the sun was rising; and the routed army came pouring into the streets of Bridgewater. The uproar, the blood, the gashes, the ghastly figures which sank down and never rose again, spread horror and dismay through the town. The pursuers, too, were close behind. During that day the conquerors continued to chase the fugitives. The neighbouring villagers long remembered with what a clatter of horsehoofs and what a storm of curses the whirlwind of cavalry swept by. Before evening five hundred prisoners had been crowded into the parish church of Weston Zoyland. Eighty of them were wounded; and five expired within the consecrated walls. Great numbers of labourers were impressed for the purpose of burying the slain. A few, who were notoriously partial to the vanquished side, were set apart for the hideous office of quartering the captives. The tithing men of the neighbouring parishes were busied in setting up gibbets and providing chains. All this while the bells of Weston Zoyland and Chedzoy rang joyously; and the soldiers sang and rioted on the moor amidst the corpses. For the farmers of the neighbourhood had made haste as soon as the event of the fight was known, to send hogsheads of their best cider as peace offerings to the victors.

Feversham passed for a goodnatured man: but he was a foreigner, ignorant of the laws and careless of the feelings of the English. He was accustomed to the military license of France. A considerable number of prisoners were immediately selected for execution. Among them was a youth famous for his speed. Hopes were held out to him that his life would be spared if he could run a race with one of the colts of the marsh. The space through which the man kept up with the horse is still marked by well-known bounds on the moor, and is about three quarters of a mile. Feversham was not ashamed, after seeing the performance, to send the wretched performer to the gallows. The next day a long line of gibbets appeared on the road leading from Bridgewater to Weston Zoyland. On each gibbet a prisoner was suspended. Four of the sufferers were left to rot in irons.

Thomas Babington Macaulay, *History of England from the Accession of James II,*
Volume 1 (1848)

1689–1690 War of the English Succession: Battle of the Boyne

When James, Duke of York, a Roman Catholic, succeeded to the throne on the death of his brother, Charles II in 1685, there were some fears that Catholicism would be restored with continental help – mainly from Louis XIV. The severe repression of the Monmouth Rebellion only six months after the succession increased anxiety. Several leading public figures gained the support of William, stadholder of the Netherlands – a Protestant monarch who was married to Charles I's daughter, Mary – to counter James's efforts. William accepted what was, in effect, an invitation to become King of England. He landed in November and marched on London. King James II fled to France.

In March 1689, during a Jacobite rising in Scotland (see Killicrankie), James landed in Ireland. William arrived in Ireland leading an army of between 35,000 and 40,000 men to match James's force of 21,000. The final engagement of the War of the English Succession was the Battle of the Boyne, fought on 1 July 1690, when William's superior cavalry enveloped James's forces. This account is from the diary of Revd Rowland Davies, who was chaplain to one of William's cavalry regiments at the Boyne:

June 30th – At two in the morning we decamped again, and marched towards Drogheda, where we found King James encamped on the other (side) of the Boyne; we drew up all our horse in a line opposite him within cannon-shot, and as his Majesty passed our line they fired six shot at him, one whereof fell and struck off the top of the Duke of Wurtemberg's pistol, and the whiskers off his horse, and another tore the King's coat on the shoulder. We stood open during at least twenty shot, until, a man and two horses being killed among the Dutch Guards, we all retired into a trench behind us, where we lay safe while much mischief was done to other regiments, and in the evening drew off and encamped behind the hill.

July 1st – About six in the morning the Earl of Portland marched up the river almost to the bridge of Slane, with the right wing, consisting of twenty-four squadrons of horse and dragoons and six regiments of foot, and at two fords we passed the river where there were six squadrons of the enemy to guard the pass; but, at the first firing of our dragoons and three pieces of cannon that marched with us, they all ran away killing nothing but one of our dragoon's horses. As soon as we passed the river, we saw the enemy marching towards us, and that they drew up on the side of a hill in two lines; the river on their right, and all their horse on the left wing: their foot appeared very numerous, but in horse we far exceeded. Whereupon the Earl of Portland drew us up also in two lines, intermixing the horse and foot by squadron and battalion, and sent away for more foot to enforce us; and thus the armies stood for a considerable time, an impassable bog being between them. At length six regiments of foot more joined us, and we altered our line of battle, drawing all our horse into the right wing; and so outflanking the enemy we marched round the bog and engaged them, rather pursuing than fighting them, as far as Duleek. In the interim Count Solmes with the foot forced the pass under our camp and marched over the river with the Blue Dutch regiment of Guards; no sooner were they up the hill but the enemy's horse fell on them, ours with the King being about half a mile lower passing at another ford. At the first push the front rank only fired and then fell on their faces, loading their muskets again as they lay on the ground; at the next charge they fired a volley of three ranks; then, at the next, the first rank got up and fired again, which being received by a choice squadron of the enemy, consisting mostly of officers, they immediately fell in upon the Dutch as having spent all their front fire; but the two rear ranks drew up in two platoons and flanked the enemy across, and the rest, screwing their swords into their muskets, received the charge with all imaginable bravery and in a minute dismounted them all. The Derry Regiment also sustained them bravely, and as they drew off maintained the same ground with a great slaughter. His Majesty then came up and charged at the head of the Enniskilling horse, who deserted him at the first charge, and carried with them a Dutch regiment that sustained them; but the King's blue troop of Guards soon supplied their place, and with them he charged in person and routed the enemy, and coming over the hill near Duleek appeared on our flank, and, not being known at first, made all our forces halt and draw up again in order, which gave the enemy time to rally also, and draw up on the side of the hill, a bog and river being between us, and then they fired two pieces of cannon on us, but did no mischief; but, as soon as our foot and cannon came up, they marched on, and we after them, but, our foot being unable to march as they did, we could not come up to fight again, but, on the night coming on, were forced to let them go; but had we engaged half an hour sooner, or the day held an hour longer, we had certainly destroyed that army. However we killed the Lord Dungane, Lord Carlingford, Sir Neal O'Neal, and about three thousand others, and lost Duke Schomberg, Dr. Walker, Colonel Caillimotte, and about three hundred more. We took Lieutenant-General Hamilton and several officers and soldiers prisoners, and, it being very dark, were forced to lie in the field all night with our horses in our hands.

July 2nd – In the morning as soon as it was light we returned to Duleek, where our foot was, and sent a detachment to bring up our baggage from the last camp. In the afternoon six troops of horse and three regiments of foot that came from Munster to join King James appeared on the flank and alarmed us, and, sending two spies to discover who we were, we took and hanged them, the rest marching back without any engagement.

Rowland Davies, Journals, Volume LXVIII (1857)

1702–1713 War of the Spanish Succession

Fought between France, Bavaria and Spain, and Britain, Austria, Prussia, Holland, Denmark and Portugal, this was a struggle over the balance of power in Europe. The ostensible cause was the death of Charles II of Spain in 1700, without leaving a direct heir. His throne was left to a grandson of Louis XIV. A union between France and Spain was something the major Protestant powers of Europe and their allies would not accommodate.

The conflict produced three brilliant commanders – Marlborough, Prince Eugene and the Duke of Berwick. Marlborough's great victories were at Blenheim (1704), Ramillies (1706), Oudenarde (1708) and Malplaquet (1709).

After Blenheim, on 14 August 1704, he wrote to his wife, Sarah, Duchess of Marlborough:

We have cut off great numbers of them, as well in the action as in the retreat, besides upwards of twenty squadrons of the French, which I pushed into the Danube, where we saw the greater part of them perish. Monsieur Tallard, with several of his general officers being taken prisoners at the same time, and in the village of Blenheim, which the enemy had entrenched and fortified, and where they made the greatest opposition, I obliged twenty-six entire battalions, and twelve squadrons of dragoons, to surrender themselves prisoners at discretion. We took likewise all their tents standing, with their cannon and ammunition, as also a great number of standards, kettle-drums, and colours in the action, so that I reckon the greatest part of Monsieur Tallard's army is taken or destroyed.

The bravery of all our troops on this occasion cannot be expressed, the Generals, as well as the officers and soldiers, behaving themselves with the greatest courage and resolution. The horse and dragoons were obliged to charge four or five several times. The Elector and Monsieur de Marsin were so advantageously posted, that Prince Eugene could make no impression on them, till the third attack, near seven at night, when he made a great slaughter of them. But being near a woodside, a great body of Bavarians retired into it, and the rest of that army retreated towards Lawringen, it being too late, and the troops too much tired to pursue them far.

Sir George Murray, *Letters and Dispatches of John Churchill,*
First Duke of Marlborough (1845)

The war had a deleterious effect on the French economy. Voltaire wrote:

The bitter winter of 1709 reduced the nation to despair. The olive trees, which are a great source of revenue in the south of France, perished, and nearly all the fruit trees were killed by the frost. All hopes of harvest were blighted. Stocks were extremely low. Grain, which could be obtained at great expense from the sea ports of the Levant and from Africa, were liable to be seized by the enemy's fleets, to oppose which there were scarcely any ships left. The distress occassioned by this winter was felt all over Europe; but the enemy had greater resources. The Dutch especially, who had been for long the factors of other nations, had sufficient stores to be able to keep the flourishing armies of the Allies in plenty, whilst the French troops, reduced in numbers, and disheartened, seemed doomed to perish from want. The King sold his gold plate for four hundred thousand francs. The highest lords sent their silver plate to the mint. For some months nothing but black bread was eaten in Paris. Several families even at Versailles lived on oaten bread.

Voltaire, *Le Siècle de Louis XIV* (1751), translated by Martyn P. Pollack (1961)

1709 Battle of Malplaquet

The most slaughterous engagement of the eighteenth century — the Battle of Malplaquet — was fought on 11 September 1709. More than 36,000 men were killed:

As soon as the French advanced to prevent the investment of Mons, the Allies moved to attack them near to the woods of Blangies and the village of Malplaquet.
    The Allies' army numbered about eighty thousand combatants, and

that of Marshal Villars about seventy thousand. The French carried with them eighty pieces of cannon, the Allies one hundred and forty. The Duke of Marlborough commanded the right wing, composed of the English and German troops in the pay of England. Prince Eugene commanded in the centre; Tilly and a certain Count Nassau were on the left, together with the Dutch.

(11 September, 1709) Marshal Villars took over the command of the left wing himself and relinquished the right to Marshal Boufflers. He had hurriedly entrenched his army, a manœuvre probably well adapted to his troops, who were in inferior numbers, had long been unsuccessful, and were half of them fresh recruits, and adapted still more to the fortunes of France, in that a total defeat would have driven her to her last extremities. Some historians have blamed the general for his disposition of the army. 'He should have crossed a wide cleft,' they said, 'instead of leaving it in front of him.' Those who pass such armchair judgments on what takes place on the field of battle must be held guilty of excessive cleverness.

All that I know is from the marshal's own words, that when the soldiers, who had been without bread for a whole day, at length received some, they threw part of it away, so that they could rush more swiftly into the fight. Not for several centuries has there been a battle so obstinately fought and so long prolonged, and none more sanguinary. I shall say nothing more about this battle than what is admitted by all the world. The enemy's left wing, where the Dutch fought, was almost completely routed, and pursued at the point of the bayonet. On the right Marlborough maintained a tremendous struggle. In order to withstand Marlborough's attack, Marshal Villars drew a few troops from his centre, and then this centre was also attacked. The entrenchments which guarded it were carried. The regiments of guards who were defending them were unable to resist. The marshal himself, hastening from the left wing to the centre, was wounded, and the battle was lost. The field was strewn with nearly thirty thousand dead and dying.

One could hardly walk, save on piled-up corpses, which were thickest where the Dutch had fought. France lost hardly more than eight thousand men in the battle. Her enemies left about twenty-one thousand dead and wounded, but as the centre had been broken through and the two wings cut off, it was the defeated side which had inflicted the heaviest slaughter.

Voltaire, *Le Siècle de Louis XIV* (1751), translated by Martyn P. Pollack (1961)

1739–1742 War of Jenkins's Ear

This war was fought over colonial rivalries in the West Indies and American colonies. Its cause was the claimed brutality of Spanish customs officials when searching British trading vessels. One British seamen claimed to have had an ear torn off during a search.

The Scottish novelist Tobias Smollett served as a surgeon's mate in the war and wrote this account of the disastrously mismanaged siege of Cartagena in 1741:

> The sick and wounded were squeezed into certain vessels, which there obtained the name of hospital ships, though methinks they scarce deserved such a creditable title, seeing few of them could boast either a surgeon, nurse or cook; and the space between the decks was so confined that the miserable patients had not room to sit upright in their beds. Their wounds . . . being neglected, contracted filth and putrefaction, and millions of maggots were hatched amidst the corruption of their sores. This inhuman disregard was imputed to the scarcity of surgeons; though it is well known, that every great ship in the fleet could have spared one at least for this duty; an expedient which could have been more than sufficient to remove this shocking inconvenience. But, perhaps, the general was too much of a gentleman to ask a favour of this kind from his fellow chief, who on the other hand, would not derogate so much from his own dignity, as to offer such assistance unasked; for I may venture to affirm, that, by this time, the Demon of Discord, with her sooty wings, had breathed her influence upon our counsels; and it might be said of these great men . . . as of Caesar and Pompey, the one could not brook a superior, and the other was impatient of an equal . . .

> Tobias Smollett, *Roderick Random* (1748)

1740–1748 War of the Austrian Succession

On the face of it a dispute between Maria Theresa and the Elector of Bavaria over the Hapsburg succession, this was yet another war fought over the balance of power. Britain was involved against France and Spain, but at the same time had to face the Jacobite rebellion of 1745. The war turned Prussia into a major European power and made Frederick the Great a household name. It was concluded by the Peace of Aix-la-Chapelle; Handel's *Royal Fireworks Music* was commissioned for the celebrations in London.

1743 Battle of Dettingen

Fought in Bavaria on 27 June 1743, Dettingen was the last occasion on which a British sovereign (George II) commanded troops in battle, and ended in a British victory in which the French were driven into the river Main.

This account is by the sixteen-year-old James Wolfe (later hero of the Heights of Abraham), then an adjutant to the 12th Foot, the Suffolk Regiment:

> We advanced towards one another; our men in high spirits, and very impatient for fighting, being elated with beating the French Horse, part of which advanced towards us; while the rest attacked our Horse, but were soon driven back by the great fire we gave them. The Major and I (for we had neither Colonel nor Lieutenant-Colonel), before they came near, were employed in begging and ordering the men not to fire at too great a distance, but to keep it till the enemy should come near us; but to little purpose. The whole of them fired when they thought they could reach them which had like to have ruined us. We did very little execution with it. As soon as the French saw we presented, they all fell down, and when we had fired, they all got up and marched close to us in tolerable good order and gave us a brisk fire, which put us into some disorder and made us give way a little, particularly ours and two or three more Regiments, who were in the hottest of it. However, we soon rallied again and attacked them with great fury, which gained us a complete victory and forced the enemy to retire in great haste. 'Twas luck that we did give way a little, for our men were loading all the while, and it gave room for an Austrian Regiment to move into an interval, rather too little before, who charged the enemy with great bravery and resolution.

> *Life and Correspondence of Major General James Wolfe*, edited by E. Wright (1864)

1745 Battle of Fontenoy

On 11 May 1745 an Allied army commanded by the Duke of Cumberland failed in its attempt to relieve Tournai, with losses of 6,500. This account is from a letter written by Charles James Hamilton, a sixteen-year-old volunteer in the 3rd Dragoons, to his aunt, Lady Murray:

From ye Army
12th May 1745

Dear Aunt,

I would have writ to you since I came to ye field but really I have not had time; I have not had time to sleep this six days but what I got

on ye ground, & nothing to cover me but ye Skies. We have had a most bloody battle with ye french; yesterday we begun at 5 in ye morning & left off at 2 in ye afternoon, all wch time ye french kept cannonading us; I was forced to be very civil & make a great many bows to ye balls, for they were very near me, for both my right & Left hand men were killed, & all round me there were men & horses tumbling about, but thank god none touched me. We could do nothing but stand there & be knocked on ye head, for they had a great many batterys & three times ye number of cannon yt we had, & besides that they were entrenched up to ye ears that we could not hurt them; we fir'd upon a Little village very Smartly where they had a Battery; The Foot were very sadly cut to Pieces, for ye french Put grape shot into their cannon & cut them down as just if they were sheering corn. There is a great many officers killed in ye Infantry; in ye Welch Fusiliers, only two came of ye field Without a Wound. My Lord Charles Hay & Charles Ross are both killed, & Andrew Sandilands very ill, Wounded & a great many others but you will hear a more Perfect account of it soon, & what number of men, is not yet known; we have a Cornett missing in our Regiment so we think he is Kill'd & a captain Wounded; there is not an Officer in My Lord Stair's, hurt. I Long'd for ym to come to it Sowrd in hand, but they durst not do yt. I had my horse shot just in ye knee with Musket ball, & I am afraid he will always be Lame. I was forced to go of ye field & get my other horse. I did not regard ye small Bullets after ye cannon Balls in ye Least tho they came bussing about me Like Bees, & I had got just by one of ye Standards Where they came very fast for they Were Shooting at ye Standards Like Mad, but at Last we were Obliged to retreat for their was no Standing their cannon as they were intrench'd, for we could not see anything Scarce but their bits of white Paper in their hats, but I hope we shall be revenged of them for this trick. Ye General is very well & sends his compliments to you, I just writ ys to Let you know I am well. I recollected yt I must die some time or Other, & if my time was not come I was as safe ther as any Where Else. Pray My duty to mama, Grand-mama, Love to my Brothers & sisters & service to every body Else
    & am Dear Aunt your most Dutyfull Nephew
Charles James Hamilton.

Colonel Charles Field, *Echoes of Old Wars: Personal and Unofficial Letters, and Accounts of Bygone Battles, both by Land and Sea: by Those Who Were There 1513–1854* (1934)

1745–1746 Jacobite Rebellion

Charles Edward Louis Philip Casimir, the Young Pretender (grandson of James II, and often known as Bonnie Prince Charlie), sailed from Belleisle and reached the Hebrides in August 1745; he unfurled his standard at Glenfinnan. The bulk of the British army was at this time in service on the continent. The rebel army entered Edinburgh early in September. Before their contemplated invasion of England, the rebel army met and defeated an English army of 3,000 under Sir John Cope at Prestonpans.

Battle of Prestonpans

This battle, fought on 20 September 1745, lasted scarcely five minutes. The English infantry was wholly routed by the charge of the Highlanders. This account of the compassionate behaviour of the Young Pretender is by his Adjutant-General, Sir John O'Sullivan:

> The Dragoons, in their flight, threw away their Standards, the foot their Colours; one found in one place, another in another, but the people of the country took away a great many of them, there were eighty-four officers made prisoners, of all ranks and about fourteen hundred private men . . . .
>
> But when people began to be cool, they reflected on the danger the Prince exposed himself to, notwithstanding what he had promised. . . . The Prince answered that he was obliged to them all, for the care and tenderness they had of him, that he only did what he ought to do, and that he would never forget their behaviour that day. They then proposed him to refresh and repose himself, that he had great need of it; 'No,' says he, with a tender heart and in a most feeling way, 'I can't rest until I see my own poor men taken care of, and the other wounded too, for they are the King's subjects as well as we, and it's none of their fault if they are led on blindly', upon which he immediately sent orders, to the neighbouring villages, upon pain of military execution that houses and everything necessary should be provided for the wounded, and that the inhabitants should come with spades and other instruments to bury the dead. He spoke to the surgeons, first to dress the Highlanders, and afterwards to neglect nothing for the others; he neither would eat or drink until he saw people set about this.

James Allardyce, *Historical Papers Relating to the Jacobite Period* (1895)

1746 Culloden

The Jacobite rebels invaded England in November 1745, but after initial successes — including the capture of Carlisle and Manchester — they were driven back by English forces commanded by the Duke of Cumberland.

Culloden (16 April 1746) was the last battle of the rising. English artillery and disciplined infantry broke the Highland ranks. The rebels lost 1,000 dead and 1,000 prisoners — most of whom were killed out of hand.

Prince Charles was indecisive throughout the engagement, as this account by his aide-de-camp records:

It was evident our destruction would become inevitable, if the English got possession of the enclosure. The Prince saw this from the eminence where he was posted, and sent his aide-de-camp six or seven times, ordering Lord George to take possession of it. He saw that his orders were not executed, but yet he never quitted his place on the eminence. This was a critical moment when he ought to have displayed the courage of a grenadier, by immediately advancing to put himself at the head of his army, and commanding himself those manoeuvres which he wished to be executed. He would never have experienced disobedience on the part of his subjects who had exposed their lives and fortunes to establish him on the throne of his ancestors, and who would have shed for him the last drop of their blood. There are occasions when a general ought to expose his person, and not remain beyond the reach of musketry, and surely there never was a more pressing occasion for disregarding a few shots than the one in question, as the gain or loss of the battle depended on it. In the desperate expedition on which he had entered, though it was proper that he should guard against danger, he ought to have done so in a manner which showed that life or death was equally indifferent to him, conducting himself with valour and prudence, according to circumstances. But he was surrounded by Irish confidants, whose baseness of soul corresponded to the obscurity of their birth. The natives of Ireland are generally supposed, in England, to have a great confusion of ideas, and they are in general very bad counsellors. But the Prince blindly adopted their opinions.

As far as I could distinguish, at the distance of twenty paces, the English appeared to be drawn up in six ranks, the three first being on their knees, and keeping up a terrible running fire on us . . .

James Johnstone ('Chevalier de Johnstone'), Memoirs (1820)

VII

INDIA AND NORTH AMERICA

1756–1763 Seven Years War

This war was waged by France, Sweden, Saxony and Austria in the hope of crushing the growing power of Prussia. England was already engaged in conflict with France in India and North America, and supported Prussia against her continental enemies.

1756 Black Hole of Calcutta

This account is by one of the few to survive the notorious imprisonment inflicted by Suraj-ud-Daula, the Subadhar of Bengal, upon the remnants of the garrison at Calcutta:

> Imagine, if possible, the situation of one hundred and forty-six wretches crammed together in a cube of about eighteen feet, in a close sultry night in Bengal, shut up to the eastward and the southward by dead walls, and by a wall and door to the north, open only to the westward by two windows, strongly barred with iron . . .
>
> We had been imprisoned but a few minutes, when everyone fell into a perspiration so profuse that it brought on a raging thirst, which increased as the body was drained of its moisture. Various expedients were thought of . . . every man put off his clothes . . . every hat was waved about . . . it was proposed that every man should sit down. This expedient was several times put in practice, and at each time many of the poor creatures, who could not immediately recover their legs as others did when the word was given to rise, fell down and were instantly trod to death or suffocated.
>
> . . . every man's thirst grew intolerable and respiration diffi-cult . . . many insults were addressed to the guard to provoke them to fire in upon us and so end our misery . . . 'Water! Water!' became

the general cry . . . I foresaw it would prove the ruin of the small chance left us . . .

The water appeared . . . We had no means of conveying it into the prison but by hats forced through the bars . . . But, though we brought full hats through the bars, there ensued such violent struggles . . . that before it reached the lips of any one there would be scarcely a small teacup left in them . . .

The confusion now became general and horrid. Several quitted the other window . . . to force their way to the water, and many from the further part of the room pressed down those in their way and trampled them to death . . .

But my thirst was rather increased by the water, so I determined to drink no more . . . and kept my mouth moist, from time to time, by sucking the perspiration out of my shirt-sleeves and catching the drops as they fell . . . from my head and face.

Many to the right and left sank with the violent pressure and were soon suffocated, for now a steam arose from the living and the dead . . .

When the day broke, and the gentlemen found that no entreaties could prevail to get the door opened, it occurred to one of them . . . to make a search for me, in hope I might have influence to gain a release from this scene of misery . . .

At this juncture the suba (the viceroy of Bengali), who had received an account of the havoc death had made amongst us, sent one of his Jemmautdaars to enquire if the chief survived. They showed me to him; told I had appearance of life remaining; and believed I might recover if the door was opened very soon. This answer being returned to the suba, an order came immediately for our release, it being then near six in the morning.

The fresh air at the window soon brought me to life . . . The weakness of the survivors made it a difficult task to remove the dead pile from against the door, and it was more than twenty minutes before we obtained a passage out for one at a time . . . of the one hundred and forty-six persons confined in this den of horrors, one hundred and twenty-three had perished during the night.

John Zephaniah Holwell, *A Narrative of the Black Hole of Calcutta* (1758)

1757 Plassey

This was the great victory of Robert Clive over Suraj-ud-Daula which made the British East India Company masters of Bengal. Clive's forces totally routed the combined Indian and French forces. This is the account Clive sent to the Company's directors on 26 July 1757:

About noon the enemy drew off their artillery, and retired to their camp . . . We immediately sent a detachment accompanied with two field-pieces, to take possession of a tank with high banks, which was advanced about three hundred yards above our grove, and from which the enemy had considerably annoyed us with some cannon managed by Frenchmen. This motion brought them out a second time; but on finding them make no great effort to dislodge us, we proceeded to take possession of one or two more eminences lying very near an angle of their camp . . . They made several attempts to bring out their cannon, but our advance field-pieces played so warmly and so well upon them that they were always drove back. Their horse exposing themselves a good deal on this occasion, many of them were killed, and among the rest four or five officers of the first distinction, by which the whole army being visibly dispirited and thrown into some confusion, we were encouraged to storm both the eminence and the angle of their camp, which were carried at the same instant, with little or no loss . . . On this a general rout ensued; and we pursued the enemy six miles, passing upwards of forty pieces of cannon they had abandoned, with an infinite number of carriages filled with baggage of all kinds. Suraj-ud-Daulah escaped on a camel, and reaching Moorshedabad early next morning, despatched away what jewels and treasure he conveniently could, and he himself followed at midnight with only two or three attendants.

It is computed there are killed of the enemy about five hundred. Our loss amounted to only twenty-two killed and fifty wounded, and those chiefly blacks. During the warmest part of the action we observed a large body of troops hovering on our right, which proved to be our friends; but as they never discovered themselves by any signal whatsoever, we frequently fired on them to make them keep their distance. When the battle was over they sent a congratulatory message, and encamped in our neighbourhood that night. The next day Meer Jaffier paid me a visit, and expressed much gratitude at the service done him, assuring me in the most solemn manner that he would faithfully perform his engagement to the English.

Robert Clive, *Report to the Select Committee of the Court of Directors of the East India Company* (26 July 1757)

1757 Battle of Rossbach

Rossbach was one of Frederick II's greatest victories – his force of 22,000 defeated a combined French and Austrian army of 41,000. The Prussian cavalry was commanded by General von Seidlitz. In this account Carlyle refers to French/Austrian forces as 'Dauphiness or Soubise-Hildurghausen Army'.

> Friedrich's artillery goes at a murderous rate; had come in view, over the hill-top, before Seidlitz ended – 'nothing but the muzzles of it visible' (and the fire-torrents from it) to us poor French below. Friedrich's lines; or rather his one line, mere tip of his left wing, – only seven battalions in it, five of them under Keith from the second or reserve line; whole centre and right wing standing 'refused' in oblique rank, invisible, *behind* the Hill, – Friedrich's line, we say, the artillery to its right, shoots-out in mysterious Prussian rhythm, in echelons, in potences, obliquely down the Janus-Hill side; straight, rigid, regular as iron clockwork; and strides towards us, silent, with the lightning sleeping in it: – Friedrich has got the flank of Dauphiness, and means to keep it. Once and again and a third time, poor Soubise, with his poor regiments much in an imbroglio, here heaped on one another, there with wide gaps, halt being so sudden, – attempts to recover the flank, and pushes-out this regiment and the other, rightward, to be even with Friedrich. But sees with despair that it cannot be; that Friedrich with his echelons, potences and mysterious Prussian resources, pulls himself out like the pieces of a prospect-glass, piece after piece, hopelessly fast and seemingly no end to them; and that the flank is lost . . .
>
> The French line is in front, next the Prussians: poor Generals of Dauphiness are panting to retrieve themselves. But with regiments jammed in this astonishing way, and got collectively into the lion's throat, what can be done? Steady, rigid as iron clockwork, the Prussian line strides forward; at forty-paces distance delivers its first shock of lightning, bursts into platoon fire; and so continues, steady at the rate of five shots a minute, – hard to endure by poor masses all in a coil. 'The artillery tore-down whole ranks of us,' says the Würtemberg Dragoon; 'the Prussian musketry did terrible execution.'

Thomas Carlyle, Frederick the Great (1865)

1759 Battle of Minden

Fought on 1 August 1759 in terrible weather, Minden was a victory for the Allies, but a very costly one for the British regiments who took most of the pounding. French forces numbered 54,000 with 170 guns, and the Hanoverians, Prussian and British armies totalled 42,500 with 190 guns. Although French lines were broken, the failure of the Allied cavalry to follow up allowed them to withdraw in good order, with losses of over 7,000. Of the Allies' 2,760 losses, half were British. This account is from a letter written from hospital two weeks after the battle by Thomas Thompson, a company commander in the Hampshire Regiment.

We marched towards Minden about two miles, found many regiments preparing and all the English on their march; at length the scene appeared, a Battery of six guns began to play on the camp we had left very smartly.

We proceeded about a mile further, joined the Brunswick troops of Infantry and our own and got into a regular line of Battle march. Everything was still quiet before us until we got about half a mile further when we discovered the enemy with the greatest advantage over us, being already formed in Battle array ready to receive us. On the immediate sight of us they opened a battery of eighteen heavy cannon which from the nature of the ground (which was a plain) flanked this regiment in particular every foot we marched, their cannon was ill served at first, but they soon felt us and their shot took place so fast, that every officer imagined the battalion would be taken off before we could get up to give a fire, notwithstanding we were then within a quarter of a mile of their right wing and absolutely running up to the mouth of their cannon in front.

I saw heads, legs and arms taken off, flying into the front, a fire every moment, my right hand file of men not more than a foot from me were all by one ball dashed to pieces and their blood flying all over me, this I must confess staggered me not a little, but on my receiving a contusion in the bend of my right arm by a spent musket shot, it steadied me immediately, all apprehensions of hurt vanished, revenge and the care for the company I commanded took place and I was *then* much more at ease than at *this* time.

Just at this time I got my wound, after having been hit three times before by spent balls, but this seared me like a red hot iron, found myself fainting and quitting the Regt: after having called for a fresh officer, but found no one to supply my place, several being (gone off) wounded already dead. I had not got four rods in the rear, but I heard the battalion fire which pleased me so much in my agony, that I stood stupefied looking on them, many poor soldiers praying, begging me to come off, after a few moments recovered my senses, and found I had no further business there and made the best of my way, which

133

was slow enough, over about a mile of common where the balls came as thick as in front, by this time a soldier of the regiment slightly wounded in the leg, came up offering me his assistance, while supporting me his left leg was carried away by a cannon ball, the wind of which fairly turned me round, but did not hurt me otherwise. The poor man is since dead. The common was strewed with dead and wounded men and horses, on the leeward side of those horses quite dead, lay wounded soldiers that could not get any further to shelter them from the small shot. The action came on in such a hurry that we did not know where to look for the Surgeons. . . . .

I hope to have the satisfaction to hear from you soon the more letters from a family the greater comfort. To whom as well as to other friends, I beg my best respects.

From Sir, Your obedient Servant
Thos. Thomson.

P.S. — I hope the nation is now satisfied as there was plenty of blood for their money.

Letter dated 14 August 1759, quoted in *The Hampshire Regimental Journal*,
Vol. VII, June 1922

1759 Quiberon Bay

Fought in a terrible gale on 20 November 1759, this engagement between the English fleet under Admiral Edward Hawke — twenty-three sails of the line and ten frigates, with twenty-one French line of battle ships and three frigates — drove the French into Quiberon Bay on the Brittany coast and put paid to France as a naval power for the rest of the century.

On the 20th about half an hour after eight in the morning, the *Maidstone* frigate let fly her top-gallant sails, which was a signal for discovering a fleet; at nine, not a doubt was left, of the happy hour being arrived which we had six months been impatiently expecting. We ascertain'd them to be the French squadron, of 21 sail of the line and three smaller ships; and that they were chasing Captain Duff's frigates and bombs; the destruction of which was one object of their destination. Upon their having a distincter view of our ships they gave over the chase, and appear'd to be forming a line to receive us. From the equality of combatants, we concluded the action would be very great, and general; but I may venture to assert, there was not an Englishman from high to low, who did not assure himself of victory.

Upon our advancing, Marshal Conflans chang'd his plan, and put right before the wind towards the shore, seeking safety in his flight. At this critical time Sir Edward paid no regard to lines of battle but every ship was directed to make the best of her way towards the enemy: the admiral told his officers he was for the old way of fighting, to make downright work with them. At noon our headmost ships were pretty near them, and between one and two, the *Warspite* and *Dorsetshire* began to fire, and were then abreast of the Cardinal rocks. Presently after the *Revenge, Resolution, Torbay, Magnanime, Swiftsure, Montagu* and *Defiance*, came into action. The firing now became very alert on both sides, and there was no distinguishing any longer English colours from French. M. Du Vergen, the French rear-admiral, in the *Formidable*, bore a very fierce cannonade from the *Resolution*; but upon the *Royal George's* coming up, they hauled down their flag and struck to Sir Edward Hawke. This was only a point of honour, the *Resolution* having the merit of subduing them. The *Royal George* continued advancing, and Sir Edward gave orders to his master to carry him close alongside of M. Conflans in the *Soleil Royal*. The French admiral seem'd to have the same ambition on his part, and it was a glorious sight to behold the blue and the white flags both at the maintopmast head bearing down to each other. The *Royal George* passed the *Torbay* which was closely engaged with the *Thesee* of 74 guns, and who soon afterwards sent that unfortunate ship to the bottom. On the other side was the *Magnanime*, who kept an incessant fire on one of the largest of the French ships, and in the end obliged her to strike. She afterwards ran ashore, and was burnt. The two commander-in-chiefs were now very near, and M. Conflans gave the English admiral his broadside; the *Royal George* returned the uncivil salutation but after two or three discharges of this kind, the marshal of France declined the combat and sheered off. The French vice-admiral likewise gave Sir Edward his broadside, and soon followed the example of his superior. Another and another acted the same part; the fifth ship escaped not so well; Sir Edward poured his whole fire into her at once, and repeating the same, down she went along side of him. The *Royal George's* people gave a cheer, but it was a faint one; the honest sailors were touched at the miserable fate of so many hundreds of poor creatures. The blue flag was now encountered with seven ships at the same time, and appeared to be in the very centre of the French rear. Every observer pitied the *Royal George*, to see her singly engaged against so many of the enemy. It seems indeed a kind of degradation to so noble a ship to be pitied; but really her situation would have been lamentable, if the enemy had preserved any degree of composure, or fired with any sort of direction; but their confusion was so great, that of many hundreds of shot, I do not believe that more than 30 or 40 struck the ship. Sir Charles Hardy in the *Union*, with the *Mars*, *Hero*, and several other ships were crowding to the admiral's assistance, when the retreat of the French, covered by the obscurity of the evening, put an end to the engagement. Happy circumstance for the enemy, as an hour's daylight more would have brought on their total ruin.

This battle was fought so near the coast of Brittany, that ten thousand persons upon the shore were the sad witnesses of the white flag's disgrace.

The Gentleman's Magazine (December 1759)

1759 Battle of Quebec

English attempts to prevent French domination of North America were finally realized at the battle of Quebec on 13 September 1759, when General James Wolfe gained the advantage over the French after getting his troops up on to the Plains of Abraham above Quebec. This account is by Captain John Knox, one of Wolfe's officers.

. . . we then faced to the right, and marched towards the town by files, till we came to the plains of Abraham; an even piece of ground which Mr Wolfe had made choice of, while we stood forming upon the hill. Weather showery: about six o'clock the enemy made their appearance upon the heights, between us and the town; whereupon we halted, and wheeled to the right, thereby forming the line of battle . . . The enemy had now likewise formed the line of battle, and got some cannon to play on us, with round and canister shot; but what galled us most was a body of Indians and other marksmen they had concealed in the corn opposite to the front of our right wing . . . but Colonel Hale . . . advanced some platoons . . . which, after a few rounds, obliged these skulkers to retire. We were now ordered to lie down, and remained some time in this position. About eight o'clock we had two pieces of short brass six-pounders playing on the enemy, which threw them into some confusion . . . About ten o'clock the enemy began to advance briskly in three columns, with loud shouts and recovered arms, two of them inclining to the left of our army, and the third towards our right, firing obliquely at the two extremities of our line, from the distance of one hundred and thirty, until they came within forty yards; which our troops withstood with

136

the greatest intrepidity and firmness, still reserving their fire, and paying the strictest obedience to their Officers: this uncommon steadiness, together with the havoc which the grape-shot from our field-pieces made among them, threw them into some disorder, and was most critically maintained by a well-timed, regular and heavy discharge of our small arms, such as they could no longer oppose; hereupon they gave way, and fled with precipitation, so that, by the time the cloud of smoke was vanished, our men were again loaded, and profiting by the advantage we had over them, pursued them almost to the gates of the town, and the bridge over the little river, redoubling our fire with great eagerness, making many Officers and men prisoners. The weather cleared up, with a comfortably warm sunshine . . . Our joy at this success is inexpressibly damped by the loss we sustained of one of the greatest heroes which this or any other age can boast of – General James Wolfe, who received his mortal wound as he was exerting himself at the head of the grenadiers of Louisbourg . . .

After our late worthy general, of renowned memory, was carried off wounded, to the rear of the front line, he desired those who were about him to lay him down; being asked if he would have a Surgeon, he replied, 'It is needless; it is all over with me'. One of them then cried out, 'They run, see how they run'. 'Who runs?' demanded our hero, with great earnestness, like a person roused from sleep. The Officer answered, 'The enemy, Sir, Egad they give way everywhere'. Thereupon the General rejoined, 'Go one of you, my lads, to Colonel Burton; tell him to march Webb's regiment with all speed down to Charles's river, to cut off the retreat of the fugitives from the bridge'. Then, turning to his side, he added, 'Now; God be praised, I will die in peace:' and thus expired.

John Knox, *The Journals of John Knox* (1800)

1775–1783 *The American Revolution*

'There. I guess King George will be able to read that.'

(John Hancock, on signing the Declaration of Independence, 4 July 1776)

The philosophical, economic and political differences between Britain and the American colonies were brought to crisis by a series of Acts affecting taxation.

Hostilities broke out at Lexington on 19 April 1775.

1775 Bunker's Hill

This battle, fought on the heights overlooking Boston harbour on 17 June 1775, has profound psychological importance – it was the first time an American colonial army had fought a pitched battle with a regular English army, and had been able to hold their own until their ammunition ran out.

This account is by Lieutenant James Waller, Adjutant 1st Marine Battalion:

My dear Brother

Amidst the hurry and confusion of a camp hastily pitched in the field of battle, I am sat down to tell you I have escaped unhurt, where many, very many, have fallen. The public papers will inform you of the situation of the ground and the redoubt that we attacked on the heights of Charlestown. I can only say that it was a most desperate and daring attempt, and it was performed with as much gallantry and spirit as was ever shown by any troops in any age.

Two companies of the first battalion of Marines, and part of the 47th Regiment, were the first that mounted the breast-work: and you will not be displeased when I tell you that I was with those two companies, who drove their bayonets into all that opposed them. Nothing could be more shocking than the carnage that followed the storming this work. We tumbled over the dead to get at the living, who were crowding out of the gorge of the redoubt, in order to form under the defences which they had prepared to cover their retreat. In these breast-works they had artillery, which did so much mischief; but these they were obliged to abandon, being followed closely by the Light Infantry, who suffered exceedingly in the pursuit. The rebels had 5,000 to 7,000 men, covered by a redoubt, breast-works, walls, hedges, trees and the like; and the number of the corps under General Howe, (who performed this gallant business) did not amount to 1,500. We gained a complete victory, and entrenched ourselves that night, where we lay under arms, in the front of the field of battle. We lay the next night on the ground, and the following day encamped. The officers have not their marquees, but are obliged to lie in soldier's tents, they being more portable in case of our advancing.

We had of our corps one major, 2 captains, and 3 lieutenants killed; 4 captains and 3 lieutenants wounded; 2 serjeants and 21 rank and file killed, and 3 serjeants and 79 privates wounded; and I suppose, upon the whole, we lost, killed and wounded, from 800 to 1,000 men. We killed a number of the rebels, but the cover they fought under made their loss less considerable than it would otherwise have been. The army is in great spirits, and full of rage and ferocity at the rebellious rascals, who both poisoned and chewed the musket balls, in order to make them the more fatal. Many officers have died of their wounds, and others very ill: 'tis astonishing what a number of officers were hit on this occasion; but the officers were particularly aimed at.

Paul Harris Nicolas, *Historical Records of the Royal Marine Forces* (1844)

1777 Stillwater

The decisive battle of the war, in which an English force of 6,000 under General Burgoyne was defeated by the Colonial army under General Gates.

This account records the adventures of Major John Dyke Acland, of Burgoyne's staff, who was wounded and taken prisoner. His wife set out to rescue him, after appealing for help from his commanding officer. Burgoyne wrote to the Colonial Commander, General Gates:

'Sir, – Lady Harriet Acland, a lady of the first distinction of family, rank, and personal virtues, is under such concern on account of Major Ackland, her husband, wounded and a prisoner in your hands, that I cannot refuse her request to commit her to your protection. Whatever general impropriety there may be in persons of my situation and yours to solicit favours, I cannot see the uncommon perseverance in every female grace, and the exaltation of character of this lady, and her very hard fortune, without testifying that your attentions to her will lay me under obligations. I am, sir, your obedient servant, J. Burgoyne.' She set out in an open boat upon the Hudson, accompanied by Mr Brudenell, the chaplain, Sarah Pollard, her waiting-maid, and her husband's valet, who had been severely wounded, while searching for his master upon the battle-field. It was about sunset when they started, and a violent storm of rain and wind, which had been increasing since the morning, rendered the voyage tedious and perilous in the extreme. It was long after dark when they reached the American outposts; the sentinel heard their oars, and hailed them. Lady Harriet returned the answer herself. The clear, silvery tones of a woman's voice amid the darkness, filled the soldier on duty with superstitious fear, and he called a comrade to accompany him to the river bank. The errand of the voyagers was made known, but the faithful guard, apprehensive of treachery, would not allow them to land until they sent for Major Dearborn. They were invited by that officer to his quarters, where every attention was paid to them, and Lady Harriet was comforted by the joyful tidings that her husband was safe. In the morning she experienced parental tenderness from General Gates, who sent her to her husband, at Poor's quarters, under a suitable escort. There she remained until he was removed to Albany.

Carlo Botti, Storia della Guerra d'Independenza degli Stati d'America (1809)

1792 Cannonade of Valmy

The French victory over the invading Austrian and Prussian armies laid the foundations of the success of the French Revolution. Among the invading army was the German poet Goethe, who wrote this account:

I had heard so much of the cannon-fever, that I wanted to know what kind of thing it was. *Ennui*, and a spirit which every kind of danger excites to daring, nay even to rashness, induced me to ride up quite coolly to the outwork of La Lune. This was again occupied by our people; but it presented the wildest aspect. The roofs were shot to pieces; the corn-shocks scattered about, the bodies of men mortally wounded stretched upon them here and there; and occasionally a spent cannon-ball fell and rattled among the ruins of the tile roofs.

Quite alone, and left to myself, I rode away on the heights to the left, and could plainly survey the favourable position of the French; they were standing in the form of a semicircle, in the greatest quiet and security; Kellerman, then on the left wing, being the easiest to reach.

I fell in with good company on the way, officers of my acquaintance, belonging to the general staff and the regiment, greatly surprised to find me here. They wanted to take me back again with them; but I spoke to them of particular objects I had in view, and they left me, without further dissuasion, to my well-known singular caprice.

I had now arrived quite in the region where the balls were playing across me: the sound of them is curious enough, as if it were composed of the humming of tops, the gurgling of water, and the whistling of birds. They were less dangerous, by reason of the wetness of the ground; wherever one fell, it stuck fast. And thus my foolish experimental ride was secured against the danger at least of the balls rebounding.

In the midst of these circumstances, I was soon able to remark that something unusual was taking place within me. I paid close attention to it, and still the sensation can be described only by similitude. It appeared as if you were in some extremely hot place, and, at the same time, quite penetrated by the heat of it, so that you feel yourself, as it were, quite one with the element in which you are. The eyes lose nothing of their strength or clearness; but it is as if the world had a kind of brown-red tint, which makes the situation, as well as the surrounding objects, more impressive. I was unable to perceive any agitation of the blood; but everything seemed rather to be swallowed up in the glow of which I speak. From this, then, it is clear in what sense this condition can be called a fever. It is remarkable, however, that the horrible uneasy feeling arising from it is produced in us solely through the ears; for the cannon-thunder, the howling, and crashing of the balls through the air, is the real cause of these sensations.

Johann Wolfgang Goethe, *Campaign in France 1792*, translated by G. F. Farie (1822)

1794 Battle of Ushant

This Anglo-French naval engagement is known as the 'glorious first of June' although the English failed in their objective of preventing the French from shipping supplies to America. The English fleet, commanded by Admiral Richard Howe, intercepted the French in the Atlantic, four hundred miles off Ushant, after trailing them for days. The supply fleet continued on its way, but the English inflicted terrible damage on its French escort. This account is from a letter home written by Lieutenant James Smith dated 3 June 1794:

On Friday and until Saturday evening we were in so thick a fog that we could scarce distinguish each other, but the fog clearing up then, the enemy were seen to leeward, when Lord Howe formed the line, but very prudently deferred the engagement till next morning as it was then near sunset. On Sunday morning the 1st June the signal was made to break the enemy's line and engage them close. The *Royal George*, seeing that a French three-decker would fall to the lot of one of our seventy-fours as the line was then formed, changed stations with her, and the whole fleet bore down, the enemy lying to receive us in very good order. The *Royal George* led the rear, and first broke through the line by throwing a very heavy fire into the bows of an 80-gun ship on her starboard (right) quarter, and then completely raking the *Terrible* (the three-decker) on her larboard or left quarter. She then ran close up to the *Terrible* and engaged her for some time, but the Frenchman did not choose to stand it, and, being less damaged in her rigging, made off. The line was soon most completely broken. The *Queen Charlotte* dismasted an 80-gun ship, and so completely raked her in three broadsides that she lost 350 men killed or wounded.

In short, after a most severe action, six French ships are taken totally dismasted, four sunk, and six towed away by their fleet totally dismasted. In two hours after the action began I counted seven Frenchmen with not a stick standing above their decks. Of our ships, the *Marlborough* and the *Defence* are totally dismasted, the *Royal George* nearly so, but we are now in tolerable order again; the *Queen* very much damaged and behaved most gallantly. The French fought with desperate bravery and great rascality . . . One Frenchman fired into another who had struck; another struck, having been fired into by their own ships for striking; a third was sunk by the *Royal Sovereign*, and a fourth sank after she was in our possession. One fired into us in a rascally manner. Another fired into the *Phaeton* in an equally rascally manner, and killed five men; and another would have been blown up by her captain after surrendering if the crew had permitted it. This villainous behaviour disgraces the gallant and desperate spirit with which they fought. 180 prisoners are on board us from the *Juste*, which was so raked by the *Queen Charlotte* that they say they lost 350 killed and wounded. It could not be otherwise – their 80-gun ships had 1,000, and their first-rates 1,500 men, and we were so close to them they must have fallen by hundreds. Our loss is trifling in comparison – 20 killed and 76 wounded . . .

T. Sturges Jackson, *Logs of the Great Sea Fights 1794–1805*
(1899)

142

VIII

THE NAPOLEONIC WARS

1799–1815 Napoleonic Wars

1805 Battle of Trafalgar

The most celebrated English naval victory, Trafalgar destroyed Napoleon's planned invasion of England and established English naval supremacy for a century. It is also remembered for the death of England's greatest naval hero, Admiral Horatio Nelson. This account is from the dispatch sent to the Admiralty by Admiral Collingwood:

Such a battle could not be fought without sustaining a great loss of men. I have not only to lament, in common with the British navy and the British nation, in the fall of the Commander-in-Chief, the loss of a hero whose name will be immortal and his memory ever dear to his country, but my heart is rent with the most poignant grief for the death of a friend to whom, by many years' intimacy and a perfect knowledge of the virtues of his mind, which inspired ideas superior to the common race of men, I was bound by the strongest ties of affection; a grief to which even the glorious occasion in which he fell does not bring the consolation which perhaps it ought. His Lordship received a musket ball in his left breast, about the middle of the action, and sent an officer to me immediately, with his last farewell, and soon after expired. I have also to lament the loss of those excellent officers, Captains Duff of the *Mars* and Cooke of the *Bellerophon*; I have yet heard of none others. I fear the numbers that have fallen will be found very great when the returns come to me, but it having blowed a gale of wind ever since the action, I have not yet had it in my power to collect any reports from the ships.

This account is allegedly by Robert Guillemard, who, it is claimed, fired the shot which killed Nelson:

In less than half an hour our vessel, without having hauled down her

143

colours, had in fact surrendered. Her fire had gradually slackened, and then ceased altogether. The mutilated bodies of our companions encumbered the two decks, which were covered with shot, broken cannon, matches still smoaking, and shattered timbers. One of our thirty-six pounders had burst towards the close of the contact. The thirteen men placed at it had been killed by the splinters, and were heaped round its broken carriage. The ladders that led between the different decks were shattered and destroyed; the mizzen-mast and main-mast had fallen, and encumbered the decks with blocks and pieces of rigging. Of the boats placed forward, or hung on the sides of our vessel, there remained nothing but some shattered planks. Not more than a hundred and fifty men survived out of a crew of about eight hundred, and almost all these were more or less severely wounded. Captain Lucas was one of the number.

It was five o'clock when the action ceased. I went over the ship where everything presented a prospect of desolation . . .

In the evening English long-boats came to take away the remainder of our crew, to be divided among the vessels of the fleet; and I was taken on board the *Victory*. There I learned the death of Nelson: he had been wounded on the right shoulder by a ball, which penetrated obliquely, and broke the spine of the back . . .

He whose death is regretted by an entire nation, he whose death is deplored by old sailors, usually little susceptible of sentiments of attachment, should necessarily inspire some interest, even in an enemy; hence, as a man, I could not help sharing in some degree the affliction that prevailed on board the *Victory*; while as a Frenchman, I had reason to rejoice at an event that had delivered my country from one of her most dangerous enemies. At any rate, from the moment in which he received his wound, and the position of the wound itself, I could not doubt for a moment that I was the author . . . But though the shot that had brought down this admiral had rendered a service to my country, I was far from considering it an action of which I had a right to boast.

Adventures of a French Sergeant from 1805 to 1823 (1826)

1809 Corunna

Napoleon joined his French army in Spain in November 1808, and after capturing Madrid he turned north west to meet the British, under Sir John Moore, advancing from Corunna. After the siege of Saragossa he believed Spain was under French control and he left Marshal Soult to deal with the remaining British. Moore's forces retreated to the coast. The French attempt to prevent the British evacuation by sea reached its climax in the Battle of Corunna, 16 January 1809. Soult's army — 20,000 — was resisted by Moore's forces — 15,000. The British safely embarked. Both armies lost about 1,000 men. Sir John Moore died in the engagement and was buried in the ramparts at Corunna. The event has been rendered immortal in Charles Wolfe's poem, based on the account in the *Annual Register*:

THE BURIAL OF SIR JOHN MOORE
AFTER CORUNNA

Not a drum was heard, not a funeral note,
    As his corse to the rampart we hurried;
Not a soldier discharged his farewell shot
    O'er the grave where our hero we buried.

We buried him darkly at dead of night,
    The sods with our bayonets turning,
By the struggling moonbeam's misty light
    And the lanthorn dimly burning.

No useless coffin enclosed his breast,
    Not in sheet or in shroud we wound him;
But he lay like a warrior taking his rest
    With his martial cloak around him.

Few and short were the prayers we said,
    And we spoke not a word of sorrow;
But we steadfastly gazed on the face that was dead,
    And we bitterly thought of the morrow.

We thought, as we hollow'd his narrow bed
    And smoothed down his lonely pillow,
That the foe and the stranger would tread o'er his head,
    And we far away on the billow!

Lightly they'll talk of the spirit that's gone,
    And o'er his cold ashes upbraid him —
But little he'll reck, if they let him sleep on
    In the grave where a Briton has laid him.

But half of our heavy task was done
    When the clock struck the hour for retiring;
And we heard the distant and random gun
    That the foe was sullenly firing.

Slowly and sadly we laid him down,
From the field of his fame fresh and gory;
We carved not a line, and we raised not a stone,
But we left him alone with his glory.

Charles Wolfe: *The Burial of Sir John Moore After Corunna*
first published in the *Newry Telegraph* (1817).

1810 Peninsula Campaign

Wives and camp followers accompanied the forces during the prolonged Peninsula Campaign 1807–1814.

At the battle of Rolica, Portugal, 17 August 1808, Rifleman Harris saw the pathetic scenes of a wife who had lost her husband in the battle administer the service for the dead as well as she could:

> The Rifles, indeed, fought well this day, and we lost many men. They seemed in high spirits, and delighted at having driven the enemy before them. Joseph Cochan was by my side, loading and firing very industriously, about this period of the day. Thirsting with heat and action, he lifted his canteen to his mouth.
>
> 'Here's to you, old boy,' he said as he took a pull at its contents. As he did so a bullet went through the canteen, and perforating his brain killed him in a moment . . .
>
> When the roll was called after the battle, the females who missed their husbands came along the front of the line to inquire of the survivors whether they knew anything about them. Among other names I heard that of Cochan called, in a female voice . . . and I observed the poor woman who had called it, as she stood sobbing before us and apparently afraid to make further inquiries about her husband . . . as I looked at the poor sobbing creature before me I felt unable to tell her of his death. At length Captain Leech observed her, and called out to the company: 'Does any man here know what has happened to Cochan? If so, let him speak out at once.'
>
> Upon this order I immediately related what I had seen . . . After a while Mrs Cochan appeared anxious to see the spot where her husband fell . . . She trusted, notwithstanding what I had told her, to find him yet alive . . .
>
> 'Go then,' said the captain, 'and show the poor woman the spot, as she seems desirous of finding the body.'
>
> I accordingly took my way over the ground we had fought upon, she following and sobbing after me; and quickly reaching the spot, where her husband's body lay, I pointed it out to her. She now

discovered all her hopes were in vain. She embraced the stiffened corpse, and after rising and contemplating his disfigured face for some minutes, with hands clasped and tears streaming down her cheeks, she took a prayer book from her pocket, and kneeling down repeated the service for the dead over the body. When she had finished she appeared a good deal comforted; and I took the opportunity of beckoning to a pioneer I saw near with some other men, and together we dug a hole and quickly buried the body. Mrs Cochan then returned with me to the company to which her husband had been attached . . . The company . . . was now her home; and she marched and took equal fortune with us to Vimieria . . . and then went with us to Lisbon, where she succeeded in procuring a passage to England.

Sir John Kincaid, 'Recollections of Rifleman Harris', in
Adventures in the Rifle Brigade (1830)

If wives remained safely at home while their menfolk served abroad on the continent, moments of terrible parting had to be endured, such as the scene as a young soldier leaves for service in Spain in 1810:

One young couple never went to bed, but sat the whole night on their berth, with their only child between them, alternately embracing it and each other, and lamenting their cruel fortune. I never witnessed in my life a more affecting scene. The poor fellow tried to assume some firmness but in vain: some feeling expression from her would throw him off his guard, and at last his grief became quite uncontrollable. When the first bugle sounded, he got up and prepared his things. Here a new source of grief sprang up. In laying aside the articles which he intended to leave, and which they had used together, the idea seemed fixed in her mind that they would never use them in that way again; and as she put them aside, she watered them with her tears. Her teapot, her cups, and everything they had in common — all had the apostrophe of sorrow. He tried to persuade her to remain in the barracks, as we had six miles to travel to the place of embarkation; but she said she would take the last moment of his company she could.

John Donaldson, *Recollections of an Eventful Life* (1852)

1811 Battle of Albuera

This is an account from the bloody engagement at Albuera on 16 May 1811, when an Allied force of 35,000 was suddenly assaulted by a French army of 25,000. Spanish and Portuguese troops fled the field but

English infantry steadfastly held their ground. Losses were huge – the French lost 8,000, the Allies 7,640.

A few lines, my dearest Mother, I, in haste sit down and write, to say, that under the protection of Almighty God, I have escaped unhurt in one of the severest actions that ever was contested between France and England; to describe the Horrors that were witnessed on the ever memorable 16th of May would be impossible, but as the part the unfortunate 1st Brigade of the 2 Division took on that day might be a little interesting to you, I will relate it as far as I am able.

I think it was about 10 o'clock a.m. when the French menaced an attack on our left; we immediately moved to support it. It proved, however, to be a feint, and the Right of the Line was destined to be the spot (Oh, never to be effaced from my mind) where Britons were to be repulsed; 3 solid columns attacked our regiment alone. We fought them till we were hardly a Regiment. The Commanding Officer was shot dead, and the two Officers carrying the Colours close by my side received their mortal wounds. In this shattered state, our Brigade moved forward to charge. Madness alone would dictate such a thing, and at that critical period Cavalry appeared in our rear. It was then that our men began to waver, and for the first time (and God knows I hope the last) I saw the backs of English soldiers turned upon French. Our Regiment once rallied, but to what avail! we were independent of Infantry: out-numbered with Cavalry. I was taken prisoner, but re-taken by the Spanish Cavalry.

Oh, what a day was that. The worst of the story I have not related. Our Colours were taken. I told you before the 2 Ensigns were shot under them; 2 Sergeants shared the same fate. A Lieutenant seized a Musket to defend them, and he was shot to the heart; what could be done against Cavalry?

Adieu, my Dear Mother, for the present. Give my most affectionate and kindest love to my Father, Annie, William and all at home, and believe me to be your most affectionate Son.

[Signed] G. Crompton,
A miserable Lt. of the unfortunate 66th Regt.

P.S. – The Fuziler Brigade afterwards came on, also the other Brigades in the Division with some Spaniards and Portuguese beat back the French and gained a complete Victory.

Journal of the Society of Army Historical Research

1812 Ben Battle — A Hero of Badajos,
17 March 1812

FAITHLESS NELLY GRAY:
A PATHETIC BALLAD

Ben Battle was a soldier bold,
    And used to war's alarms;
But a cannon ball took off his legs,
    So he laid down his arms!

Now as they bore him off the field,
    Said he, 'Let others shoot,
For here I leave my second leg,
    And the Forty-second Foot!'

The army-surgeons made him limbs:
    Said he — 'They're only pegs:
But there's as wooden members quite
    As represent my legs!'

Now Ben he loved a pretty maid,
    Her name was Nelly Gray;
So he went to pay her his devours
    When he'd devoured his pay!

But when he called on Nelly Gray,
    She made him quite a scoff;
And when she saw his wooden legs,
    Began to take them off!

'O Nelly Gray! O Nelly Gray!
    Is this your love so warm?
The love that loves a scarlet coat,
    Should be more uniform!'

She said, 'I loved a soldier once,
    For he was blithe and brave;
But I will never have a man
    With both legs in the grave!

'Before you had those timber toes,
    Your love I did allow,
But then, you know, you stand upon
    Another footing now!'

149

'O Nelly Gray! O Nelly Gray!
  For all your jeering speeches,
At duty's call I left my legs
  In Badajos's *breaches*!'

'Why then,' said she, 'you've lost the feet
  Of legs in war's alarms,
And now you cannot wear your shoes
  Upon your feats of arms!'

'Oh, false and fickle Nelly Gray,
  I know why you refuse: –
Though I've no feet – some other man
  Is standing in my shoes!

'I wish I ne'er had seen your face;
  But now a long farewell!
For you will be my death: – alas!
  You will not be my *Nell*!'

Now when he went home from Nelly Gray,
  His heart so heavy got –
And life was such a burthen grown,
  It made him take a knot!

So round his melancholy neck
  A rope he did entwine,
And, for his second time in life,
  Enlisted in the Line!

One end he tied around a beam,
  And then removed his pegs,
And, as his legs were off, – of course
  He soon was off his legs!

And there he hung till he was dead
  As any nail in town, –
For though distress had cut him up,
  It could not cut him down!

A dozen men sat on his corpse,
  To find out why he died –
And they buried Ben at four cross-roads,
  With a *stake* in his inside!

Thomas Hood

1812 Retreat from Moscow

Napoleon invaded Russia in June 1812. Although the Grand Army numbered 460,000, the campaign was ultimately a disaster. They occupied Moscow in September, and fired it. Failing to inflict severe damage on enemy forces, with his supply lines inadequate, troop morale declining, and the winter closing in, Napoleon decided to retreat at the end of October.

The Grand Army was constantly harassed by Russian forces as it escaped back along the route it had triumphantly travelled in June. Accounts of his engineers building pontoon bridges for crossings, and freezing to death as they worked part-submerged in icy waters, are the stuff of nightmare. When Napoleon left his army to return to Paris, a mere 10,000 troops survived.

This account is from the memoirs of a sergeant of infantry who survived the retreat, dying at the age of eighty-one in 1867:

I cannot possibly describe all the sufferings, anguish, and scenes of desolation I had seen and passed through, nor those which I was fated still to see and endure; they left deep and terrible memories, which I have never forgotten.

This was 25 November, perhaps about seven o'clock in the morning, and as yet it was hardly light. I was musing on all I had seen, when the head of the column appeared. Those in advance seemed to be Generals, a few on horseback, but the greater part on foot. There were also a great number of other officers, the remnant of the Doomed Squadron and Battalion formed on the 22nd, and barely existing at the end of three days. Those on foot dragged themselves painfully along, almost all of them having their feet frozen and wrapped in rags or in bits of sheepskin, and all nearly dying of hunger. Afterwards came the small remains of the Cavalry of the Guard. The Emperor came next, on foot, and carrying a stick. He wore a large cloak lined with fur, a dark-red velvet cap with black fox fur on his head. Murat walked on foot at his right, and on his left Prince Eugène, Viceroy of Italy. Next came the Marshals, Berthier — Prince of Neufchâtel — Ney, Mortier, Lefebvre, with other Marshals and Generals whose corps had been nearly annihilated.

The Emperor mounted a horse as soon as he passed: so did a few of those with him, the greater part of them having no more horses to ride. Seven or eight hundred officers and non-commissioned officers followed, walking in order and perfect silence, and carrying the eagles of their different regiments, which so often had led them to victory. This was all that remained of 60,000 men . . .

I had more than an hour to wait before the column had passed by, and after that there was a long train of miserable wretches following the regiments mechanically. They had reached the last stage of destitution, and could not hope to get across the Berezina, although we were now so near it. Then I saw the remains of the Young Guard, skirmishers, flankmen, and some of the light companies, escaped from Krasnoi. All these regiments mingled together marched in perfect order. Behind them came the artillery and several waggons. The bulk of the artillery, commanded by General Nègre, had already passed. Next came the Fusilier-Chasseurs. Their numbers were greatly diminished. Our regiment was still separated from me by some pieces of artillery, drawn by poor beasts with no power left in them . . .

I never remember in all my life having such a terrible longing for sleep, and yet we were obliged to go on. My friends supported me under the arms again, telling me to go to sleep. This we did for each other in turn, for sleep overcame us all. Frequently it happened that we stopped short, all three of us having gone off. The cold, fortunately, was much less that day, otherwise most of us might have been frozen to death.

In the middle of the night we reached Borisov. The Emperor stayed in a country house on the right of the road, and the Guard bivouacked round it . . .

The next day (the 26th) we took up a position on the banks of the Berezina. The Emperor was at Studianka, a little village on a hill in front.

We saw the brave *pontonniers* working hard at the bridges for us to cross. They had worked all night, standing up to their shoulders in ice-cold water, encouraged by their General. These brave men sacrificed their lives to save the army. One of my friends told me as a fact that he had seen the Emperor himself handing wine to them.

The first bridge was finished at two o'clock in the afternoon. It was a painful and difficult piece of work, as the trestles sank continually in the mud. Marshal Oudinot's corps crossed immediately to attack the Russians, who had tried to prevent our passage. The cavalry of the 2nd Corps had already swum across, not waiting for the bridge to be finished, and every man took a foot soldier behind him. The second bridge, for the artillery and cavalry, was finished at four o'clock . . .

Directly we arrived at the banks of the river I lay down wrapped up in my fur, and then found myself trembling all over with fever. I was delirious for a long time . . .

On the next day (the 27th) I felt rather better, but terribly weak. That day the Emperor crossed the Berezina with part of the Guard, and about a thousand men belonging to Marshal Ney's corps. Our regiment remained on the banks . . .

We were a medley of Frenchmen, Italians, Spaniards, Portuguese, Croats, Germans, Poles, Romans, Neapolitans, and even Prussians. I saw some canteen men whose wives and children were in great despair, weeping. We noticed that the men seemed to suffer more, both morally and physically, than the women. The women bore their sufferings and privations with an astonishing courage, enough to reflect shame on certain men, who had no courage and resignation to endure their trials. Very few of these women died, except those who fell into the Berezina in crossing the bridge, or some who were suffocated.

Memoirs of Adrien-Baptiste-François Bourgogne, translated by J. W. Fortescue (1926)

1813 Battle of Nivelle

Private Wheeler of the 51st Regiment of Foot left a valuable series of letters recounting his experiences in Wellington's army. After being wounded at the Battle of Nivelle in the Peninsula Campaign on 10 November 1813, Wheeler managed to find shelter in a hedge. He was attended to by the regimental surgeon and then proceeded to a farmhouse which had been used to store food and drink, but had now been ransacked by soldiers and camp followers. There, he saw sights of drunkenness and compassion:

. . . drinking and smoking, others rolling about, some half and others dead drunk, while a great many lay stretched out as if dead. Women, too, who had followed up the rear of the army, had forgot they had come up in the laudable pursuit of seeking their husbands and had freely partaken of the damnable poison until they had transformed themselves into something more like fiends than angels of mercy . . .

In one place you could see a lovely young woman supporting the head of her dying husband on her bosom, anxiously awaiting the last gasp for life, then again your eye would meet with one in bitter anguish, bewailing her loss, fondly clinging to the cold remains of all that was dear to her, and many more were running about mad, unconscious of where they were going or what they were doing, these had received news of their husbands' deaths in some distant part of the field.

The Letters of Private Wheeler 1809–28, edited by B. H. Liddell Hart (1951)

1815 Battle of Waterloo

This was the last battle of Napoleon's 'Hundred Days', fought in wet weather, on 18 June 1815.

Napoleon commanded an army of 80,000, with 246 guns. The Allied armies consisted of 24,000 British, 43,000 Dutch and Belgian troops with 156 guns.

Wellington's positions were well chosen, along the line of hills covering the route to Brussels, affording cover for his troops from French artillery. He held two advanced posts – two farms, La Haye Sainte and Hougemont.

The Allied infantry held against several French assaults, accompanied by ferocious artillery fire. By six o'clock in the evening, the French had captured La Haye Sainte, but the arrival of the Prussians under Bluecher saved the day.

As Wellington was to say, it was a close run thing. The British lost 15,000, the Prussians 7,000 (Dutch and Belgian losses were small, as they left the field early in the day). The French lost 25,000 – killed, wounded or taken prisoner. About 15,000 horses were killed.

This account, by a British Army surgeon, gives some interesting close-ups of the actions and reactions during the battle. The contest had been raging for some time before he was ordered to the village of Mont Saint-Jean, where the wounded were sent.

At last we got up to them, and were informed that the services of only one medical officer were required, and, being the junior, it fell to my lot to remain . . . The regiment was halted and we were sheltered from all but shell firing by hugging the bank of a sunken road or lane, and here I received orders as to how I was to act when they engaged the enemy, and was informed of all that had occurred since we parted. It was a terrible roll of killed and wounded; but the violent death of so many of their comrades did not seem in any way to affect the spirits of the men, who during this short interval talked most unconcernedly of the fate of their companions, describing the death of one man whose head had been taken clean off by a round shot, as if he had only lost a finger. The canteen of gin passed round from lip to lip familiarly as if they were sitting in an alehouse, instead of on horseback waiting for an order to be again engaged. They were laughing and joking, made light of the weariness of themselves and horses, and declared they would yet be avenged for the loss of their comrades . . .

I had not been ten minutes in the village, indeed had hardly commenced giving my assistance, when the Colonel of my regiment was brought in desperately wounded, he telling me it had occurred almost immediately after I had left his side. A round shot had shattered his leg, and entering the horse's abdomen, killed it on the spot. As the wounded limb was on the side near which I had been riding, it is not improbable that had I remained I also should have suffered. The leg was only suspended by a few muscles and the bone in splinters. Amputation, and that at once, was the only chance.

I got the Colonel placed in a room where there were several other wounded officers, and separating the foot from its connections, told him he must undergo the operation of amputation. Then after obviating all danger from hæmorrage, I endeavoured to get him removed to a more suitable place for the operation, so removing a door from an outhouse, we placed him upon it . . . With the aid of my door and six men we got the Colonel to the village of Waterloo, about one mile distant, and sought for accommodation, but every house and cottage was crowded. Men and officers intermingled; many of whom as yet had not received surgical aid, and among these, to my great grief, I came across my dear young friend, Lieutenant Buckley of my regiment. He had received a bullet wound in the stomach, the missile had passed through his liver and came out through his back causing great hæmorrage. I hurriedly dressed the wound and gave him all the hopes possible, but did not conceal my misgivings. It was a melancholy sight to find a youth of his age, perhaps nineteen or twenty, cut off in the very opening of life, and this his first battle. He had done his duty, and acted as bravely as the oldest soldier, and now dying, he behaved and spoke as became a Christian. I loved him well, but I had to leave him and rejoin the Colonel, for whom as yet no place of comfort could be found. At length we were obliged to be satisfied with a miserable room and a more miserable bed or pallet in a small public house, where there was only one other wounded officer. It suited our purpose, and the people of the house were civil and obliging. Towards nine o'clock the firing from both armies slackened, and soon after we had the satisfaction of knowing that the French army was in full retreat, pursued by the Prussians.

Thomas Gibney, *Eighty Years Ago, or, The Recollections of an Old Army Doctor* (1896)

This is Wellington's own account, from a letter dated 19 June 1815 to Earl Bathurst:

The enemy collected his army, with the exception of the 3rd corps, which had been sent to observe Marshal Blücher, on a range of heights in our front, in the course of the night of the 17th and yesterday morning, and at about 10 o'clock he commenced a furious attack upon our post at Hougoumont. I had occupied that post with a detachment from General Byng's brigade of Guards, which was in position in its rear; and it was for some time under the command of Lieut. Colonel Macdonnell, and afterwards of Colonel Home; and I am happy to add, that it was maintained throughout the day with the utmost gallantry by these brave troops, notwithstanding the repeated efforts of large bodies of the enemy to obtain possession of it.

This attack upon the right of our centre was accompanied by a very heavy cannonade upon our whole line, which was destined to support the repeated attacks of cavalry and infantry, occasionally mixed, but sometimes separate, which were made upon it. In one of these the enemy carried the farm house of La Haye Sainte, as the detachment of the light battalion of the German Legion, which occupied it, had expended all its ammunition; and the enemy occupied the only communication there was with them.

The enemy repeatedly charged our infantry with his cavalry, but these attacks were uniformly unsuccessful; and they afforded opportunities to our cavalry to charge, in one of which Lord E. Somerset's brigade, consisting of the Life Guards, the Royal Horse Guards, and 1st dragoon guards, highly distinguished themselves, as did that of Major General Sir W. Ponsonby, having taken many prisoners and an eagle.

These attacks were repeated till about 7 in the evening, when the enemy made a desperate effort with cavalry and infantry, supported by the fire of artillery, to force our left centre, near the farm of La Haye Sainte, which, after a severe contest, was defeated; and, having observed that the troops retired from this attack in great confusion, and that the march of General Bülow's corps, by Frischermont, upon Planchenois and La Belle Alliance, had begun to take effect, and as I could perceive the fire of his cannon, and as Marshal Prince Blücher had joined in person with a corps of his army to the left of our line by Ohain, I determined to attack the enemy, and immediately advanced the whole line of infantry, supported by the cavalry and artillery. The attack succeeded in every point: the enemy was forced from his positions on the heights, and fled in the utmost confusion, leaving behind him, as far as I could judge, 150 pieces of cannon, with their ammunition, which fell into our hands.

I continued the pursuit till long after dark, and then discontinued it only on account of the fatigue of our troops, who had been engaged during 12 hours, and because I found myself on the same road with

Marshal Blücher, who assured me of his intention to follow the enemy throughout the night.

Herbert Maxwell, *Life of Wellington* (1900)

Napoleon's letter to the Prince Regent:

Exposed to the factions which distract my country and to the enmity of the greatest Powers of Europe, I have ended my political career, and I come, like Themistocles, to throw myself upon the hospitality of the British people. I put myself under the protection of their laws, which I claim from your Royal Highness, as the most powerful, the most constant, and the most generous of my enemies.

Rochefort, 13 July 1815

Translation from the original, held in the Royal Archives, Windsor

IX

EARLY COLONIAL CONFLICTS

1831–1842 First Afghan War: Retreat from Kabul

The North West Frontier was for generations an area of concern to British colonial/imperial interests. During an uprising the British garrison in Kabul surrendered, and Major General William Elphistone's force of 4,500 troops and 12,000 refugees (wives, children, civilian staff) were promised safe conduct to India.

But in January they were attacked and massacred by tribesmen at the Khyber Pass. Only a few survived. This account is from the journals of Lady Florentia Sale, wife of Colonel Robert Henry Sale, defender of Jalalabad:

The ladies were mostly travelling in camel-panniers and were mixed up with the baggage and column in the pass; here they were heavily fired on and many camels were killed. On one camel were, in one pannier, Mrs Boyd and her youngest boy Hugh, and in the other Mrs Mainwairing and her infant, scarcely three months old, and Mrs Anderson's eldest child. This camel was shot. Mrs Boyd got a horse to ride, and her child was put on another behind a man, who, being shortly after unfortunately killed, the child was carried off by the Afghans. Mrs Mainwairing, less fortunate, took her own baby in her arms. Mary Anderson was carried off in the confusion. Meeting with a pony laden with treasure, Mrs Mainwairing endeavoured to mount and sit on the boxes, but they were upset, and in the hurry pony and treasure were left behind, and the unfortunate lady pursued her way on foot, until after a time an Afghan asked her if she was wounded, and told her to mount behind him. This apparently kind offer she declined, being fearful of treachery, alleging as an excuse that she could not sit behind him on account of the difficulty of holding her child when so mounted. This man shortly after snatched her shawl off her shoulders, and left her to her fate.

Mrs Mainwairing's sufferings were very great; she not only had to walk a considerable distance with her child in her arms through the deep snow, but had also to pick her way over the bodies of the dead, and dying, and wounded, both men and cattle, and constantly to cross the streams of water, wet up to the knees, pushed and shovelled about by men and animals, the enemy keeping up a sharp fire, and several persons being killed close to her. She, however, got safe to camp with her child . . .

Poor Sturt was laid on the side of a bank, with his wife and myself beside him. It began snowing heavily; Johnson and Bygrave got some coarse blanket thrown over us.

Dr Bryce came and examined Sturt's wound and he dressed it, but I saw by the expression of his countenance that there was no hope. He afterwards kindly cut the ball out of my wrist, and dressed both my wounds. Half of a Sipahee's pall had been pitched, in which the ladies and their husbands took refuge. We had no one to scrape the snow off the ground in it. Captain Johnson and Mr Mein first assisted poor Sturt over to it, and then carried Mrs Sturt and myself through the deep snow. Mrs Sturt's bedding (saved by the nurse riding on it, whom we kept up close with ourselves) was now a comfort to my poor wounded son. He suffered dreadful agony all night, and intolerable thirst, and most grateful did we feel to Mr Mein for going out constantly to the stream to procure water; we had only a small vessel to fetch it in, which contained but a few mouthfuls. To sleep in such anxiety of mind and intense cold was impossible. There were nearly thirty of us packed together, without room to turn.

The Sepoys and camp-followers, half-frozen, tried to force their way, not only into the tent, but actually into our beds, if such resting places can be so called . . . a pelisse of sheepskin half spread on the snow, and the other half wrapped over one. Many poor wretches died round the tent in the night. The light company of the 54th Native Infantry, which left Kabul thirty-six hours previously eighty strong, was reduced to eighteen. This is only one instance which may fairly be taken as a general average of the destruction of our force.

Florentia Sale, Journals (1843)

Only one man survived this terrible exploit. Lady Sale and her child were among the ninety-five prisoners taken by Akbar Khan and held at Kabul, who were dramatically rescued in September 1842 by Sir Richmond Shakespear as part of Sir George Pollock's punitive invasion of Afghanistan.

1849 Second Sikh War: Chilianwallah

The Second Sikh War was fought to put down continued unrest in the Punjab, despite British victories at Moodkee, Ferozeshah and Sabraon. A British force of 10,000 under Sir John Littler, stationed at Lahore, failed to contain the situation, and Viscount Gough was dispatched to subdue the risings led by Chutter Singh, and his son, Shere Singh – who had amassed a force of 40,000. This account of the Battle of Chilianwallah on 14 January 1849 is from Gough's own report:

Having learned from my spies, and from other sources of information, that Shere Singh still held with his right the villages of Lukhneewallah and Futteh Shah-ke-Chuck, having the great body of his force at the village of Lolianwallah, with his left at Russool, on the Jhelum, strongly occupying the southern extremity of a low range of difficult hills intersected by ravines, which extended nearly to that village, I made my arrangements accordingly that evening, and communicated them to the commanders of the several divisions; but, to ensure correct information as to the nature of the country, which I believed to be excessively difficult and ill adapted to the advantage of a regular army, I determined upon moving on this village, Chilianwallah, to reconnoitre.

On the morning of the 13th the force advanced. I made a considerable detour to my right, partly in order to distract the enemy's attention, but principally in order to get as clear as I could of the jungle, on which it would appear the enemy mainly relied.

We approached the village about twelve o'clock, and I found on a mound close to it a strong picket of the enemy's cavalry and infantry, which we at once dispersed, obtaining from the mound a very extended view of the country before us, and the enemy drawn out in battle array, he having, either during the night or that morning, moved out of his several positions and occupied the ground in our front, which, although not a dense, was a difficult jungle, his right in advance of Futteh Shah-ke-Chuck, and on his left the furrowed hills before described.

The day being so far advanced, I decided upon taking up a position in the rear of the village, in order to reconnoitre my front, finding that I could not turn the enemy's flanks, which rested upon a dense jungle extending nearly to Hailah . . .

The engineer department had been ordered to examine the country before us, and the quarter-master general was in the act of taking up ground for the encampment when the enemy advanced some horse artillery and opened fire on the skirmishers in front of the village. I immediately ordered them to be silenced by a few rounds from our heavy guns, which advanced to an open space in front of the village. The fire was instantly returned by nearly the whole of the enemy's field artillery, thus exposing the positions of his guns, which the jungle had hitherto concealed.

It was now evident that the enemy intended to fight, and would probably advance his guns so as to reach the encampment during the night.

I therefore drew up in order of battle, Sir Walter Gilbert's division on the right, flanked by Brigadier Pope's brigade of cavalry, which I strengthened by the 14th Light Dragoons, well aware that the enemy was strong in cavalry upon his left. To this were attached three troops of horse artillery, under Lieutenant Colonel Grant. The heavy guns were in the centre.

Brigadier Campbell's division formed the left, flanked by Brigadier White's brigade of cavalry, and three troops of horse artillery, under Lieutenant Colonel Brind. The field batteries were with the infantry divisions . . .

Letters and Dispatches of Field Marshal Sir Hugh Gough (1865)

The battle of Chilianwallah was fought between Gough's Anglo-Indian force of 12,000 with sixty guns and a Sikh army of 40,000 with sixty-two guns. It was hotly contested, but eventually the Sikhs were driven from the field after three hours of fighting. Gough's losses were severe − 2,300. Gough further lost four guns and five stands of colours. The insurrection was finally put down at the battle of Gujarat, 22 February 1849, after which the entire Punjab was annexed, putting an end to the Sikh state.

1854–1856 Crimean War

'Highlanders, you will on Monday embark for the purpose of meeting the enemies of your Country. Soldiers have nothing to do with the causes of quarrels, their duty is to fight; but in this instance you have a noble cause to fight for, the protection of the weak by the strong. You will be led by Lord Raglan, a man who was at the right hand of the Duke of Wellington, a man who knows how to lead you to victory as well as you know how to fight to obtain it . . . '

(Major-General Sir Harry Smith, during the inspection of the 93rd Sutherland Highlanders at Plymouth Hoe before their embarkation for the Crimean campaign on the *Himalaya*, March 1854)

The real causes of the Crimean War were deep-seated international rivalries. British Russophobes were particularly anxious about the extension of Russian influence into the Mediterranean and the north-western area of India. Russian suppression of the Hungarian revolt (1848–9) and the Tsar's declared intention to partition Turkish territory were seen as danger signals. Tensions reached a crisis in April 1853 when Russia claimed protectorate over Christian subjects of the Ottoman (Turkish) Empire. The next month Tsar Nicholas I ordered the occupation of Moldavia and Wallachia (modern Romania). Russian and French relations had been strained by the dispute over the privileges of Catholic and Orthodox monks at the Holy Places in Palestine. A British fleet was sent to the Dardanelles in June, where it was joined by a French squadron. The Turks declared war on 23 September. On 30 November the Turkish fleet was destroyed at Sinope. British public opinion was singularly belligerent. Britain and France jointly declared war in March 1854.

This account of day-to-day life in the trenches before Balaclava is from the letters and journals of Captain Hedley Vicars of the 97th Regiment, who was killed at Sebastopol in 1855:

December 1 1854

I have just returned from another night in the trenches. The rain is descending in torrents. Last night, whilst standing opposite an embrasure, serving out to my men their allowance of grog, a shell whizzed over my head within a foot. The men made a most humble salaam, but I soon got them on their legs again, by threatening to withhold the spirits. The enemy gave us a few more shots, one of which hit the ground so near as to send the gravel into my face.

The accounts of the Russians killing our wounded officers and men are too true, – confirmed by all here. Poor Sir Robert Newman was left wounded on the ground during the temporary retreat of his regiment, the Grenadier Guards; when they returned, he was found stabbed through the head and body in several places.

It is stated that 20,000 French have landed at Eupatoria, and, as a set off to this, that 30,000 more Russians have entered the Crimea; but, whatever their numbers may be, with God's help, we are sure to beat them. They surprised us at Inkermann, but yet we repulsed them with great slaughter; the British bayonet settled the business; they fight well though; in that battle it was a regular hand-to-hand encounter. A Sergeant of the Scots Fusilier Guards told me that he saw a Guardsman and a Russian both dead, with each other's bayonets transfixed in their bodies. Campbell, a young officer of the 30th, who was in the 97th at Canterbury, had four or five balls in his clothes; one of them took off the tail of his red coat, in which was his purse, containing nine pounds! The night before last, one of my beautiful dreams was dispelled by a shaking of my tent, and in answer to 'Who is there?' I received the reply, 'Please, Sir, a staff-officer has just ridden into the camp to bid us be ready at a moment's notice; the Russians are moving on our right flank.' 'All right,' said I, and commending myself to my Heavenly Father, fell fast asleep again, knowing I was all ready for a moment's notice. However, we heard no more of it. While I write, musketry is hard at work and cannon roaring. Our fellows say the Russian cheer is a pitiful whine, very unlike the British war-shout!

Memorials of Captain Hedley Vicars, Ninety-Seventh Regiment (1856)

Battle of Balaclava

One of the most notorious engagements of the Crimean War, the Battle of Balaclava was fought on 25 October 1854, Prince Mentschikov commanded a Russian army of 30,000, which drove the Turks out of Kadikoi and then entered the valley of Balaclava. The Russians were driven back by the Heavy Brigade, under General Sir James Yorke Scarlett.

Alexander William Kinglake, scholar, traveller and author, accompanied the British forces to the Crimea. This is his account of the charge of the Heavy Brigade:

From the time when the 'three hundred' had fairly closed with the enemy, but there was but little recourse to carbine or pistol; and the movement of the horses within the column being necessarily slight . . . there resulted little sound from their tramp. The clash of sabres overhead had become so steady and ceaseless, and its sound so commingled with the jangle of cavalry accoutrements proceeding from thousands of horsemen, that upon the whole it was but little expressive of the numberless separate conflicts in which each man was holding to life with the strength of his own right arm.

In regard to the use men made of their voices, there was a marked difference between our people and the Russian horsemen. The islanders hurled out, whilst they fought, those blasts of malediction, by which many of our people in the act of hard striving are accustomed to evoke their full strength; whilst the Russians in general fought without using articulate words. Nor, instead, did they utter any truculent, theological yells of the kind which, some few days later, were destined to be heard on the battle-field. They had not, as yet, been sanctified. It was not until the 4th of November that the army of the Tsar underwent that fell act of consecration which whetted his people for the morrow, and prepared those strange shrieks of doctrinal hate which were heard on the ridges of Inkerman. But although abstaining from articulate speech and from fierce yells, the grey-mantled horseman in general was not therefore mute. He sometimes evolved, whilst he fought, a deep gurgling, long-drawn sound, close akin to an inchoate roar; or else . . . a sustained and continuous 'zizz' of the kind that is made with clenched teeth; and to the ears of those who were themselves engaged in the fight, the aggregate of the sounds coming thus from the mouths of the Russians was like that of some factory in busy England, where numberless wheels hum and buzz. And meanwhile, from those masses of Russian horsemen who stood ranged in such parts of the column as to be unable to engage in bodily contact, there rose a low murmur of that indefinite kind which attests the presence of a crowd without disclosing its humour . . . the collective roar which ascended from this thicket of intermixed combatants had the unity of sound which belongs to the moan of a distant sea.

Alexander William Kinglake, The Invasion of the Crimea (1868)

The celebrated charge of the Light Brigade happened in mid-morning. Lord Raglan had a commanding view of the entire valley from his position, and thought he perceived a Russian attempt to remove captured British gunnery. He sent orders to Lord Lucan, commander of the cavalry division, that the cavalry were to see to it that the guns were not removed from the fortifications. Lucan did not see any opportunity for such action, and did nothing.

Raglan waited half an hour and sent another message:

'Lord Raglan wishes the cavalry to advance rapidly to the front, follow the enemy, and try to prevent the enemy carrying away the guns. Troop of horse artillery may accompany. French cavalry is on your left. Immediate.'

This message as delivered and interpreted led to the Light Brigade's charging Russian gun emplacements at the end of the valley, head-on. They were shelled from both sides all the way. This is an eye-witness account:

Captain Nolan appears to have totally misunderstood the instructions he had just before received: 'the guns' in the written order, of course, alluded to those the enemy had captured in the redoubts, and which it was thought they were carrying away, and the direction which he

165

[Nolan] pointed out to Lord Lucan was quite contrary to that intended by Lord Raglan . . . Lord Lucan appears to have considered that he was bound to charge the enemy . . . He consequently communicated with Lord Cardigan, and desired him to form the Light Brigade into two lines . . . to the horror of all of us on the heights above, we saw our handful of light cavalry advance downwards towards the Russian batteries . . . It consisted of scarce 700 horses, although composed of no less than five different regiments. In the first line were four squadrons of the 13th Light Dragoons and 17th Lancers; in the second were four squadrons of the 4th Light Dragoons and 11th Hussars . . . in their rear was one squadron of the 8th Hussars, as a sort of reserve. As they started into a trot, poor Nolan galloped some way in front of the brigade, waving his sword and encouraging his men by voice and gesture. Before they had gone any distance the enemy's guns opened on them at long range. Nolan was the first man killed: some grape-shot hit him in the chest: his horse turned and carried him to the rear through our advancing squadrons. His screams were heard far above the din of battle, and he fell dead from his saddle near the spot where the order had been given for the charge. The pace of our cavalry increased every moment, until they went thundering along the valley, making the ground tremble beneath them. The awful slaughter that was going on, from the fire the enemy poured into them, apparently did not check their career. On they went, headlong to the death, disregarding aught but the object of their attack.

Lieutenant-Colonel Somerset Gough Calthorpe, *Letters From Headquarters* (1856)

Casualties were considerable: there were 122 wounded, 156 killed and missing; and 335 horses were killed. The Russians took many prisoners.

THE CHARGE OF THE LIGHT BRIGADE

Half a league, half a league,
Half a league onward,
All in the valley of Death
Rode the six hundred.
'Forward, the Light Brigade!
Charge for the guns!' he said:
Into the valley of Death
Rode the six hundred.

'Forward, the Light Brigade!'
Was there a man dismayed?

Not though the soldier knew
  Some one had blundered:
Theirs not to make reply,
Theirs not to reason why,
Theirs but to do and die:
Into the valley of Death
  Rode the six hundred

Cannon to right of them,
Cannon to left of them,
Cannon in front of them
  Volleyed and thundered;
Stormed at with shot and shell,
Boldly they rode and well,
Into the jaws of Death,
Into the mouth of Hell
  Rode the six hundred.

Flashed all their sabres bare,
Flashed as they turned in air
Sabring the gunners there,
Charging an army, while
  All the world wondered:
Plunged in the battery-smoke
Right through the line they broke;
Cossack and Russian
Reeled from the sabre-stroke
  Shattered and sundered.
Then they rode back, but not,
  Not the six hundred.

Cannon to right of them,
Cannon to left of them,
Cannon behind them
  Volleyed and thundered;
Stormed at with shot and shell,
While horse and hero fell,
They that had fought so well
Came through the jaws of Death
Back from the mouth of Hell,
All that was left of them,
  Left of six hundred.

Alfred, Lord Tennyson (1854)

Battle of Inkerman

This battle was fought in thick fog on 5 November 1854, with some very close hand-to-hand fighting. The arrival of French reinforcements caused the Russians to withdraw. This account of some tense moments is by a sergeant of the Royal Marine Light Infantry:

I was one of eight told off to two stretchers; we had two killed instantly, our drummer having his drum shot away from his arm, and a piece of his trousers from the back part of the legs without getting a scratch; our lot was now in extended order advancing towards the edge of a steep ravine which separated us from the Russians. I got rather confused wandering about with the stretcher in the rear, and, not liking the job, I called to a comrade, 'Come on, Harry, let us join the mob.' The last I saw of the stretcher was one fellow dragging it after him . . . As our position was the extreme left, it was a particularly warm quarter, the guns from the Russian shipping in the harbour on our left making a cross fire of artillery. We got what cover we could as we replied to the tempest of bullets that came across that ravine. We saw the plumes of an English battery bobbing above the brushwood on our right, where they unlimbered and opened fire on the six guns in our front, which very soon rid us of their presence. I heard one hurrah on our side, which came from the 88th Connaught Rangers in one of their mad charges against the masses opposed to them. They were very strong in the field, having seven companies engaged. They suffered heavily that day, maintaining one portion of the character that Wellington gave the Regiment in the Peninsula, viz., 'You are the greatest ruffians and the best soldiers that I have.'

. . . Whilst still waiting orders to return to camp, we witnessed a fight between a rifleman and a Russian. The former was bringing the latter in a prisoner. The rifleman was a strapping young fellow about 5 ft. 10 in., but the Russian was a giant, and refusing to give up his sword, they had a scuffle for it, the Russian throwing his adversary away from him as though he were a child, every time he attempted to take it. We could easily have shot the Russian, but an officer of the Rifles shouted, 'Let them fight it out, I'll back my man wins.' The young rifleman changed his tactics, and began to give it to the Russian with his fists, when he had it all his own way, and the Muscovite – who was quite at sea in this mode – was fain to surrender.

Sergeant Turner, 'Memories of an Old Soldier', in *Globe and Laurel*, Journal of the Royal Marines (1904)

1857 Indian Mutiny

The Afghan campaigns and the Crimean War had eroded the myth of British military invincibility. Rumours that cartridges were smeared with fat from cows (which insulted Hindus) and fat from pigs (which insulted Muslims) provided the spark which inflamed British India in May 1857.

In three weeks the entire Ganges basin was aflame. There were fewer than 40,000 British troops there to contain the situation against a population of 40,000,000. Cawnpore and Lucknow were besieged.

When the garrison defence surrendered they were promised safe conduct to Allahabad, but were massacred as they left by boat. Their women and children were then put to death.

This account is by Richard Barter, Adjutant of the 75th Gordon Highlanders, who was among the rescuers who pursued the mutineers and reached Cawnpore in October 1857:

> We reached Cawnpore, the scene of the Nana Sahib's massacre of the poor defenceless European men, women and children. Just outside the place we halted near a fine house which was, however, empty, and while waiting for the order to march on, we strolled into it. Even there there had been murder if one could judge by the crimson stain where blood had spurted on the wall and by the smear of a bloody hand. Our Camp was pitched at each side of the road, and that evening we all paid the now-famous well etc. a visit as well as the house close to it in which before their massacre the women and children were confined. The house was a small one, being as well as I can now remember one long room with a verandah in front and rear and the back verandah looked into a courtyard or zenana compound, on the other three sides of which were walls with a door leading out of that on the left to the path to the well. In the courtyard itself grew a babul tree and near the well between it and the house were three or four large trees and some low scrubby thicket of thorny shrubs. The inside of the house was of course bare of furniture and there was no matting or carpet on the floor, but instead blood, thick clotted blood looking like Russia leather, with which the walls also for three or four feet from the ground were spattered, and in some places smeared as if a great spout of it had gushed out on them, while here and there were marks where the murderers had dried their bloody hands by rubbing them against the walls in which were also deep sword cuts, as if some poor victim had dodged aside from the blow. There were also several pencil inscriptions, noting the date of arrival there, and memoranda of deaths of friends or relatives, or short prayers for help. Bonnets, slippers, hats, stays and various other articles of female clothing, with tresses

and plaits of hair were scattered about with fragments of books, most, if not all of them Bibles and prayer books. Some of the bonnets and hats were hanging from the beams in the back verandah, which as well as the back yard was covered thick with clotted blood. All the way to the well was marked by a regular track along which the bodies had been dragged and the thorny bushes had entangled in them scraps of clothing and long hairs. One of the large trees to the left of this track going to the well had evidently had children's brains dashed out against its trunk, for it was covered thick with blood and children's hair matted into the coarse bark, and an eye, glazed and withered could be plainly made out pasted into the trunk. A few paces on and you stood by the well itself, now the receptacle of all these poor mangled bodies. It looked old and going fast to decay for the bricks and mortar had given way and crumbled in many places round the low edge, I think it must have been dry or very nearly so. After peering into it for some time until the eyes had become accustomed to the gloom, you could see members of human bodies, legs and arms sticking up browned and withered like those of a mummy. But there was no putrid smell or anything of that kind that I could perceive. Those dead arms of our murdered country people seemed to be making a mute appeal to us from the darkness below; far more eloquent than words they called to Heaven for vengeance on the ruthless perpetrators of untold atrocities, and many a vow was registered over that well never to spare should they be met with hand to hand in the approaching struggle for the Relief of Lucknow, but four short marches now lay between us and that city where we knew the garrison with a crowd of women and children, were daily subject to the attacks of the Cawnpore, and thousands of similar ruffians all eager to repeat the horrors of the place where we now stood; but we had to curb our impatience to go to their relief and had days still to wait the coming of Sir Colin Campbell, the new Commander-in-Chief, who with a large force was now pushing up country.

Richard Barter, *The Siege of Delhi – Mutiny Memories of an Old Officer* (1869)

1857 Relief of Lucknow

A force commanded by Generals Sir Henry Havelock and Sir James Outram relieved the besieged Residency at Lucknow on 26 September 1857.

One enduring Victorian legend recounts the dream of one of the besieged at Lucknow, who predicts that the relief columns of Highlanders will enter the citadel to the skirl of pipes:

THE PIPES AT LUCKNOW:
AN INCIDENT OF THE SEPOY MUTINY

Pipes of the misty moorlands,
  Voice of the glens and hills;
The droning of the torrents,
  The treble of the rills;
Not the braes of bloom and heather,
  Nor the mountains dark with rain,
Nor maiden bower, nor border tower,
  Have heard your sweetest strain!

Dear to the Lowland reaper,
  And plaided mountaineer, −
To the cottage and the castle
  The Scottish pipes are dear; −
Sweet sounds the ancient pibroch
  O'er mountain, loch, and glade;
But the sweetest of all music
  The pipes at Lucknow played.

Day by day the Indian tiger
  Louder yelled, and nearer crept;
Round and round the jungle-serpent
  Near and nearer circles swept.
'Pray for rescue, wives and mothers, −
  Pray to-day!' the soldier said;
'To-morrow, death's between us
  And the wrong and shame we dread.'

Oh, they listened, looked and waited,
  Till their hope became despair;
And the sobs of low bewailing
  Filled the pauses of their prayer.
Then up spake a Scottish maiden,
  With her ear unto the ground:
'Dinna ye hear it? − dinna ye hear it?
  The pipes o' Havelock sound!'

Hushed the wounded man his groaning;
  Hushed the wife her little ones;
Alone they heard the drum-roll
  And the roar of Sepoy guns.

But to sounds of home and childhood
    The Highland ear was true; –
As her mother's cradle-crooning
    The mountain pipes she knew.

Like the march of soundless music
    Through the vision of the seer,
More of feeling than of hearing,
    Of the heart than of the ear,
She knew the droning pibroch,
    She knew the Campbell's call:
'Hark! hear ye no MacGregor's,
    The grandest o' them all!'

Oh, they listened, dumb and breathless,
    And they caught the sound at last;
Faint and far beyond the Goomtee
    Rose and fell the piper's blast!
Then a burst of wild thanksgiving
    Mingled woman's voice and man's;
'God be praised! – the march of Havelock!
    The piping of the clans!'

Louder, nearer, fierce as vengeance,
    Sharp and shrill as swords at strife,
Came the wild MacGregor's clan-call,
    Stinging all the air to life.
But when the far-off dust-cloud
    To plaided legions grew,
Full tenderly and blithesomely
    The pipes of rescue blew!

Round the silver domes of Lucknow,
    Moslem mosque and Pagan shrine,
Breathed the air to Britons dearest,
    The air of Auld Lang Syne.
O'er the cruel roll of war-drums
    Rose that sweet and homelike strain;
And the tartan clove the turban,
    As the Goomtee cleaves the plain

Dear to the corn-land reaper
    And plaided mountaineer, –

To the cottage and the castle
  The piper's song is dear.
Sweet sounds the Gaelic pibroch
  O'er mountain, glen, and glade;
But the sweetest of all music
  The pipes at Lucknow played!

John Greenleaf Whittier

X

THE AMERICAN CIVIL WAR

1861–1865 American Civil War

'This is essentially a people's contest . . . whose leading object is to elevate the conditions of men – to lift artificial weights from all shoulders – to clear the paths of laudable pursuit for all – to afford all, an unfettered start, and a fair chance, in the race of life.'

(Abraham Lincoln, Message to Congress, 4 July 1861)

The American Civil War, sometimes called 'the irrepressible conflict', seemed inevitable for a long time, yet was a long time in coming. The Missouri Compromise of 1820 and the Compromise of 1850 merely postponed a major confrontation. This came in 1860 when Abraham Lincoln was elected President. Although Lincoln was not an Abolitionist, he regarded slavery as morally repugnant and was opposed to its extension into new territories. As slavery was an essential part of the economic infrastructure of the South, the election of Lincoln was perceived as a danger signal to the Southern states. On 20 December 1860 South Carolina seceded, and was followed by six other states. Lincoln sent reinforcements to Federal troops at Fort Sumter and Confederate troops fired on the Fort on 12 April 1861, thus precipitating the Civil War. As the conflict escalated, more states left the Union and eventually the Confederacy numbered eleven states.

Although familiar to us through costume dramas, films and popular illustrations (particularly those by Currier and Ives) as an 'old-fashioned' war, the American Civil War, which featured mass armies, rapid-fire rifles, the introduction of iron-clad battleships and modern transport and communications, was the first of the 'modern' wars – certainly as far as mass slaughter was concerned. The Battle of Antietam, fought on 17 September 1862, was described by R. E. Dupuy and T. N. Dupuy in *The Compact History of the Civil War* (1960) as 'the bloodiest one-day battle of the entire war'. In this engagement, the Confederate forces of 50,000 sustained 13,000 casualties, with the Union army of 70,000 suffering 12,400 casualties. At Gettysburg on 1–3 July 1863 the Confederate army of 70,200 suffered 20,000 casualties and the Union army of 90,000 suffered 23,000 casualties.

The Union had all the advantages – stable government, manpower (twice that of the Confederacy), industrialization and control of the seas. Initially, however, the Southern states were more successful in battle, and it was not until the battles of Vicksburg and Gettysburg in July 1863 that the Confederacy began to show serious signs of weakening. The Union's naval blockade of the South and the gradual military supremacy of Grant and Sherman eventually exacted their toll. The Confederate war effort was dissipated by successive defeats, desertion and internal division. Lee surrendered to Grant at Appomattox on 9 April 1865.

In his late twenties Samuel Clemens (Mark Twain) served briefly in a group of Confederate volunteers in Missouri. After a few hours of marching and training, the small body of rookies go through the motions of campaigning, hoping they will not actually come across any Union soldiers. Camping, foraging and cooking all present them with severe difficulties. After many false alarms a figure on horseback appears and they prepare for action. He is fired upon and killed. They sincerely regret his death. He was not even in uniform. He was a stranger. No one ever found out who he was.

> The thought of him got to preying upon me every night; I could not get rid of it. I could not drive it away, the taking of that unoffending life seemed such a wanton thing. And it seemed an epitome of war; that all war must be just that – the killing of strangers against whom you feel no personal animosity; strangers whom, in other circumstances, you would help if you found them in trouble, and who would help you if you needed it. My campaign was spoiled. It seemed to me that I was not rightly equipped for this awful business; that war was intended for men, and I for a child's nurse . . .
>
> The rest of my war experience was of a piece with what I have already told of it. We kept monotonously falling back upon one camp or another, and eating up the country. I marvel now at the patience of the farmers and their families. They ought to have shot us . . .
>
> The thoughtful will not throw this war paper of mine lightly aside as being valueless. It has this value: it is a not unfair picture of what went on in many and many a militia camp in the first months of the rebellion, when the green recruits were without discipline, without the

steadying and heartening influence of trained leaders; when all their circumstances were new and strange, and charged with exaggerated terrors, and before the invaluable experience of actual collision in the field had turned them from rabbits into soldiers. If this side of the picture of that early day has not before been put into history, then history has been to that degree incomplete, for it had and has its rightful place there. There was more Bull Run material scattered through the early camps of this country than exhibited itself at Bull Run. And yet it learned its trade presently, and helped to fight the great battles later. I could have become a soldier myself if I had waited. I had got part of it learned; I knew more about retreating than the man that invented retreating.

Mark Twain, *History of a Campaign that Failed* (1865)

BALL'S BLUFF: A REVERIE

One noonday, at my window in the town,
    I saw a sight — saddest that eyes can see —
Young soldiers marching lustily
        Unto the wars,
With fifes, and flags in mottoed pageantry;
    While all the porches, walks, and doors
Were rich with ladies cheering royally.

They moved like Juny morning on the wave,
    Their hearts were fresh as clover in its prime
    (It was the breezy summer time),
        Life throbbed so strong,

How should they dream that Death in a rosy clime
    Would come to thin their shining throng?
Youth feels immortal, like the gods sublime.

Weeks passed; and at my window, leaving bed.
    By night I mused, of easeful sleep bereft,
    On those brave boys (Ah War! thy theft);
        Some marching feet
Found pause at last by cliffs Potomac cleft;
    Wakeful I mused, while in the street
Far footfalls died away till none were left.

Herman Melville (1861)

177

Mary Boykin Chesnut (1823–1886) was the wife of a prosperous slaveholder and senator from South Carolina. She was a believer in State's Rights, but deeply sympathised with black people. Her social circle contained leading members of South Carolina's establishment, including Jefferson Davis, the Confederate President. Her diaries are remarkable documents and preserve the real world of which *Gone with the Wind* was only a fantasy version:

May 19 [1861] Back in Montgomery. Mrs Fitzpatrick said Mr [Jefferson] Davis is too gloomy for her. He says we must prepare for a long war and unmerciful reverses at first, because they are readier for war, and so much stronger numerically. Men and money count so in war. 'As they do everywhere else,' said I, doubting her accurate account of Mr Davis's spoken words, though she tried to give it faithfully. We need patience and persistence. There is enough and to spare of pluck and dash among us; the do-and-dare style.

[May 27, 1861] Johnny [Mary Chesnut's nephew] has gone as a private in Gregg's regiment. He could not stand it at home any longer. Mr Chesnut was willing for him to go, because those sandhill men said: 'This is a rich man's war,' and that the rich men could be officers and have an easy time, and the poor ones be privates. So he said: 'Let the gentlemen set the example; let them go in the ranks.' So John Chesnut is a gentleman private. He took his servant with him, all the same.

[June 10, 1861] The war is making us all tenderly sentimental. No casualties yet, no real mourning, nobody hurt; so it is all parade, fuss and fine feathers. There is no imagination here to forestall woe, and only the excitement and wild awakening from everyday stagnant life is felt; that is, when one gets away from the two or three sensible men who are still left in the world.

In Charleston, a butcher has been clandestinely supplying the Yankee fleet outside of the Bar with beef. They say he gave the information which led to the capture of the *Savannah*. They will hang him. Mr Petigru alone, in South Carolina, has not seceded. When they pray for our President, he gets up from his knees. He might risk a prayer for Mr Davis, though I doubt if it would do Mr Davis any good. Mr Petigru is too clever to think himself one of the righteous, whose prayers avail so overly much. Mr Petigru's disciple, Mr Bryan, followed his example. Mr Petigru has such a keen sense of the ridiculous, he must be laughing in his sleeve at the hubbub this untimely trait of independence has raised.

Harper's Ferry has been evacuated, and we are looking out for a battle at Manassas Station. I am always ill. The name of my disease is a longing to get away from here, and go to Richmond. Good Lord, forgive me! Your commandment I cannot keep. How can I honor what is so dishonorable, or respect what is so little respectable, or love what is so utterly unlovely. Then I must go, indeed; go away from here.

[June 28, 1861] In Mrs Davis's drawing-room last night, the President took a seat by me on the sofa where I sat. He talked for nearly an hour. He laughed at our faith in our own prowess. We are like the British; we think every Southerner equal to three Yankees at least, but we will have to be equivalent to a dozen now. After his experience of the fighting qualities of Southerners in Mexico, Mr Davis believes that we will do all that can be done by pluck and muscle, endurance and dogged courage, dash and red-hot patriotism, and yet his tone was not sanguine. There was a sad refrain running through it all. For one thing, either way, he thinks it will be a long war. That floored me at once. It has been too long for me already. Then he said that before the end came we would have many a bitter experience. He said only fools doubted the courage of the Yankees, or their willingness to fight when they saw fit. And now we have stung their pride, we have roused them till they will fight like devils. He said Mr Chesnut's going as aide-de-camp to Beauregard was a mistake, and that he ought to raise a regiment of his own.

[July 11, 1861] The spy, so called, gave us a parting shot. She said Beauregard arrested her brother so that he might take a fine horse aforesaid brother was riding. Why? Beauregard could have at a moment's notice any horse in South Carolina – or Louisiana, for that matter – at a word. The brother was arrested and sent to Richmond, and 'will be acquitted as they always are,' said Brewster. They send them first to Richmond to see and hear everything there; then they acquit them, and send them out of the country by way of Norfolk to see everything there. But after all, what does it matter? The Yankees have no need of spies. Our newspapers keep no secrets hid. The thoughts of our hearts are all revealed. Everything with us is open and above board. At Bethel, the Yankees fired too high, and every daily is jeering them about it even now. They'll fire low enough next time, but no newspaper man will be there to get the benefit of their improved practice! Alas!

[September 19, 1861] Mr Chesnut and Uncle John, both *ci-devant* [heretofore] Union men, are now utterly for State's Rights.

. . . An iron steamer has run the blockade at Savannah. We raise our wilted heads like flowers after a shower. This drop of good news revives us.

September 24 [1861] The men who went to Society Hill (the

Witherspoon home) have come home again with nothing very definite. William and Cousin Betsey's old maid, Rhody, are in jail; strong suspicion but as yet no proof of their guilt. The neighborhood is in a ferment. Evans and Wallace say these Negroes ought to be burnt. Lynching proposed! But it is all idle talk. They will be tried as the law directs, and not otherwise. John Witherspoon will not allow anything wrong or violent to be done. He has a detective there from Charleston.

Hitherto I have never thought of being afraid of Negroes. I had never injured any of them; why should they want to hurt me? Two thirds of my religion consists in trying to be good to Negroes, because they are so in our power, and it would be so easy to be the other thing. Somehow today I feel that the ground is cut away from under my feet. Why should they treat me any better than they have done Cousin Betsey Witherspoon?

Kate and I sat up late and talked it all over. Mrs Witherspoon was a saint on this earth, and this is her reward. Kate's maid Betsey came in − a strong-built, mulatto woman − dragging in a mattress. 'Missis, I have brought my bed to sleep in your room while Mars' David is at Society Hill. You ought not to stay in a room by yourself these times.' She went off for more bed gear. 'For the life of me,' said Kate gravely, 'I cannot make up my mind. Does she mean to take care of me, or to murder me?' I do not think Betsey heard, but when she came back she said: 'Missis, as I have a soul to be saved, I will keep you safe. I will guard you.' We know Betsey well, but has she soul enough to swear by? She is a great stout, jolly, irresponsible, unreliable, pleasant-tempered, bad-behaved woman, with ever so many good points. Among others, she is so clever she can do anything, and she never loses her temper; but she has no moral sense whatever.

That night, Kate came into my room. She could not sleep. The thought of those black hands strangling and smothering Mrs Witherspoon's grey head under the counterpane haunted her; we sat up and talked the long night through.

[October 7, 1861] An appalling list of foreigners in the Yankee army, just as I feared; a rush of all Europe to them, as soon as they raised the cry that this war is for the extirpation of slavery. If our people had read less of Mr Calhoun's works, and only read the signs of the times a little more; if they had known more of what was going on around them in the world.

[October 13, 1861] I was shocked to hear that dear friends of mine refused to take work for the soldiers because their seamstresses had their winter clothes to make. I told them true patriotesses would be willing to wear the same clothes until our siege was raised. They did not seem to care. They have seen no ragged, dirty, sick and miserable soldiers lying in the hospital, no lack of woman's nursing, no lack of woman's tears, but an awful lack of a proper change in clean clothes. They know nothing of the horrors of war. One has to see to believe. They take it easy, and are not yet willing to make personal sacrifices. The time is coming when they will not be given a choice in the matter. The very few stay-at-home men we have are absorbed as before in plantation affairs; cotton-picking, Negro squabbles, hay stealing, saving the corn from the freshet. They are like the old Jews while Noah was building the Ark.

Woe to those who began this war, if they were not in bitter earnest. Lamar (L. Q. C., and the cleverest man I know) said in Richmond in one of those long talks of ours: 'Slavery is too heavy a load for us to carry.'

[October 25, 1861] The Yankees' principal spite is against South Carolina. Fifteen war steamers have sailed — or steamed — out against us. Hot work will be cut out for us whenever they elect to land. They hate us, but they fear us too. They do not move now until their force is immense; overwhelming is their word. Enormous preparations and a cautious approach are the lessons we taught them at Manassas.

November 6 [1861] Mr Chesnut has gone to Charleston, and Kate to Columbia, on her way to Flat Rock. Partings are sorrowful things now.

As for the dunderheads here, I can account for their stolidity only in one way. They have no imagination. They cannot conceive what lies before them. They can only see what actually lies under their noses. To me it is evident that Russell, the Times [of London] correspondent, tries to tell the truth, unpalatable as it is to us. Why should we expect a man who recorded so unflinchingly the wrong-doing in India, to soften matters for our benefit, sensitive as we are to blame. He described slavery in Maryland, but says that it has worse features further South; yet his account of slavery in Maryland might stand as a perfectly accurate picture of it here. God knows I am not inclined to condone it, come what may. His work is very well done for a stranger who comes and in his haste unpacks his three P's — pen, paper, and prejudices — and hurries through his work.

A Diary from Dixie 1861–65, edited by Ben Ames Williams (1949)

The Red Badge of Courage

Stephen Crane, who wrote one of the great masterpieces of war literature – *The Red Badge of Courage* (1895) – had no personal experience of war, something that is difficult to believe when reading his work. In page after page there are passages which become printed on the readers' minds and become absorbed into the furniture of their future thinking:

> The men dropped here and there like bundles. The captain stretched out in the position of a tired man resting . . . The babbling man was grazed by a shot that made the blood stream widely down his face. He clapped both hands to his head. 'Oh!' he said, and ran . . .
>
> Under foot there were a few ghastly forms motionless. They lay twisted in fantastic contortions. Arms were bent and heads were turned in incredible ways. It seemed that the dead men must have fallen from some great height . . . They looked to be dumped out upon the ground from the sky . . .
>
> (from *The Red Badge of Courage*)

Almost incredibly, Crane learned the skills which made him famous from reading Tolstoy and books about the Civil War.

In *The Red Badge of Courage: An Episode of the American Civil War*, the young hero, Henry Fleming, endures his first experience of war. He starts out fired, anxious to participate and show what he is made of, but then suffers severely from his first taste of war's realities, believing he is a coward. He learns to bear up as a result of his experiences, of which one of the most overwhelming is having to witness the horrible sufferings of his wounded friend, Jim Conklin, as he retreats with the wounded:

> . . . he was amid wounds. The mob of men was bleeding . . .
>
> At times he regarded the wounded soldiers in an envious way. He conceived persons with torn bodies to be peculiarly happy. He wished that he, too, had a wound, a little red badge of courage.
>
> The spectral soldier was at his side like a stalking reproach. The man's eyes were still fixed in a stare into the unknown . . . As he went on, he seemed always looking for a place, like one who goes to choose a grave.
>
> Something in the gesture of the man as he waved the bloody and pitying soldiers away made the youth start as if bitten . . .
>
> 'Gawd! Jim Conklin!'
>
> The tall soldier made a little commonplace smile. 'Hello, Henry,' he said.

The youth swayed on his legs and glared strangely. He stuttered and stammered. 'Oh, Jim — oh, Jim — oh, Jim — '

The tall soldier held out his gory hand. There was a curious red and black combination of new blood and old blood upon it. 'Where yeh been, Henry?' he asked. He continued in a monotonous voice, 'I thought mebbe yeh got keeled over. There's been thunder t' pay t'-day. I was worryin' about it a good deal.'

The youth still lamented. 'Oh, Jim — oh, Jim — oh, Jim — '

'Yeh know,' said the tall soldier, 'I was out there.' He made a careful gesture. 'An', Lord, what a circus! An, b'jiminey, I got shot — I got shot. Yes, b'jiminey, I got shot.' He reiterated this fact in a bewildered way, as if he did not know how it came about.

The youth put forth anxious arms to assist him, but the tall soldier went firmly on as if propelled. Since the youth's arrival as a guardian for his friend, the other wounded men had ceased to display much interest. They occupied themselves again in dragging their own tragedies toward the rear.

Suddenly, as the two friends marched on, the tall soldier seemed to be overcome by a terror. His face turned to a semblance of gray paste. He clutched the youth's arm and looked all about him, as if dreading to be overheard. Then he began to speak in a shaking whisper:

'I tell yeh what I'm 'fraid of, Henry — I'll tell yeh what I'm 'fraid of. I'm 'fraid I'll fall down — an' then yeh know — them damned artillery wagons — they like as not 'll run over me. That's what I'm 'fraid of — '

The youth cried out to him hysterically: 'I'll take care of yeh, Jim! I'll take care of yeh! I swear t' Gawd I will!'

'Sure — will yeh, Henry?' the tall soldier beseeched.

'Yes — yes — I tell yeh — I'll take care of yeh, Jim!' protested the youth. He could not speak accurately because of the gulpings in his throat.

But the tall soldier continued to beg in a lowly way. He now hung babelike to the youth's arm. His eyes rolled in the wildness of his terror. 'I was allus a good friend t' yeh, wa'n't I, Henry? I've allus been a pretty good feller, ain't I? An' it ain't much t' ask, is it? Jest t' pull me along outer th' road? I'd do it fer you, wouldn't I, Henry?'

He paused in piteous anxiety to await his friend's reply.

The youth had reached an anguish where the sobs scorched him. He strove to express his loyalty, but he could only make fantastic gestures.

However, the tall soldier seemed suddenly to forget all those fears. He became again the grim, stalking specter of a soldier. He went stonily forward. The youth wished his friend to lean upon him, but

183

the other always shook his head and strangely protested. 'No – no – no – leave me be – leave me be – '

His look was fixed again upon the unknown. He moved with mysterious purpose, and all of the youth's offers he brushed aside. 'No – no – leave me be – leave me be – '

The youth had to follow.

Presently the latter heard a voice talking softly near his shoulders. Turning he saw that it belonged to the tattered soldier. 'Ye'd better take 'im outa th' road, pardner. There's a batt'ry comin' helitywhoop down th' road an' he'll git runned over. He's a goner anyhow in about five minutes – yeh kin see that. Ye'd better take 'im outa th' road. Where th' blazes does he git his stren'th from?'

'Lord knows!' cried the youth. He was shaking his hands helplessly.

He ran forward presently and grasped the tall soldier by the arm. 'Jim! Jim!' he coaxed, 'come with me.'

The tall soldier weakly tried to wrench himself free. 'Huh,' he said vacantly. He stared at the youth for a moment. At last he spoke as if dimly comprehending. 'Oh! Inteh th' fields? Oh!'

He started blindly through the grass.

The youth turned once to look at the lashing riders and jouncing guns of the battery. He was startled from this view by a shrill outcry from the tattered man.

'Gawd! He's runnin'!'

Turning his head swiftly, the youth saw his friend running in a staggering and stumbling way toward a little clump of bushes. His heart seemed to wrench itself almost free from his body at this sight. He made a noise of pain. He and the tattered man began a pursuit. There was a singular race.

When he overtook the tall soldier he began to plead with all the words he could find. 'Jim – Jim – what are you doing – what makes you do this way – you'll hurt yerself.'

The same purpose was in the tall soldier's face. He protested in a dulled way, keeping his eyes fastened on the mystic place of his intentions. 'No – no – don't tech me – leave me be – leave me be – '

The youth, aghast and filled with wonder at the tall soldier, began quaveringly to question him. 'Where yeh goin', Jim? What you thinking about? Where you going? Tell me, won't you, Jim?'

The tall soldier faced about as upon relentless pursuers. In his eyes there was a great appeal. 'Leave me be, can't yeh? Leave me be fer a minnit.'

The youth recoiled. 'Why, Jim,' he said, in a dazed way, 'what's the matter with you?'

The tall soldier turned and, lurching dangerously, went on. The youth and the tattered soldier followed, sneaking as if whipped, feeling unable to face the stricken man if he should again confront them. They began to have thoughts of a solemn ceremony. There was something ritelike in these movements of the doomed soldier. And there was a resemblance in him to a devotee of a mad religion, blood-sucking, muscle-wrenching, bone-crushing. [They could not understand.] They were awed and afraid. They hung back lest he have at command a dreadful weapon.

At last, they saw him stop and stand motionless. Hastening up, they perceived that his face wore an expression telling that he had at last found the place for which he had struggled. His spare figure was erect; his bloody hands were quietly at his side. He was waiting with patience for something that he had come to meet. He was at the rendezvous. They paused and stood, expectant.

There was a silence.

Finally, the chest of the doomed soldier began to heave with a strained motion. It increased in violence until it was as if an animal was within and was kicking and tumbling furiously to be free.

This spectacle of gradual strangulation made the youth writhe, and once as his friend rolled his eyes, he saw something in them that made him sink wailing to the ground. He raised his voice in a last supreme call.

'Jim — Jim — Jim — '

The tall soldier opened his lips and spoke. He made a gesture. 'Leave me be — don't tech me — leave me be — '

There was another silence while he waited.

Suddenly, his form stiffened and straightened. Then it was shaken by a prolonged ague. He stared into space. To the two watchers there was a curious and profound dignity in the firm lines of his awful face.

He was invaded by a creeping strangeness that slowly enveloped him. For a moment the tremor of his legs caused him to dance a sort of hideous hornpipe. His arms beat wildly about his head in expression of implike enthusiasm.

His tall figure stretched itself to its full height. There was a slight rending sound. Then it began to swing forward, slow and straight, in the manner of a falling tree. A swift muscular contortion made the left shoulder strike the ground first.

The body seemed to bounce a little way from the earth. 'God!' said the tattered soldier.

The youth had watched, spellbound, this ceremony at the place of meeting. His face had been twisted into an expression of every agony he had imagined for his friend.

He now sprang to his feet and, going closer, gazed upon the pastelike face. The mouth was opened and the teeth showed in a laugh.

As the flap of the blue jacket fell away from the body, he could see that the side looked as if it had been chewed by wolves.

The youth turned, with sudden, livid rage, toward the battle-field. He shook his fist. He seemed about to deliver a philippic.

'Hell — '

The red sun was pasted in the sky like a [fierce] wafer.

The tattered man stood musing.

'Well, he was reg'lar jim-dandy fer nerve, wa'n't he;' said he finally in a little awestruck voice. 'A reg'lar jim-dandy.' He thoughtfully poked one of the docile hands with his foot. 'I wonner where he got 'is stren'th from? I never seen a man do like that before. It was a funny thing. Well, he was a reg'lar jim-dandy.'

The youth desired to screech out his grief. He was stabbed, but his tongue lay dead in the tomb of his mouth . . .

Stephen Crane, *The Red Badge of Courage* (1895)

1863 Battle of Gettysburg

The Battle of Gettysburg was fought in July 1863 between the Federal forces, the Army of the Potomac (88,000) under General Meade, and the Confederate forces, the Army of Virginia (75,000) under Robert E. Lee. The Union army had recently been defeated by Stonewall Jackson at Chancellorsville on 2 May, after which Lee launched his second major assault on the North. He moved up the Shenandoah Valley and through into Pennsylvania. He was followed by Meade whose army engaged his on 1 July.

The conflict lasted three days, with Meade holding ground at first, in spite of severe losses, and then driving the Confederates from the field.

The battle was covered for the *New York Times* by Sam Wilkeson. His son, Lieutenant Bayard Wilkeson, who served in the Artillery of the Union Army, was killed in the battle. Wilkeson spent many hours searching for him, eventually finding that he had been wounded during the defence of a knoll early in the battle; left unattended, the son had died of his wounds.

Who can write the history of a battle whose eyes are immovably fastened on a central figure of transcendingly absorbing interest — the dead body of an oldest born son, crushed by a shell in a position where a battery should never have been set, and abandoned in a building where surgeons dared not to stay?

The battle of Gettysburg. I am told that it commenced on the first day of July, a mile north of the town, between two weak brigades and some doomed artillery and the whole force of the Rebel army.

What remains to say of the fight? It straggled surlily over the middle of the horseshoe on the west, grew big and angry on the heel at the southwest, lasted there to eight o'clock in the evening when the fighting Six Corps went joyously by as a reinforcement through a wood bright with coffee pots on the fire. I leave the details to my friend and associate. My pen is heavy.

Oh, you dead, who at Gettysburg have baptised with your blood the second birth of freedom in America, how you are to be envied. I rise from a grave whose wet clay I have passionately kissed and I look up and I see Christ spanning this battlefield with his feet and reaching fraternal and loving up to heaven. His right hand opens the gates of Paradise – with His left, He sweetly beckons to those mutilated, bloody, swollen forms to ascend.

Sam Wilkeson, New York Times (4 July 1863)

1863 Abraham Lincoln: The Address at Gettysburg

Abraham Lincoln's speech at the dedication of the cemetery at Gettysburg is among the most celebrated examples of oratory. Yet when Lincoln actually delivered his address at the ceremony of 19 November 1863, it made little immediate impact, overshadowed by the florid two-hour oration performed by Edward Everett, the most renowned speaker in America. The crowd were still stunned from Everett's rhetoric when Lincoln stood to speak his famous words. Lincoln's speech took barely two minutes and as he sat down he observed that the address would 'not scour', referring to wet soil not folding properly from the plough. Nevertheless, newspaper publicity soon passed his words into immortality and they have come to enshrine the fundamental beliefs which bound a vast nation together:

Four score and seven years ago our fathers brought forth on this continent, a new nation, conceived in Liberty, and dedicated to the proposition that all men are created equal.

Now we are engaged in a great civil war, testing whether that nation, or any nation so conceived and so dedicated, can long endure. We are met on a great battle-field of that war. We have come to dedicate a portion of that field, as a final resting place for those who here gave their lives that that nation might live. It is altogether fitting and proper that we should do this.

But, in a larger sense, we can not dedicate – we can not consecrate – we can not hallow – this ground. The brave men, living and dead, who struggled here, have consecrated it, far above our poor power to add or detract. The world will little note, nor long remember what we say here, but it can never forget what they did here. It is for us the living, rather, to be dedicated here to the unfinished work which they who fought here have thus far so nobly advanced. It is rather for us to be here dedicated to the great task remaining before us – that from these honored dead we take increased devotion to that cause for which they gave the last full measure of devotion – that we here highly resolve that these dead shall not have died in vain – that this nation, under God, shall have a new birth of freedom – and that government of the people, by the people, for the people, shall not perish from the earth.

Abraham Lincoln, 'Gettysburg Address' (1863)

1865 Walt Whitman as witness to Civil War

Walt Whitman left Brooklyn in 1862 for Washington DC to seek his brother, who had been wounded in the Civil War. He spent some months looking after the wounded, and his military experiences form the background to many of the most vivid moments in *Drum Taps* published in 1865.

CAVALRY CROSSING A FORD

A line in long array where they wind betwixt green islands,
They take a serpentine course, their arms flash in the sun – hark to the
    musical clank,
Behold the silvery river, in it the splashing horses loitering stop to
    drink,
Behold the brown-faced men, each group, each person a picture, the
    negligent rest on the saddles,
Some emerge on the opposite bank, others are just entering the ford
    – while,
Scarlet and blue and snowy white,
The guidon flags flutter gayly in the wind.

188

THE AMERICAN CIVIL WAR

BIVOUAC ON A MOUNTAIN SIDE

I see before me now a traveling army halting,
Below a fertile valley spread, with barns and the orchards of summer,
Behind, the terraced sides of a mountain, abrupt, in places rising high,
Broken, with rocks, with clinging cedars, with tall shapes dingily seen,
The numerous camp-fires scatter'd near and far, some away up on the
    mountain,
The shadowy forms of men and horses, looming, large-sized, flickering,
And over all the sky — the sky! far, far out of reach, studded, breaking
    out, the eternal stars.

VIGIL STRANGE I KEPT ON THE FIELD ONE NIGHT

Vigil strange I kept on the field one night;
When you my son and my comrade dropt at my side that day,
One look I but gave which your dear eyes return'd with a look I shall
    never forget,
One touch of your hand to mine O boy, reach'd up as you lay on the
    ground,
Then onward I sped in the battle, the even-contested battle,
Till late in the night reliev'd to the place at last again I made my way,
Found you in death so cold dear comrade, found your body son of
    responding kisses, (never again on earth responding,)
Bared your face in the starlight, curious the scene, cool blew the
    moderate night-wind,
Long there and then in vigil I stood, dimly around me the battlefield
    spreading,
Vigil wondrous and vigil sweet there in the fragrant silent night,
But not a tear fell, not even a long-drawn sigh, long, long I gazed,
Then on the earth partially reclining sat by your side leaning my chin
    in my hands,
Passing sweet hours, immortal and mystic hours with you dearest
    comrade — not a tear, not a word,
Vigil of silence, love and death, vigil for you my son and my soldier,
As onward silently stars aloft, eastward new ones upward stole,
Vigil final for you brave boy, (I could not save you, swift was your
    death,
I faithfully loved you and cared for you living, I think we shall surely
    meet again,)
Till at latest lingering of the night, indeed just as the dawn appear'd,
My comrade I wrapt in his blanket, envelop'd well his form,
Folded the blanket well, tucking it carefully over head and carefully
    under feet,

And there and then and bathed by the rising sun, my son in his grave,
  in his rude-dug grave I deposited,
Ending my vigil strange with that, vigil of night and battle-field dim,
Vigil for boy of responding kisses, (never again on earth responding,)
Vigil for comrade swiftly slain, vigil I never forget, how as day
  brighten'd
I rose from the chill ground and folded my soldier well in his blanket,
And buried him where he fell.

Walt Whitman, Drum Taps (1865)

1865 General Robert E. Lee's Farewell Address to his Troops

Headquarters Army of Northern Virginia
10th April 1865

After four years of arduous service marked by unsurpassed courage
and fortitude the Army of Northern Virginia has been compelled to
yield to overwhelming numbers and resources.

I need not tell the survivors of so many hard fought battles, who
have remained steadfast to the last, that I have consented to this result
from no distrust of them. But feeling that valor and devotion could
accomplish nothing that could compensate for the loss that would
have accompanied the continuance of the contest, I determined to
avoid the useless sacrifice of those whose past services have endeared
them to their country.

By the terms of the agreement Officers and men can return to their
homes and remain there until exchanged. You will take with you the
satisfaction that proceeds from the consciousness of duty faithfully
performed and I earnestly pray that a merciful God will extend to you
his blessing and protection.

With an unceasing admiration of your constancy and devotion to
your country and a grateful remembrance of your kind and generous
consideration of myself, I bid you all an affectionate farewell.

XI

US–INDIAN WARS

1860–1890 US–Indian Wars

The name 'Indian Wars' usually refers to the final stages in the closing decades of the nineteenth century of the struggle between the white settlers and the indigenous Indian population of the United States. A systematic attempt was made by the federal government, using the US Cavalry, to press back the various tribes of plains, prairie and mountain Indians. This was finally achieved after the Civil War, but the process goes back to the seventeenth century when Europeans first began to settle in America.

The Civil War spread railroad technology which brought thousands of settlers into the West. The size and organization of the federal army increased proportionately. The market for western beef grew rapidly. In 1865 the Apache and Navajo Indians submitted to the authorities and accepted sanctuary in reservations. Treaties and promises were broken and trust between the Indians and the white man continued to decline. The Indian position was well stated by Chief Ten Bears of the Comanches, at the Council of Medicine Lodge Creek in 1867:

Two years ago, I came upon this road, following the buffalo, that my wives and children might have their cheeks plump and their bodies warm. But the soldiers fired on us. And since that time there has been a noise like thunder, and we have not known which way to go.

So it was on the Canadian River. Nor have we been made to cry only once. The blue dressed soldiers . . . came from out the night when it was dark and still. And for campfires they lit our lodges. Instead of hunting game, they killed my braves . . .

So it was in Texas. They made sorrow come in our camps . . . But there are things that you have said to me that I do not like. They are not sweet like sugar, but bitter like gourds. You said you wanted to put us on reservations, to build us houses, and make us medicine lodges. I do not want them. I was born on the prairie, where the wind blew free and there was nothing to break the light of the sun. I was born where there were no fences and everything drew a free breath. I want to die there and not inside walls. I know every stream and every wood between the Rio Grande and the Arkansas. I have hunted and lived over that country. I live like my fathers before me and like them, I live happily.

When I was at Washington the Great White Father told me that all the Comanche land was ours, and that nobody would stop us from living on it. So why do you ask us to leave the rivers, and the sun, and the wind, and live in houses? Do not ask us to give up the buffalo for the sheep. The young men have heard talk of this, and it has made them sad and angry. Do not speak of it anymore . . .

The Sioux continued to fight until 1868 and then accepted reservations in Dakota Territory.

Massacres at Washita and Grant Camp are typical of the dreadful skirmishes which characterize these final stages of the confrontation between the white man and the Amerindian.

1868 Washita River Massacre

General George Armstrong Custer, in command of several companies of US Cavalry, massacred two hundred Indians at their village on the Washita River. The victims believed they were protected by having signed the Treaty of Medicine Lodge. Custer personally shot their livestock – ponies and dogs – sitting by his camp-fire, taking aim, and deliberately terrorizing the Indian survivors who were compelled to watch. A member of his staff, Captain Frederick W. Benteen, wrote a letter describing the scene to a friend of his, who had it printed in newspapers in St. Louis and New York:

That which cannot be taken away must be destroyed. Eight hundred ponies are to be put to death. Our chief exhibits his close sharpshooting and terrifies the crowd of frightened captured squaws and papooses by dropping the straggling ponies in death near them. Ah! he is a clever marksman! Not even do the poor dogs of the Indians escape his eye and aim, as they drop dead or limp howling away . . . The plunder having been culled over is hastily piled; the wigwams are pulled down and thrown on it, and soon the whole is one blazing mass . . . The last pony is killed. The huge fire dies out, and as the brave band of the 7th Cavalry strikes up the air 'Ain't I

Glad To Get Out Of The Wilderness' we slowly pick our way across the creek over which we charged so gallantly in the early morn. Take care! Do not trample on the dead bodies of that woman and child lying there.

1871 Camp Grant Massacre

On 28 April 1871 a party of leading citizens from Tucson, Arizona, led by William Sanders Oury, a lawyer, rancher and former Mayor of Tucson, together with a group of Papagos (traditional enemies of the Apaches), formed a raiding party and shot and clubbed to death 125 unarmed Apaches who had been granted asylum at Camp Grant since February. Thirty young Apache boys and girls were abducted and later sold to slavery in Mexico. Fewer than eight of the victims were men; most of the slaughtered were women and children. Many of the women had been mass-raped.

First Lieutenant Royal E. Whitman, the commander of Camp Grant, described what he found at the scene of the massacre in his report:

The camp was burning and strewn with their dead and mutilated women and children. I immediately mounted a party of about twenty soldiers and citizens and sent them with the post surgeon, with a wagon to bring in any wounded, if any could be found. The party returned late in the p.m. having found no wounded and without having been able to communicate with any of the survivors. Early the next morning I took a similar party, with spades and shovels, and went out and buried all the dead in and immediately about the camp . . . While at the work many of them came to the spot and indulged in their expressions of grief, too wild and terrible to be described.

Many of the men, whose families have been killed, when I spoke to them and expressed sympathy for them, were obliged to turn away, unable to speak, and too proud to show their grief. The women whose children had been killed or stolen were convulsed with grief, and looked at me appealingly, as though I was their last hope on earth. Children who two days before had been full of fun and frolic kept at a distance, expressing wondering horror . . .

This incident was reported in the Denver press under the headline:

VICTORY FOR PEACE

We give this act of the citizens of Arizona most hearty and unqualified endorsement. We congratulate them on the fact that permanent peace arrangements have been made with so many, and we only regret that the number was not double. Camp Grant is the last of those victories for civilization and progress which have made Sand Creek, Washita . . . and other similar occurrences famous in western history. It was just and right and fully demanded by circumstances of the times.

(President Ulysses Grant threatened that Arizona would be put under martial law unless those responsible were put on trial. They were tried and found not guilty of murder.)

1874 Sand Creek Massacre

In Autumn 1874 a numerous band of Arapaho and Cheyenne Indians travelled to Fort Lyon, Colorado, in order to sign a peace treaty. After signing, they received supplies and were allowed to set up camp at Sand Creek, forty miles from the fort.

A few days afterwards they were attacked without warning by a company of Colorado Volunteers under the command of Colonel John M. Chivington. While still asleep in their tents they were massacred. Two hundred men, women and children (maybe more) were shot, clubbed and butchered. Women were raped, and children had their brains dashed out. Fingers and ears were removed in order to obtain jewellery, while limbs and genitalia were hacked off and later exhibited at Denver. It was Colonel Chivington's orders that the victims be scalped. The Denver newspapers carried this account:

Among the brilliant feats of arms in Indian warfare, the recent campaign of our Colorado Volunteers will stand in history with few rivals, and none to exceed it in final results . . . All acquitted themselves well, and Colorado soldiers have again covered themselves with glory.

1877 Chief Joseph: 'I'll fight no more forever'

The Gold Rush to the Black Hills in 1875 brought trouble to Dakota as the land on which the Indians had been settled was now sought by

)rospectors. During this dispute the Battle of the Little Big Horn)ccurred on 25 June 1876 when General Custer and 264 of his men were massacred. The fierce Apache leader Geronimo was captured in 1886, and in the North-West the Nez Perce Indians conducted a superb retreat in the face of US military advances but were finally defeated in 1877. They accepted reservation accommodation in Oklahoma.

Our Chiefs are killed . . . The old men are all dead . . . The little children are freezing to death. My people, some of them have run away to the hills and have no blankets, no food, No one knows where they are, perhaps freezing to death. I want to have time to look for my children and see how many of them I can find. Maybe I can find them among the dead. Hear me, my chiefs. My heart is sick and sad. From where the sun now stands I will fight no more forever'

Chief Joseph (Hinmaton-Yalakit: Thunder Rolling in the Mountains) (1840–1904), Speech to the Nez Perce tribe, after their surrender to General Nelson A. Miles at the Battle of Bear Paw Mountains, Montana (30 September–25 October 1877)

1890 The Ghost Dance and Wounded Knee

The Paiute religious leader Wovoka proclaimed the faith of the Ghost Dance. It was an Indian millennarian movement which incorporated several traditional religions and a selection of Christian beliefs. Wovoka had a vision in which Christ appeared to him and told him that He had forsaken the white man for his lies, cruelties and unworthiness. He was now the Messiah of the Indians. They were promised that if they lived according to His moral laws, forsaking whisky and laxity, the white man would be destroyed in a holocaust. America would be restored to the condition it was before the white man arrived. All the Indians who had been killed by the white man would be resurrected. The message appealed particularly to those tribes – Sioux, Cheyenne, Arapaho – who had most recently surrendered and come in to the reservations. The Ghost Dance would make them impervious to the white man's bullets. The message of the Dance was transcribed and translated thus:

The whole world is coming,
A nation is coming, a nation is coming,
The Eagle has brought the message to the tribe,
The father says so, the father says so.
Over the whole earth they are coming.
The buffalo are coming, the buffalo are coming,
The Crow has brought the message to the tribe,
The father says so, the father says so.

The last battle of the Indian Wars was the massacre of the Sioux at Wounded Knee, South Dakota, on 29 December 1890, when 300 defenceless men, women and children were shot by US Cavalry. The firing was so indiscriminate that the soldiers killed twenty-five and wounded thirty-nine of their own men by mistake.

One eye-witness, Louise Weasel Bear, said:

'We tried to run, but they shot us like we were buffalo. I know there are some good white people, but the soldiers must be mean to shoot children and women. Indian soldiers would not do that to white children.'

XII

FRANCO–PRUSSIAN WAR

1870 Battle of Sedan

This was the decisive battle of the Franco-Prussian War. On 1 September 1870, a French army of 20,000 with 564 guns was defeated by the Prussian army of 200,000 and 750 guns. The French surrendered, with Napoleon III taken prisoner. One of the highlights of the battle was the charge of the Chasseurs d'Afrique. The battle – and this catastrophic charge – feature in Zola's novel *La Débacle*:

When, with heroic obstinacy, the third charge was made, Prosper found himself mixed up with some Hussars and Chasseurs de France. The regiments were mingling; there was now only a huge wave of horsemen which incessantly broke and re-formed, carrying whatever it met along with it. Prosper no longer had any idea of anything; he had surrendered himself to his horse, brave Zephyr, whom he was so fond of, and who seemed maddened by a wound in the ear. At present he was in the centre; other horses reared and fell around him; some men were thrown to the ground as by a hurricane, whilst others, though shot dead, remained in the saddle, and continued charging, showing but the whites of their eyes. And, this time, again, another two hundred yards having been covered, the stubble in the rear of the squadrons was littered with dead and dying. There were some whose heads had sunk deep into the soil. Others, who had fallen on their backs, gazed at the great round sun with terrified eyes starting from their sockets. Then there was a big black horse, an officer's charger, whose belly had been ripped open, and who vainly strove to rise with the hoofs of both forelegs caught in his entrails. Whilst the foe redoubled his fire, the wings whirled once again, and fell back, to return, however, to the charge with desperate fury.

It was, indeed, only the fourth squadron, at the fourth onslaught, that reached the Prussian lines. Prosper, with his sabre uplifted, smote the helmets and the dark uniforms that he saw through the smoky mist. Blood flowed, and on noticing that Zephyr's mouth was ensanguined, he imagined that it was through having bitten the foe. So frightful was the clamour becoming, that he could no longer hear himself shout, and yet his throat was being almost torn away by the yells that issued from it. Behind the first Prussian line, however, there was yet another one, then another, and then another. Heroism remained of no avail; those deep masses of men were like lofty herbage amid which horses and horsemen disappeared. Mow them down as you might, there were always thousands left standing. The firing continued with such intensity, the muzzles of the needle guns were so close, that uniforms were set on fire. All foundered, sank down among the bayonets; chests were transpierced, and skulls were split. Two-thirds of those regiments of horsemen were to remain on the field, and of that famous charge there would abide but the memory of the glorious madness of having attempted it. And, all at once, Zephyr, in his turn, was struck by a bullet full in the chest, and fell to the ground, crushing under him Prosper's right thigh, the pain of which was so acute that the Chasseur fainted.

Emile Zola, *La Débacle*, translated by Ernest Alfred Vizetelly (1892)

XIII

IMPERIAL WARFARE

1873–1874 Ashanti War

This was a typical Victorian punitive colonial expedition. Its commander, the Empire's troubleshooter, Sir Garnet Wolseley, actually
recorded that the purpose was 'to leave marks of our power or
vengeance' as he ordered the destruction of Coomassie, the capital.

'The whole scheme of Ashantee [Ashanti] politics,' wrote Sir Garnet
to Lord Kimberley, 'is so based upon treachery, that the king does not
understand any other form of negotiation, or believe it possible that
others can have honest intentions.'

'Nothing was left us,' he added, 'but to leave marks of our power or
vengeance, which would long be remembered. No more utterly
atrocious government than that which has thus, perhaps, fallen, ever
existed on the face of the earth . . . Their capital was a charnel-house;
their religion a combination of cruelty and treachery; their policy the
natural outcome of their religion.'

Before the final order went forth to destroy Coomassie, it was
evident that the king was making cunning efforts to obtain both guns
and powder from the town for further efforts against us.

The decision of Sir Garnet Wolseley was, without doubt, a wise
one. For the past five days the troops had undergone heavy work,
with almost continual fighting. The knowledge that Coomassie was
so near kept every man's spirit high; but a march beyond it might
have proved a serious trial, and the coming rains were a source of
keen anxiety. Though it would have been gratifying, according to
European ideas, to have secured, by treaty, the payment of a certain
sum of money, and freedom of trade, it would not have had the same
effect upon the tribes in that part of Africa as the destruction of
Coomassie.

That 'charnel-house' destroyed, its palace blown up, would be emblems of defeat and terror never to be forgotten, while the northern tribes, so long cut off from the coast by the Kings of Ashantee, were certain to open for themselves a path to the Atlantic.

During the night of the 5th, a strong party of Engineers had been at work mining the palace in every quarter, while a prize committee had been engaged in actively searching it, selecting and packing up all that was worth conveying away. What became of the reputed hoards of secret gold in the sepulchres of the Osai kings, none ever knew; but few articles of value were brought away by the troops.

'When it became known that we were to start for the sea, every face brightened; and although a long and monotonous march lay before us, every one felt that the fatigue could be encountered, and the continual fight against fever maintained successfully, if we were but on our way home.'

At six o'clock, the bugles sounded, and the advanced guard began to move off – the main body following an hour after. The Royal Highlanders remained as a rear-guard, to cover the Engineers and burning party. A hundred Engineers and labourers, armed with palm-leaf torches, began the work of deliberate destruction; and, though many expressed grave fears that the recent deluges of rain might prevent the thatch and wood from burning, the troops had soon the satisfaction of seeing mighty volumes of smoke rolling over the further end of the city.

There was but one emotion of regret, 'that the flames did not consume the Bantama, with the temples of their hideous and atrocious Paganism, made glorious by the gore of a myriad of human victims.'

The Highlanders kept marching forward, as the work went on, and soon the commander of the Engineers with his party, came from the palace to report that the main building had been blown up, and all the rest was in flames. It was considered singular that no explosion was heard; but this was to be accounted for from the circumstance that the Engineers were short of powder, and they had been compelled to cut the walls in certain places, and only mine the corners; but they brought the whole palace down, like a house of cards.

Owing to the dampness of the materials of which the streets were composed, the volumes of smoke that rolled over the whole site of Coomassie were vast and dark; but ever and anon bright pyramids of flame could be seen to shoot upward, as the retiring troops defiled round the dismal swamp on their homeward way.

James Grant, *British Battles on Land and Sea* (1884)

1879 Zulu Wars

'Nothing could be more unpromising or more fraught with danger than the existing condition.- Of course a happy stroke of fortune might end the war at any moment, but I confess to see no probability of it under present circumstances, with a demoralised army, the men of which, in all ranks, are thoroughly sick of the war, and have lost all confidence apparently in their leaders. It is very probable that I shall find myself forced to postpone all operations till January, which would create a bad impression at home politically speaking, and would be a fearful disappointment to the Ministry; however, they have only themselves to blame for not having sent me here three months ago.'

(Major General Sir Garnet Wolseley, on being sent to retrieve the situation in Zululand after Isandhlwana, 22 January 1879)

Even after Britain annexed the Transvaal in 1877, serious border disputes continued between Boers and the Zulus, inspired by their leader, Cetewayo. The British solution was the declaration of a protectorate over Zululand, which the Zulus rejected in December 1878. War followed. A British invasion force (5,000 British troops, with 8,500 native troops) moved into Zululand on 11 January 1879.

Isandhlwana

'Fix bayonets and die like British soldiers do.'

(Last order given to the British troops at Isandhlwana)

The slaughter at Isandhlwana occurred on 22 January. Half the invading forces were away attempting to locate Cetewayo's army when the Zulus struck the camp early in the morning. Only fifty-five British and three hundred natives survived. Melton Prior, employed by the *Illustrated London News*, after seeing the camp, wrote:

I have seen dead and dying on a battlefield by hundreds and thousands; but to come suddenly on the spot where the slaughtered battalions of the 24th Regiment (South Wales Borderers) and others were lying at Isandhlwana was far more appalling. Here I saw not the bodies, but the skeletons of men whom I had known in life and health; some of whom I had known well, mixed up with the skeletons of oxen and horses, and with wagons thrown on their sides, all in the greatest confusion, showing how furious had been the onslaught of the enemy.

Rorke's Drift

Later the same day Cetewayo's army struck the base camp at Rorke's Drift. This was constructed into one of the great epic engagements of British imperialism. Late in the afternoon about eighty-five defenders (of the South Wales Borderers) drove off six attacking waves of 4,000 Zulu warriors, killing about 400 of them. The Regiment earned eight Victoria Crosses and nine Distinguished Conduct Medals. The disaster of Isandhlwana required a British triumph. This was supplied by Rorke's Drift:

> The defence of Rorke's Drift was a triumph of skill, discipline, courage and stamina but it was a very small triumph. A hundred well-armed men with unlimited ammunition and a good position held off for twelve hours a magnificently brave horde who were effectively without firearms. In any other of Britain's endemic colonial wars of the nineteenth century it would scarcely have been noticed . . . A centuries' old tradition laid down that this was the kind of thing that the British infantryman was expected to do.
>
> The Zulu onslaught must have been terrifying to see and hear but, statistically speaking, it was not very dangerous to men behind improvised fortifications . . .
>
> Rorke's Drift became a legend because it was juxtaposed with Isandhlwana. Beaconsfield, with his showman's instinct, built it up to epic proportions because it suited his policy to do so. This was not the only cause. It restored the public confidence in the advance of technology. They had been conditioned to believe that scientific progress gave Britain an automatic superiority over the more primitive races of Africa . . .
>
> It may be that the defenders of the mission station got more acclamation than would normally have come to them. It cannot be said that they got more than they deserved . . . '

Michael Glover, Rorke's Drift: A Victorian Epic (1975)

Ulundi

Ulundi was the last battle of the Zulu war. On 4 July 1879, a British force of 5,000 under Lord Chelmsford defeated 20,000 Zulus. Cetewayo was captured a few weeks later.

> On the slope towards Ulundi the shells were crashing into the black masses that were rushing forward to the encounter. Into the hordes in

front the Gatlings, with their measured volleys, were raining pitiless showers of death. But those Zulus could die – ay, they could dare and die with a valour and a devotion unsurpassed by the soldiers of any age or of any nationality. They went down in numbers; but numbers stood up and pressed swiftly and steadily on. The sharper din of our musketry fire filled the intervals between the hoarse roar of the cannon and the screams of speeding shells. Still the Zulus would not stay the whirlwind of their converging attack. They fired and rushed on, halting to fire again, and then rushing on time after time . . . For half an hour the square stood grim and purposeful, steadfastly pouring the sheet of death from every face. There was scarce any sound of human speech, save the quiet injunctions of the officers – 'fire low, men; get your aim, no wildness' – one rush came within a few yards, but it was the last effort of the heroic Zulus. Their noble ardour could not endure in the face of the appliances of civilized warfare.

Archibald Forbes, *Daily News*

1898 Battle of Omdurman

'The valour of those poor half-starved Dervishes in their patched jibbahs would have graced Thermopylae.'

(Lieutenant Colonel Charles Townsend, on witnessing the Battle of Omdurman)

The death of General Charles Gordon during the siege of Khartoum in 1885 was considered a national disgrace. Eventually, increasing French and Italian colonial interest in the area caused the British government to reconquer the Sudan. The campaign was brilliantly conducted by Horatio Kitchener and culminated in the slaughterous victory at Omdurman on 2 September 1898.

The noise of something began to creep in upon us; it cleared and divided into the tap of drums and the far-away surf of raucous war-cries. A shiver of expectancy thrilled along our army, and then a sigh of content. They were coming on. Allah help them! they were coming on.

It was now half-past six. The flags seemed still very distant, the roar very faint, and the thud of our first gun was almost startling. It may have swung forward, and a mass of white flying linen swung forward with it too. They came very fast, and they came very straight; and then presently they came no farther. With a crash the bullets leaped out of the British rifles. It began with the Guards and

Warwicks – section volleys at 2000 yards; then, as the Dervishes edged rightward, it ran along to the Highlanders, the Lincolns, and to Maxwell's Brigade. The British stood up in double rank behind their zariba; the blacks lay down in their shelter-trench; both poured out death as fast as they could load and press trigger. Shrapnel whistled and Maxims growled savagely. From all the line came perpetual fire, fire, fire, and shrieked forth in great gusts of destruction.

And the enemy? No white troops would have faced that torrent of death for five minutes, but the Bagarra and the blacks came on. The torrent swept into them and hurled them down in whole companies. You saw a rigid line gather itself up and rush on evenly; then before a shrapnel shell or a Maxim the line suddenly quivered and stopped. The line was yet unbroken, but it was quite still. But other lines gathered up again, again, and yet again; they went down, and yet others rushed on. Sometimes they came near enough to see single figures quite plainly. One old man with a white flag started with five comrades; all dropped, but he alone came bounding forward to within 200 yards of the 14th Sudanese. Then he folded his arms across his face, and his limbs loosened, and he dropped sprawling to earth beside his flag.

It was the last day of Mahdism, and the greatest. They could never get near, and they refused to hold back. By now the ground before us was all white with dead men's drapery. Rifles grew red-hot; the soldiers seized them by the slings and dragged them back to the reserve to change for cool ones. It was not a battle, but an execution.

George Warrington Steevens, *The Daily Mail* (5 September 1898)

1898 Spanish–American War

The Spanish–American War now seems highly symbolic as a conflict between the oldest European imperial power and the emerging empire of the New World, but at the time it seemed minor and highly localized, American interest had centred on the future of Cuba after native unrest under Spanish rule manifested itself in armed rebellion in 1868. American sympathy was with the rebels; US investments were also at risk, and some politicians astutely perceived Cuba's strategic value in the Caribbean. The yellow press clamoured for intervention, which finally came after the mysterious explosion sinking the US battleship *Maine* in Havana's harbour.

The Spanish–American War has been described as the 'newspaper correspondents' war *par excellence*'. By this time the mass-circulation newspaper was big business, especially in the US. There was a vast potential readership ready and anxious to consume the scandals, crises, crimes, and natural and man-made disasters which formed the staple fare of the newspapers' menu. But there was nothing to touch a good war, and no tastier item than a dispatch from the field. It made fortunes for William Randolph Hearst and Joseph Pulitzer – it has been claimed that it was these powerful newspaper proprietors who pushed the US into the war as a source of perfect copy for their newspapers. In the event, reports varied enormously in tone and attitude. This is Caspar Whitney of *Harper's Weekly* optimistically reporting from the US infantry, artillery and cavalry camps at Tampa:

If you visit them early in the morning you will witness some of the cleverest work, in all three branches of the service, that you have yet seen, even though you have watched the infantry and cavalry of Germany and the artillery of France. My observations come with the added interest to me, who have just returned from the continent with a previous idea based merely on what I had heard that our regulars were inferior to those of England, France or Germany, in mere matter of drill and general tactical efficiency. I have been most delightfully surprised by what I have seen here as compared with what I saw on the continent. . . . for alertness – for dash, speed, and accuracy in action – these United States Troops seem to me to excel anything I have ever seen in that line . . .

Caspar Whitney, 'Waiting for the World', in *Harper's Weekly* (22 May 1898)

This happy picture was contradicted by another of *Harper's* correspondents, Poultney Bigelow. He published two articles, on 22 May and 28 May, which painted a very different picture. His forthright reporting resulted in his being deprived of his credentials to accompany the US Army as a war correspondent. Nevertheless, his writing is a landmark in the reporting of modern war.

He praised the US soldier:

I have been camping with regulars, living their life, eating their food, and noting their courage and discipline . . . In all three armies of Europe there are no better soldiers, man for man, than those of the United States infantry, and nowhere have I known officers who command more cheerfully the respect and obedience of their men . . .

However, Bigelow attacked the US government for selecting such an unhealthy spot as Tampa for their encampment and for the appalling inadequacies of their uniforms, equipment and logistics:

Down here we are sweltering day and night, with the thermometer ninety-eight in the shade. Nobody dares complain for fear of appearing unpatriotic. Still, it will do us no harm to hear a little of the truth . . . Here we are thirty days after the declaration of war, and not one regiment is yet equipped with uniforms suitable for hot weather. The Cuban patriots and other cigar-makers look happy in their big Panama hats and loose linen trousers, but the US troops sweat day and night in their cowhide boots, thick flannel shirts, and winter trousers. In addition to this they wear a tunic at inspection – a piece of torture . . .

THERE WAS A CRIMSON CLASH OF WAR

There was a crimson clash of war,
Lands turned black and bare;
Women wept;
Babes ran, wondering.
There came one who understood not these things.
He said: 'Why is this?'
Whereupon a million strove to answer him.
There was such intricate clamour of tongues,
That still the reason was not.

Stephen Crane (1899)

ON A SOLDIER FALLEN IN THE PHILIPPINES

Streets of the roaring town.
Hush for him, be still!
He comes, who was stricken down
Doing the word of our will.
Hush! Let him have his state,
Give him his soldier's crown.
The grists of his trade can wait
Their grinding at the mill,
But he cannot wait for his honour, now the trumpet has been blown;
Wreathe pride now for his granite brow, lay love on his breast of
     stone.

Toll! Let the great bells toll
Till the clashing air is dim.
Did we wrong his parted soul?
We will make it up to him.

Toll! Let him never guess
What work we set him to.
Laurel, laurel, yes;
He did what we bade him do.
Praise, and never a whispered hint but that the fight he fought was
     good;
Never a word that the blood on his sword was his country's own
     heart's-blood.

A flag for the soldier's bier
Who dies that his land may live;
O, banners, banners here,
That he doubt not nor misgives!
That he heed not from the tomb
The evil days draw near
When the nation, robed in gloom,
With its faithless past shall strive.
Let him never dream that his bullet's scream went wide of its island
     mark,
Home to the heart of his darling land where he stumbled and sinned in
     the dark.

William Vaughn Moody (1901)

1899–1902 Boer War

A rugged old Boer finding one of the British soldiers wounded on the
ground, stopped under fire and bound him up. 'I feel no hatred
towards you,' he said, 'but you have no reason to fight at all. We are
fighting for our country.' He turned away, and a bullet killed him as he
turned.

The British began seriously to increase their expansion in Africa after the
acquisition of the Cape of Good Hope in 1814. Collision with the Dutch,
who had settled the Transvaal and Orange Free State, was inevitable.

Gold was discovered in the Transvaal in 1886. This brought an influx
of prospectors – many of them British subjects – who were taxed and
made to pay excessive transport fees by the Boers. Finally they appealed
to the British government. Matters came to a head when the Jameson
Raid in 1895 was interpreted as a British trick to achieve a *coup d'état*.
The Boers declared war on 12 October 1899, and were initially
successful. But after 1900 British fortunes turned. The war made
Kitchener, Roberts and Baden-Powell household names.

A War Correspondent is Captured by the Boers

Winston Churchill resigned his commission in the cavalry after serving in Kitchener's Sudan campaign, and went to South Africa as a correspondent for the *Morning Chronicle* during the early stages of the Boer crisis. He was captured in November 1899. He describes his experiences as a prisoner of war in this dispatch:

The position of a prisoner of war is painful and humiliating. A man tries his best to kill another, and finding that he cannot succeed asks his enemy for mercy. The laws of war demand that this should be accorded, but it is impossible not to feel a sense of humbling obligation to the captor from whose hand we take our lives. All military pride, all independence of spirit must be put aside. These may be carried to the grave, but not into captivity. We must prepare ourselves to submit, to obey, to endure certain things – sufficient food and water and protection during good behaviour – the victor must supply or be a savage, but beyond these all else is favour. Favours must be accepted from those with whom we have a long and bitter quarrel, from those who feel fiercely that we seek to do them cruel injustice. The dog who has been whipped must be thankful for the bone that is flung to him.

When the prisoners captured after the destruction of the armoured train had been disarmed and collected in a group we found that there were fifty-six unwounded or slightly wounded men, besides the more serious cases lying on the scene of the fight. The Boers crowded round looking curiously at their prize, and we ate a little chocolate that by good fortune – for we had had no breakfast – was in our pockets, and sat down on the muddy ground to think. The rain streamed down from a dark leaden sky, and the coats of the horses steamed in the damp. 'Voorwärts,' said a voice and, forming in a miserable procession, two wretched officers, a bare-headed, tattered correspondent, four sailors with straw hats and 'HMS Tartar' in gold letters on the ribbon – ill-timed jauntiness – some fifty soldiers and volunteers, and two or three railwaymen, we started, surrounded by the active Boer horsemen . . .

'You need not walk fast,' said a Boer in excellent English, 'take your time.' Then another, seeing me hatless in the downpour, threw me a soldier's cap – one of the Irish Fusilier caps, taken, probably, near Ladysmith. So they were not cruel men, these enemy. That was a great surprise to me, for I had read much of the literature of this land of lies, and fully expected every hardship and indignity. At length we reached the guns which had played on us for so many minutes – two strangely long barrels sitting very low on the axles of the wheels . . . We waited here near the guns for half an hour, and meanwhile the Boers searched among the wreckage for dead and wounded. A few of the wounded were brought to where we were, and laid on the ground, but most of them were placed in the shelter of one of the overturned trucks. As I write I do not know with any certainty what the total losses were . . .

After a while we were ordered to march on, and looking over the crest of the hill a strange and impressive sight met the eye. Only about 300 men had attacked the train, and I had thought that this was the enterprise of such a separate detachment, but as the view extended I saw that this was only a small part of the large, powerful forces marching south, under the personal direction of General Joubert . . .

Our captors conducted us to a rough tent which had been set up in a hollow in one of the hills, and which we concluded was General Joubert's headquarters. Here we were formed into a line, and soon surrounded by a bearded crowd of Boers cloaked in mackintosh. I explained that I was a special correspondent and a non-combatant, and asked to see General Joubert. But in the throng it was impossible to tell who were the superiors. My credentials were taken from me by a man who said he was a field cornet, and who promised that they should be laid before the general forthwith. Meanwhile we waited in the rain, and the Boers questioned us. My certificate as a correspondent bore a name better known than liked in the Transvaal. Moreover, some of the private soldiers had been talking. 'You are the son of Lord Randolph Churchill?' said a Scottish Boer abruptly. I did not deny the fact. Immediately there was much talking, and all crowded round me, looking and pointing, while I heard my name repeated on every side. 'I am a newspaper correspondent,' I said, 'and you ought not to hold me prisoner.' The Scottish Boer laughed. 'Oh,' he said, 'we do not catch lords' sons every day.' Whereat they all chuckled, and began to explain that I should be allowed to play football at Pretoria.

We tramped for six hours across sloppy fields and along tracks deep and slippery with mud, while the rain fell in a steady downpour and soaked everyone to the skin. The Boer escort told us several times not to hurry and to go our own pace, and once they allowed us to halt for a few moments. But we had neither food nor water, and it was with a feeling of utter weariness that I saw the tin roofs of Colenso rise in the distance. We were put into a corrugated iron shed near the station, the floors of which were four inches deep with torn railway forms and account books. Here we flung ourselves down exhausted, and what with the shame, the disappointment, the excitement of the morning, the misery of the present and physical weakness, it seemed that love of life was gone . . .

I could not sleep. Vexation of spirit, a cold night and wet clothes withheld sweet oblivion. The rights and wrongs of the quarrel, the fortunes and chances of the war, forced themselves on my mind. What men they were, these Boers! I thought of them as I had seen them in the morning riding forward through the rain – thousands of independent riflemen, thinking for themselves, possessed of beautiful weapons, led with skill, living as they rode without commissariat or transport or ammunition column, moving like the wind, and supported by iron constitutions and a stern, hard, Old Testament God who should surely smite the Amalekite hip and thigh. And then, above the rain storm that beat loudly on the corrugated iron, I heard the sound of a chaunt. The Boers were singing their evening psalm, and the menacing notes – more full of indignant war than love and mercy – struck a chill into my heart, so that I thought after all that the war was unjust, that the Boers were better men than we, that Heaven was against us, that Ladysmith, Mafeking and Kimberley would fall, that the Estcourt garrison would perish, that foreign powers would intervene, that we should lose South Africa, and that that would be the beginning of the end. So for the time I despaired of the Empire, nor was it till the morning sun – all the brighter after the rain storms, all the warmer after the chills – struck in through the windows that things reassumed their true colours and proportions.
1 January, 1900

Frederick Woods (editor), *Young Winston's Wars – The Original Dispatches of Winston S. Churchill, War Correspondent 1897–1900* (1972)

1899 *The Siege of Ladysmith*

The siege of Ladysmith was one of the most celebrated incidents in the Boer War. A British force of 12,000, under Sir George White, was besieged by the Boer army, under General Joubert, from 2 November 1899 until it was relieved by Sir Redvers Buller on 27 February 1900. For most of the time Ladysmith was subjected to regular bombardment, but there was a fierce pitched battle fought on 6 January 1900, when the British defended their positions against a Boer attempt to force their positions on Caesar's Camp and Waggon Hill. The Boers lost some 800 soldiers and the British 850. Many of the besieged died of disease, especially fever. This letter was written from Ladysmith by Sir George White, 10 December 1899:

I think I may commence a letter to you as Sir Redvers Buller is approaching the Tugela and we may reasonably expect some hard fighting within the next week, the result of which I hope will be the relief of Ladysmith, and the opening of our communications with the outside world from which we have been so long cut off. I have been in good health all the time but it has been weary work. I fought in the open as long as I could with a superior enemy on both sides of me. I was heartbroken over the loss of the Gloucestershire Regiment, the Royal Irish Fusiliers and the Mountain Battery and of course I now wish with all my heart I had not sent them out, but two regiments and a battery ought to have been able to hold their own against the number of Boers sent against them which, as far as I can make out, were only 750 men.

We occupy a very large position here. It is some 13 miles round. This is rendered necessary by the immense range of the enemy's guns. One big 6-in gun which annoyed us for a very long time threw a shell into our lines to a distance of over 10,000 yards from the gun. When this is repeated north, south, east and west of us, it makes it hot for us but it is remarkable how few casualties there have been. The soldiers spend the days in shelters which save them from the shells. Most of the officers and civil residents have also dug themselves shelters underground. The escapes have been marvellous. I have over and over again seen shells bursting amidst groups of soldiers and horses without hurting anyone.

There are several women and children still in Ladysmith. Thank Goodness none of the children has been hit and only one woman. A 6-in shell burst actually in the room in which this woman was sitting and blew everything to ribbons and the whole side out of the house.

Sometimes the Boer guns bombard us at night and this is distressful. The night before last my Chief of Staff, Major-General Sir Archibald Hunter led a party of 600 picked men and made a raid on Gun Hill, one of the enemy's positions round Ladysmith. He surprised the post and took three guns including one of the enemy's largest (6-in) guns.

I am so pleased not only because that gun was doing us much harm but also because Hunter is such a delightful fellow and has done so well all through the siege and previous operations. You will like to hear of our mess and manner of life. All the Headquarter Staff live in the same house which we have commandeered . . .

We have had plenty to eat and to drink and we keep very early hours. I am up about 4 o'clock every morning and we generally retire between 9 and 10 o'clock. At one time before our defences were as strong as they are now I used always to sleep in my clothes ready to turn out in a second; but now a large proportion of the Boer Army has gone south to face the relieving force on the Tugela and I turn in regularly. Most of the Regimental officers, however, have to sleep in the open with their men in strong points built of stones heaped together. There is no dearth of this class of building material in Natal. The climate is very variable; some days are very hot, about as hot as Simla in mid-June, or perhaps a little hotter. We then have a severe thunderstorm with most vivid lightning and this cools the weather down greatly.

Ladysmith is a nasty place and I fear there will be a terrible plague of enteric if we are kept much longer. Already there are 80 cases and the numbers are increasing rapidly. We had more enteric fever here last year than in any other station of the British Army and I dread the result of siege conditions this year far more than the shells and bullets of the enemy.

We have also a bad prospect of horse sickness which is very bad at Ladysmith and usually sets in about this time. The flies are a terrible nuisance. The number of horses, mules, cattle, etc., bring them in myriads. In our dining room, which is very small, we catch them on fly papers and in wire domes in millions but it does not seem to decrease their numbers. They get into everything left uncovered.

Ian Hamilton has done extremely well in this campaign and is I think sure to get a KGB (and I hope a VC) for which I have recommended him. He was very brave at Elandslaagte and General French who commanded there – I was present but did not assume command – recommended him to me, a recommendation I was of course very glad to support.

I had a bit of a fight with the Boers yesterday. Wishing to take advantage of General Hunter's successful raid on the enemy's guns I made a demonstration with the cavalry to make the enemy believe I intended to attack to the north and make him uneasy about his communications in that direction. The enemy was very quick and the cavalry were not worked quite as I wished, so we had heavier losses than I had anticipated but my object was to make them increase their force north of me and decrease their force which is between me and Sir Redvers. This purpose was effected as at least 1,000 more Boers have moved round.

I have plenty of provisions greatly due to Colonel Ward's foresight and excellent organisation. He is an admirable officer and deserves all that can be bestowed on him for his masterly arrangements. Whatever we want, we go to Ward, and he finds it for us.

Gerald Sharp, *The Siege of Ladysmith* (1976)

1899 Mafeking

The garrison at Mafeking – 700 irregulars and citizens in arms under Colonel Robert Baden-Powell – was besieged by a Boer force of 5,000 in October 1899. At a later stage of the siege the Boer force was reduced to 2,000, but Mafeking was constantly bombarded and occasionally attacked. It was eventually relieved by the cavalry of Colonel Mahon. News of the relief of Mafeking was greeted with unequalled enthusiasm at home on 17 May 1900:

. . . over the country church bells were ringing, maroons were being fired, and crowds were gathering that would not noticeably decrease, through the continuous arrival of reinforcements, for three, four and even five days. The citizens of Liverpool were 'quite delirious with joy': flights of rockets pierced the sky, and an enormous crowd outside the Town Hall greeted the Lord Mayor, who had to abandon an attempt to speak 'and contented himself with leading the rendering of the National Anthem'. At Newcastle-upon-Tyne the rockets sent up from the *Chronicle* office were seen for miles around; every village knew what they signified and cheering and singing crowds instinctively gathered together. At Bradford the factory hooters sounded. At Brighton and Leicester processions grew to proportions never seen before. At Glasgow all church bells were rung, a vast crowd sang popular airs, and the vessels in the harbour sounded whistles and sirens. In Dublin there were unprecedented scenes when the news was announced in the Theatre Royal.

There had been great gatherings of the British people before: at the state funeral of the great Duke, at the Diamond Jubilee. There had been crowds and public rejoicing at the relief of Ladysmith. But already it was apparent that a spontaneous outbreak such as was now occurring, with no official sanction about it, had never before occurred on such a scale in the entire history of the country.

By eleven o'clock London seemed to have gone altogether mad. As the theatre crowds spilled out there was pandemonium. Lamp-posts were climbed. Hats and caps were thrown wildly away. Curtains were pulled back from shining windows and people in evening-dress called to the crowds below. They waved not only flags, but every sort of thing they could get hold of, including blankets, table cloths, towels and various feminine undergarments.' *The Times* continued:

At Piccadilly Circus matters culminated . . . as the stream of omnibuses and of cabs bringing people from the theatre thickened . . . [the traffic] grew slower and slower and then ceased. The Circus was jammed with people. And then a cornet or some such instrument struck up *God Save the Queen*. Immediately thousands of voices took it up and in a twinkling every hat was off. It was a wonderful sight under the glare of the Criterion lamps. The walls around the big space were alive with cheering and gesticulating figures. The pavements and the streets blocked with them, and motionless among them the streams of omnibuses and cabs, all crowded with persons waving hats, umbrellas, flags, anything . . . I saw many cabs fairly blazing with Union Jacks; the people had obviously taken them to the theatre in anticipation. No one minded being stopped or crushed. Ladies in evening-dress were squeezed in the crowd, but only smiled happily. And over it all and throughout it all and through it all the cheers thundered on in a continuous roar like the sound of a heavy surf on a rocky shore.

At midnight crowds were still tramping across the bridges from the south bank in quest of confirmation of the news. Outside the War Office, all night, hung a small notice which read: 'No news.' And in the Commons, on the motion for the adjournment at twelve o'clock, Mr Henderwick asked the Leader of the House if he had any news to communicate to the House with reference to the reported relief of Mafeking. Mr Balfour replied: 'No, sir. The only news I have received is through the courtesy of the press. We have no official information at the War Office.' The House, in a gay and happy mood, adjourned. The news, if not convincing enough for the Government, was enough for everyone else.

The scenes in the centre of London showed no indications of ending, the crowds no inclination to disperse. It was alarming. The Victorian sense of propriety and orderliness was not happy about such behaviour. When would it all end? And where would it lead to? The city-dwellers of the new nation were not, it seemed, after all, the same men as the rural John Bulls who had peacefully lit their bonfires on the news of Waterloo. There was something frightening, something new, about such a vast concourse demonstrating, apparently unchecked and uncontrolled, with such fervour.

Express trains roaring through the countryside that night whistled loud and long at every halt and every village and every crossing. So the news was spread. Villages, long since abed, rose, and shops were opened well past midnight and bunting and cloth of red, white and blue was sold, and neighbours wakened, and toasts drunk.

Above all other emotions, even above the alarm felt by a few, one was paramount — a great and deep sense of relief. Everything would be all right, after all.

Brian Gardner, Mafeking — A Victorian Legend (1966)

1907

Rudyard Kipling attempted to characterize particularly atmospheric aspects and moments of the South African War, not previously celebrated in verse. This is his poem on the British soldiers guarding the Blood River Bridge, 1901:

BRIDGE GUARD IN THE KARROO

'. . . and will supply details to guard the Blood River Bridge.'
District Orders: Lines of Communication —
South African War.

> Sudden the desert changes,
>   The raw glare softens and clings,
> Till the aching Oudtshoorn ranges
>   Stand up like the thrones of Kings —
>
> Ramparts of slaughter and peril —
>   Blazing, amazing, aglow —
> 'Twixt the sky-line's belting beryl
>   And the wine-dark flats below.
>
> Royal the pageant closes,
>   Lit by the last of the sun —
> Opal and ash-of-roses,
>   Cinnamon, umber, and dun.
>
> The twilight swallows the thicket,
>   The starlight reveals the ridge.
> The whistle shrills to the picket—
>   We are changing guard on the bridge.
>
> (Few, forgotten and lonely,
>   Where the empty metals shine —
> No, not combatants — only
>   Details guarding the line.)

ECHOES OF WAR

We slip through the broken panel
   Of fence by the ganger's shed;
We drop to the waterless channel
   And the lean track overhead;

We stumble on refuse of rations,
   The beef and the biscuit-tins;
We take our appointed stations,
   And the endless night begins.

We hear the Hottentot herders
   As the sheep click past to the fold —
And the click of the restless girders
   As the steel contracts in the cold —

Voices of jackals calling
   And, loud in the hush between,
A morsel of dry earth falling
   From the flanks of the scarred ravine.
And the solemn firmament marches,
   And the hosts of heaven rise
Framed through the iron arches —
   Banded and barred by the ties,

Till we feel the far track humming,
   And we see her headlight plain,
And we gather and wait her coming —
   The wonderful north-bound train.

(Few, forgotten and lonely,
   Where the white car-windows shine —
No, not combatants — only
   Details guarding the line.)

Quick, ere the gift escape us!
   Out of the darkness we reach
For a handful of week-old papers
   And a mouthful of human speech.

And the monstrous heaven rejoices,
   And the earth allows again
Meetings, greetings, and voices
   Of women talking with men.

So we return to our places,
    As out on the bridge she rolls;
And the darkness covers our faces,
    And the darkness re-enters our souls.

More than a little lonely
    Where the lessening tail-lights shine.
No — not combatants — only
    Details guarding the line!

                 Rudyard Kipling

XIV

THE GREAT WAR FOR CIVILIZATION

1914–1918 The Great War

After the triumph of Prussia in the war with France in 1871 and German unification, the balance of power in Europe became precariously balanced. Germany gradually began to dominate diplomacy, and tensions increased with trade rivalry. After Bismarck left office, and German policy became dictated by the wayward ambitions of Kaiser Wilhelm II, Germany seemed more belligerent. She began building a big navy – the German army was already enormous. Britain and France began to drift into an unspecified partnership. Russia and France, with strong economic links already in place, began to cement diplomatic relations. The Ottoman Empire and the Austro-Hungarian Empire seemed to offer danger to stability. Slav peoples under Austrian domination looked to Russia for support. Wilhelm developed closer diplomatic ties with Austria.

European influence in Asia and Africa had developed considerably since the middle of the 19th century. Germany seemed to have been left behind and now began obviously demanding a place in the sun. As early as 1900 Germany had obtained the concession from Turkey to build a railway from Berlin to the Persian Gulf. In 1904 the Entente Cordiale (a colonial agreement between France and Britain) was clear evidence of the dividing of Europe into two major coalitions – Britain/France/Russia and Germany/Austria/Turkey. As early as 1905 the British Foreign Minister, Sir Edward Grey, gave a pledge to the French for British support should France be attacked by Germany, although the cabinet did not learn this until 1911. In 1907 Britain and Russia concluded an *entente* which resolved their differences in Persia and elsewhere in Asia. In 1908 Austria annexed Bosnia and Herzegovina, with tacit German support. This caused great consternation in Serbia, Montenegro and Turkey. The Balkans seemed a highly inflammable area. The Turks calmed down after Austria paid them an indemnity of over two million pounds. The fragile peace in the Balkans was broken by the war of 1912, and Austria became alarmed by Serbian victories and possible domination of Albania. Tension mounted as Austria and Russia began to mobilize for war, which was averted by the armistice of December. Further tensions resulted in another Balkan war in June 1913. The Great War broke out in 1914 when the Archduke Franz Ferdinand, heir to the throne of Austria, was killed in a Serbian assassination conspiracy during a visit to Bosnia. The Austrian government used the incident as an excuse to force a war on Serbia. They were backed to the hilt by Germany. Russia mobilized, Germany declared war on Russia on 1 August and on France on 4 August. The Germans invaded France through neutral Belgium. Britain was party to the Treaty of London signed in 1839 which guaranteed Belgian neutrality, and consequently Britain was involved in the European conflict. The German Army entered Brussels on 21 August 1914:

The entrance of the German army into Brussels has lost the human quality. It was lost as soon as the three soldiers who led the army bicycled into the Boulevard du Regent and asked the way to the Gare du Nord. When they passed the human note passed with them.

What came after them, and twenty four hours later is still coming, is not men marching, but a force of nature like a tidal wave, an avalanche or a river flooding its banks . . .

At the sight of the first few regiments of the enemy we were thrilled with interest. After for three hours they had passed in one unbroken steel-grey column we were bored. But when hour after hour passed and there was no halt, no breathing time, no open space in the ranks, the thing became uncanny, inhuman. You returned to watch it, fascinated. It held the mystery and menace of fog rolling toward you across the sea.

The grey of the uniforms worn by both officers and men helped this air of mystery. Only the sharpest eye could detect among the thousands that passed the slightest difference . . .

The infantry came in in files of five, two hundred men to each company; the Lancers in columns of four, with not a pennant missing. The quick-firing guns and field pieces were one hour at a time in passing, each gun with its caisson and ammunition wagon taking twenty seconds in which to pass.

The men of the infantry sang 'Fatherland, My Fatherland'. Between each line of song they took three steps. At times two thousand men were singing together in absolute rhythm and beat. When the melody gave way the silence was broken only by the stamp of iron-shod boots, and then again the song rose. When the singing ceased, the bands played marches. They were followed by the rumble of siege guns, the creaking of wheels, and of chains clanking against the cobblestones and the sharp bell-like voices of the bugles.

For seven hours the army passed in such solid columns that not once might a taxicab or a trolley car pass through the city. Like a river of steel it flowed, grey and ghostlike. Then, as dusk came and as thousands of horses' hoofs and thousands of iron boots continued to tramp forward, they struck tiny sparks from the stones . . .

At midnight pack wagons and siege guns were still passing. At seven this morning I was awakened by the tramp of men and bands playing jauntily . . . now for twenty six hours the grey army has rumbled by with the mystery of fog and the pertinacity of a steam roller.

Richard Harding Davis, 'The German Army Marches Through Brussels,
21 August 1914' (News Chronicle, 23 August 1914)

1914 The Times: Why We are Fighting

. . . We have refused 'quietly to stand by and witness the perpetration of the direst crime that ever stained the pages of history, and thus become participants in the sin.' We are fighting now to save a flourishing constitutional kingdom which has constantly deserved and enjoyed our friendship against a wrong no independent State could tolerate without the loss of all its most essential liberties. We are going into the war that is forced upon us as the defenders of the weak and the champions of the liberties of Europe. We are drawing the sword in the same cause for which we drew it against Philip II, against Louis XIV, and against Napoleon. It is the cause of right and honour, but it is also the cause of our own vital and immediate interests. The Netherlands and Belgium largely owe their independent existence to the instinct we have ever felt and ever acted on – that on no account whatever can England suffer the coasts of the North Sea and of the narrow seas over against her own to be at the command of a great military monarchy, be that monarchy which it may . . .

We must suffer much, but we shall know how to suffer for the great name of England and for all her high ideals, as our fathers did before us. We go into the fray without hatred, without passion, without selfish ambitions, or selfish ends. We go into it in the spirit which our fellow-subjects in the Dominions have shown with one accord – the spirit in which their King and ours has assured them that he has found fresh strength in this hour of national trial. We go into it 'united, calm, resolute, trusting in God'. That is the mood in which we, their true sons, will fight today, with the humble but firm hope that in a just and righteous cause 'the only Giver of all victory' will bless our arms.

The Times (5 August 1914)

1914 *The Declaration of War*

Some say the Declaration of War threw us into a primitive abyss of hatred and the lust for blood. Others declare that we behaved very well. I do not know. I only know the thoughts that flowed through the mind of a friend of mine when he heard the news. My friend – I shall make no endeavour to excuse him – is a normal, even ordinary man, wholly English, twenty-four years old, active and given to music. By a chance he was ignorant of the events of the world during the last days of July. He was camping with some friends in a remote part of Cornwall, and had gone on, with a companion, for a four-days' sail. So it wasn't till they beached her again that they heard. A youth ran down to them with a telegram: 'We're at war with Germany. We've joined France and Russia.'

My friend ate and drank, and then climbed a hill of gorse, and sat alone, looking at the sea. His mind was full of confused images, and the sense of strain. In answer to the word 'Germany', a train of vague thoughts dragged across his brain. The pompous, middle-class vulgarity of the building of Berlin; the wide and restful beauty of Munich; the taste of beer; innumerable quiet, glittering *cafés*; the *Ring*; the swish of evening air in the face, as one *skis* down past the pines; a certain angle of the eyes in the face; long nights of drinking, and singing, and laughter; the admirable beauty of German wives and mothers; certain friends; some tunes; the quiet length of evening over the Starnberger-See. Between him and the Cornish sea he saw quite clearly an April morning on a lake south of Berlin, the grey water slipping past his little boat, and a peasant-woman, suddenly revealed against apple-blossom, hanging up blue and scarlet garments to dry in the sun. Children played about her; and she sang as she worked . . .

A cloud over the sun woke him to consciousness of his own thoughts; and he found, with perplexity, that they were continually recurring in two periods of his life, the days after the death of his mother, and the time of his first deep estrangement from one he loved. After a bit he understood this. Now, as then, his mind had been completely divided into two parts: the upper running about aimlessly from one half-relevant thought to another, the lower unconscious half labouring with some profound and unknowable change. This feeling of ignorant helplessness linked him with those past crises. His consciousness was like the light scurry of waves at full tide, when the deeper waters are pausing and gathering and turning home. Something was growing in his heart, and he couldn't tell what. But as he thought 'England and Germany', the word 'England' seemed to flash like a line of foam. With a sudden tightening of his heart, he realized that there might be a raid on the English coast. He didn't imagine any possibility of it *succeeding*, but only of enemies and warfare on English soil. The idea sickened him. He was immensely surprised to perceive that the actual earth of England held for him a quality which he found in A − , and in a friend's honour, and scarcely anywhere else, a quality which, if he'd ever been sentimental enough to use the word, he'd have called 'holiness'. His astonishment grew as the full flood of 'England' swept him on from thought to thought. He felt the triumphant helplessness of a lover. Grey, uneven little fields, and small, ancient hedges rushed before him, wild flowers, elms and beeches, gentleness, sedate houses of red brick, proudly unassuming, a countryside of rambling hills and friendly copses. He seemed to be raised high, looking down on a landscape compounded of the western view from the Cotswolds, and the Weald, and the high land in Wiltshire, and the Midlands seen from the hills above Prince's Risborough. And all this to the accompaniment of tunes heard long ago, an intolerable number of them being hymns. There was, in his mind, a confused multitude of faces, to most of which he could not put a name. At one moment he was on an Atlantic liner, sick for home, making Plymouth at nightfall; and at another, diving into a little rocky pool through which the Teign flows, north of Bovey; and again, waking, stiff with dew, to see the dawn come up over the Royston plain. And continually he seemed to see the set of a mouth which he knew for his mother's, and A − 's face, and, inexplicably, the face of an old man he had once passed in a Warwickshire village. To his great disgust, the most commonplace sentiments found utterance in him. At the same time he was extraordinarily happy . . .

Rupert Brooke

1914 *The Good Soldier Švejk*

Švejk is among the immortal characters of war literature. He was the invention of Jaroslav Hasek, the Czech humorist and practical joker, who was able to draw on his vast experience of military service as an Austrian soldier, a Czech legionnaire in Russia and as an officer in the Red Army to produce one of the great satires of military life, *The Good Soldier Švejk*, which was published between 1921 and 1923.

Švejk is a good-natured simpleton who gets involved in the vast catastrophe of the dying days of the Austro-Hungarian Empire. He was discharged from the army for chronic simple-mindedness, but when the Great War breaks out in 1914, despite the additional handicap of arthritis, he is anxious to enlist. He is identified as a malingerer and treated accordingly:

> In these great times the army doctors took unusual pains to drive the devil of sabotage out of the malingerers and restore them to the bosom of the army.
>
> Various degrees of torture had been introduced for malingerers and suspected malingerers, such as consumptives, rheumatics, people with hernia, kidney disease, typhus, diabetes, pneumonia and other illnesses.
>
> The tortures to which the malingerers were subjected were systematized and the grades were as follows:
>
> 1. Strict diet, a cup of tea each morning and evening for three days, during which, irrespective, of course, of their complaints, aspirin to be given to induce sweating.
>
> 2. To ensure they did not think that war was all beer and skittles, quinine in powder to be served in generous portions, or so-called 'quinine licking'.
>
> 3. The stomach to be pumped out twice a day with a litre of warm water.
>
> 4. Enemas with soapy water and glycerine to be applied.
>
> 5. Wrapping up in a sheet soaked in cold water.
>
> There were stalwart men who endured all five degrees of torture and let themselves be carried off to the military cemetery in a simple coffin. But there were also pusillanimous souls who, when they reached the stage of the enema, declared that they were now well and desired nothing better than to march off to the trenches with the next march battalion.
>
> In the garrison prison Švejk was put into the sanatorium hut among pusillanimous malingerers of this very type.
>
> 'I can't stand it any longer,' said his neighbour in the next bed, who was brought in from the consulting room after having had his stomach pumped for the second time.
>
> This man was shamming short-sightedness.
>
> 'Tomorrow I'll join the regiment,' decided his other neighbour on

the left, who had just had an enema and who had been shamming deafness.

In the bed by the door a consumptive who was wrapped up in a cold wet sheet was slowly dying.

'That's the third this week,' observed his neighbour on the right. 'And what's your trouble?'

'I've got rheumatism,' answered Švejk, upon which there was a hearty guffaw all round. Even the dying consumptive, who was shamming tuberculosis, joined in the laughter.

'Don't try and climb in here with rheumatism,' a fat man warned Švejk solemnly. 'Rheumatism here doesn't mean more than a chilblain. I'm anaemic, I've lost half my stomach and five of my ribs, but no one believes me. We even had a fellow here who was deaf and dumb. For a fortnight they wrapped him up every half-hour in a cold wet sheet and every day they gave him an enema and pumped his stomach. All the nurses thought he'd won through and would go home, when the doctor prescribed him an emetic. It could have torn him in half and so he lost courage. 'I can't go on being deaf and dumb,' he said. 'My speech and hearing have returned.' All the patients urged him not to ruin himself but he insisted that he could hear and speak just like other people. And he reported to this effect at the doctor's visit next morning.'

'He kept it up for quite a long time,' remarked a man, who was pretending to have one leg four inches shorter than the other. 'Not like that chap who shammed a stroke. All they had to do was to give him three doses of quinine, one enema and a day's fasting. He confessed and by the time they started pumping out his stomach there wasn't a trace left of his stroke. The chap who held out longest of all was the one who had been bitten by a mad dog. He bit, he howled — it's true he could do it splendidly — but he just couldn't manage to foam at the mouth. We did our best to help him. Several times we tickled him for a whole hour before the doctor's visit until he had convulsions and got blue all over, but the foam wouldn't come and didn't in fact come at all. It was really terrifying. When he gave in one morning at the doctor's visit we were quite sorry for him. He stood by his bed erect as a candle, saluted and said: "Humbly report, sir, the dog I was bitten by may not have been mad after all." The doctor gave him such a queer look that he began to tremble all over and went on: "Humbly report, sir, I wasn't bitten by a dog at all. It was I who bit myself on the arm." After that confession they put him under investigation for self-mutilation on the charge that he had tried to bite off his arm to get out of going to the front.'

'All those kinds of illnesses where you have to foam at the mouth are difficult to sham,' said the fat malingerer. 'Take for instance epilepsy. We had an epileptic here who always used to tell us that one fit wasn't enough and so he put on some ten a day. He writhed in convulsions, clenched his fists, rolled his eyes wildly, flung himself about on the floor, stuck out his tongue, in short, I can tell you, it was a magnificent first-class epilepsy, the genuine thing. But suddenly he got boils, two on the neck and two on the back, and it was all over with his writhing and flinging himself about on the floor, when he couldn't move his head and wasn't able either to sit or lie down. He got fever and in delirium he let out everything at the doctor's visit. He gave us a lot of trouble over his boils, because he had to lie here with them another three days and got another diet — coffee and rolls in the morning, soup, dumplings and gravy for lunch, and porridge or soup in the evening. And with our hungry, pumped-out stomachs and strict diet we had to watch this fellow bolting the food, smacking his lips, panting and belching with repletion. In this way he broke down another three who confessed as well. They had been suffering from heart disease.'

'The best thing to sham,' said one of the malingerers, 'is insanity. There are two of our teachers lying in the ward next door and one of them shrieks out incessantly day and night: "Giordano Bruno's stake is still smouldering. Reopen the trial of Galileo." And the other one barks, first three times slowly: bow — wow — wow, then five times quickly in succession: bowwowwowwowwow, and then once more slowly, and so it goes on without a break. They've managed to keep it up for over three weeks now. Originally I wanted to be insane too, have religious mania and preach about papal infallibility, but in the end I fixed myself up with cancer of the stomach from a barber in Malá Strana for fifteen crowns.'

'I know a chimney-sweep in Břevnov,' remarked another patient. 'For ten crowns he'll give you such a fever that you'll jump out of the window.'

'That's nothing,' said another. 'In Vršovice there's a midwife who for twenty crowns will dislocate your leg so well that you'll be a cripple until your death.'

'I had my leg dislocated for ten crowns,' came a voice from the row of beds by the window, 'for ten crowns and three glasses of beer.'

'My illness has cost me more than two hundred already,' announced his neighbour, a dried-up stick. 'You tell me any poison I haven't taken. You won't find it. I'm a living repository of poisons of all kinds. I've taken mercury chloride, I've breathed in mercury fumes,

I've chewed arsenic, I've smoked opium, I've drunk tincture of opium, I've sprinkled morphine on bread, I've swallowed strychnine, I've drunk a solution of phosphorus in carbon sulphide as well as picric acid. I've destroyed my liver, my lungs, my kidneys, my gall-bladder, my brain, my heart and my intestines. No one knows what kind of illness I have.'

'The best thing to do,' explained somebody from the door, 'is to inject paraffin under the skin of your arm. My cousin was so fortunate as to have his arm cut off under the elbow and today he has no trouble for the rest of the war.'

'So you see,' said Švejk, 'everyone has to go through all that for His Imperial Majesty – even stomach-pumping and enemas . . . '

Jaroslav Hasek, *The Good Soldier Švejk* (1923), translated by Cecil Parrott (1973)

SONNET

When you see millions of the mouthless dead
Across your dreams in pale battalions go,
Say not soft things, as other men have said,
That you'll remember. For you need not so.
Give them not praise. For, deaf, how should they know
It is not curses heaped on each gashed head?
Nor tears. Their blind eyes see not your tears flow.
Nor honour. It is easy to be dead.
Say only this, 'They are dead'. Then add thereto,
'Yet many a better one has died before'.
Then, scanning all the o'ercrowded mass, should you
Perceive one face that you loved heretofore,
It is a spook. None wears the face you knew.
Great death has made all his for evermore.

Charles Hamilton Sorley

1914 – Five Poems by Rupert Brooke

These five sonnets were written by Rupert Brooke in December 1914 during his Christmas leave from the Royal Naval Division. He had assisted in the relief of the Belgians at Antwerp and was to take part in Churchill's Dardanelles operation in 1915, where he died of blood poisoning on 23 April 1915. They seem to epitomize British sentiments of the time, before the horrors of the Western Front came to dominate the idea of the war.

ECHOES OF WAR

I. PEACE

Now, God be thanked Who has matched us with His hour,
   And caught our youth, and wakened us from sleeping,
With hand made sure, clear eye, and sharpened power,
   To turn, as swimmers into cleanness leaping,
Glad from a world grown old and cold and weary,
   Leave the sick hearts that honour could not move,
And half-men, and their dirty songs and dreary,
   And all the little emptiness of love!

Oh! we, who have known shame, we have found release there,
   Where there's no ill, no grief, but sleep has mending,
   Naught broken save this body, lost but breath;
Nothing to shake the laughing heart's long peace there
   But only agony, and that has ending;
   And the worst friend and enemy is but Death.

II. SAFETY

Dear! of all happy in the hour, most blest
   He who has found our hid security,
Assured in the dark tides of the world at rest,
   And heard our word, 'Who is so safe as we?'
We have found safety with all things undying,
   The winds, and morning, tears of men and mirth,
The deep night, and birds singing, and clouds flying,
   And sleep, and freedom, and the autumnal earth.
We have built a house that is not for Time's throwing.
   We have gained a peace unshaken by pain for ever.
War knows no power. Safe shall be my going,
   Secretly armed against all death's endeavour;
Safe though all safety's lost; safe where men fall;
And if these poor limbs die, safest of all.

III. THE DEAD

Blow out, you bugles, over the rich Dead!
   There's none of these so lonely and poor of old,
   But, dying, has made us rarer gifts than gold.
These laid the world away; poured out the red
Sweet wine of youth; gave up the years to be
   Of work and joy, and that unhoped serene,
   That men call age; and those who would have been,
Their sons, they gave, their immortality.

Blow, bugles, blow! They brought us, for our dearth,
    Holiness, lacked so long, and Love, and Pain.
Honour has come back, as a king, to earth,
    And paid his subjects with a royal wage;
And Nobleness walks in our ways again;
    And we have come into our heritage.

IV. THE DEAD

These hearts were woven of human joys and cares,
    Washed marvellously with sorrow, swift to mirth.
The years had given them kindness. Dawn was theirs,
    And sunset, and the colours of the earth.
These had seen movement, and heard music; known
    Slumber and waking; loved; gone proudly friended;
Felt the quick stir of wonder; sat alone;
    Touched flowers and furs and cheeks. All this is ended.

There are waters blown by changing winds to laughter
And lit by the rich skies, all day. And after,
    Frost, with a gesture, stays the waves that dance
And wandering loveliness. He leaves a white
    Unbroken glory, a gathered radiance,
A width, a shining peace, under the night.

V. THE SOLDIER

If I should die, think only this of me:
    That there's some corner of a foreign field
That is for ever England. There shall be
    In that rich earth a richer dust concealed;
A dust whom England bore, shaped, made aware,
    Gave, once, her flowers to love, her ways to roam,
A body of England's breathing English air,
    Washed by the rivers, blest by suns of home.

And think, this heart, all evil shed away,
    A pulse in the eternal mind, no less
    Gives somewhere back the thoughts by England given;
Her sights and sounds; dreams happy as her day;
    And laughter, learnt of friends; and gentleness,
In hearts at peace, under an English heaven.

Rupert Brooke

1914 The Hun is at the Gate

Since the beginning of this war the meaning of it has in one respect considerably changed, and I hope that our people will see that it is primarily a holy war. It is manifestly a war between Christ and the Devil . . . The infernal machine which has been scientifically preparing for the last twenty-five years is now on its wild career like one of Mr Wells's inventions, and wherever it goes it will leave desolation behind it and put all material progress back for at least half a century. There was never anything in the world worthier of extermination, and it is the plain duty of civilised nations to unite to drive it back into its home and exterminate it there.

Robert Bridges, letter to *The Times* (2 September 1914)

For all we have and are,
For all our children's fate,
Stand up and take the war,
The Hun is at the gate!

Our world has passed away,
In wantonness o'erthrown.
There is nothing left to-day
But steel and fire and stone!
Though all we knew depart,
The old Commandments stand: —
'In courage keep your heart,
In strength lift up your hand.'

Once more we hear the word
That sickened earth of old: —
'No law except the Sword
Unsheathed and uncontrolled.'
Once more it knits mankind,
Once more the nations go
To meet and break and bind
A crazed and driven foe.

Comfort, content, delight,
The ages' slow-bought gain,
They shrivelled in a night.
Only ourselves remain
To face the naked days
In silent fortitude,
Through perils and dismays
Renewed and re-newed.

Though all we made depart,
The old Commandments stand: –
'In patience keep your heart,
In strength lift up your hand.'

No easy hopes or lies
Shall bring us to our goal,
But iron sacrifice
Of body, will, and soul.

There is but one task for all –
One life for each to give.
Who stands if Freedom fall?
Who dies if England live?

Rudyard Kipling, 'For All We Have and Are', *The Times* (2 September 1914)

1914 Ypres: An Epitaph on an Army of Mercenaries

This poem was written after the first Battle of Ypres (12 October to 11 November 1914). It was the last major battle on the Western Front that year. The German forces under General von Falkenhayn attacked the British Expeditionary Force under Sir John French at a point where they joined up with the Belgian forces. Initially the Germans advanced several miles. The Belgians flooded the front between Dixmunde and the sea, while the French reinforced the Allied lines; then the British counter-attacked. Another German assault followed, and the battle ended in November amid terrible weather – snow and rain. Losses were enormous – eighty per cent of the original BEF perished, 2,368 officers and 55,787 other ranks; French losses totalled 50,000 and the Germans lost 130,000 men.

Housman wrote this poem as a response to the issue the British press had made of the distinction between regular, professional soldiers and volunteer forces. Hugh McDiarmid, writing many years after the Great War, answered Housman's celebration of the professional soldiers who saved the world by fighting for their money.

EPITAPH ON AN ARMY OF MERCENARIES

These, in the day when heaven was falling,
The hour when earth's foundations fled,
Followed their mercenary calling
And took their wages and are dead.

Their shoulders held the sky suspended;
They stood, and earth's foundations stay;
What God abandoned, these defended,
And saved the sum of things for pay.

A E. Housman

1915 The New Warfare

By the beginning of 1915 a terrible situation of deadlock had been reached on the Western Front. The opposing armies faced each other in five hundred miles of trenches which extended from Switzerland to the English Channel. Each side hoped that some major push would achieve a breakthrough and lead to victory, while in fact things settled down to an obscene war of attrition. To many taking part, however, it seemed that things were tidied up a bit:

> The first few months after the war broke out confusion reigned supreme. Belgium and the north of France were one huge jumbled battlefield, rather like a public park on a Saturday afternoon . . . Friend and foe were inextricably mingled, and the direction of the goal was uncertain. If you rode into a village, you might find it occupied by a Highland regiment or a squadron of Uhlans. If you dimly discerned troops marching side by side with you in the dawning, it was by no means certain that they would prove to be your friends. On the other hand, it was never safe to assume that a battalion which you saw hastily entrenching itself against your approach was German. It might belong to your own brigade . . .
>
> Well . . . the trench system has put an end to all that. The trenches now run continuously — a long, irregular, but perfectly definite line of cleavage — from the North Sea to the Vosges. Everybody has been carefully sorted out — human beings on one side, Germans on the other . . .
>
> The result is an agreeable blend of war and peace. This week, for example, our battalion has been undergoing a sort of rest-cure a few miles from the hottest part of the firing line . . . In the morning we wash our clothes, and perform a few mild martial exercises. In the afternoon we sleep . . . under the trees in an orchard. In the evening we play football, or bathe in the canal, or lie on our backs on the grass, watching our aeroplanes buzzing home to roost, attended by German shrapnel. We could not have done this in the Autumn. Now, thanks to our trenches . . .
>
> But there are drawbacks to everything. The fact is . . . a trench is a

232

compromise. It is neither satisfactory as a domicile nor efficient as a weapon of offence. The most luxuriant dug-out; the most artistic window box — these, in spite of all biased assertions to the contrary, compare unfavourably with a flat in Knightsbridge. On the other hand, the knowledge that you are keeping yourself tolerably immune from the assaults of your enemy is heavily discounted by the fact that the enemy is equally immune from yours. In other words, 'you get no forrarder' with a trench; and the one thing which we are all anxious to do out here is to bring this war to a speedy and gory conclusion, and get home to hot meals and regular baths.

Ian Hay, *The First Hundred Thousand: Being the Unofficial Chronicle of a Unit of Kitchener's Army* (1915)

1915 Gallipoli and Egypt: Social Life at Suez

The Russians wanted a diversionary expedition to relieve Turkish pressure on the Russian armies in the Caucasus. Russia had become isolated from war supplies and the European allies. The aim was to restore the Mediterranean–Black Sea route to Russia through the Turkish straits. A relief force would combine with an attack on the Turkish forces. Troops were trained for the Dardanelles operation in Europe, where the British had stationed some 250,000 men before the war started. Here men trained, lived and desported themselves before embarking on the fateful adventure of the Gallipoli landings in February 1915. British, colonial and French troops formed a sizeable population which soon created its own often quite roisterous social life:

The town itself was full of Tommies. I think the whole of my battalion was in Suez that night, and of course the Aussies were splashing their money about. The hotels and the gardens in front, and the restaurants, were chock-full of dining and wining Tommies. Others were staggering about the streets, shouting and singing. The boys were certainly relaxing! Every kind of wine and liquor could be bought by the bottle, and the native shops did a roaring trade in silks and brooches, which the boys bought to send home as souvenirs to mothers, wives and sweethearts. There was a picture palace there too, owned by a Frenchman who, during our stay in Suez, arranged concerts and boxing and wrestling matches in his hall for the pleasure of the troops.

The natives did not seem to like the intrusion into their town and sat smoking their hookahs and scowling at us as we passed by. They certainly had no love for us and were not to be trusted. One or two of our boys who visited the town never returned to camp and were never seen again. These dirty, scowling fellows were certainly responsible for their disappearance. Our command must have thought so too, for they issued the order that every man going to town must wear belt and bayonet. During the boys' drinking orgies many of these natives were left bleeding and unconscious for their unfriendly attitude. Often drinking houses were turned into a shambles, arguments arose, tempers flared up, tables were overturned and bottles began to fly through the air alongside whirling belts, while drunken men lurched into the street, cursing and bleeding.

One evening as I sat with a chum having a drink in one of these 'pubs' and listening to a native who, standing on an empty cask, was doing his best to entertain us with a song, half a dozen drink-sodden Aussies lurched into the place. One of them, glaring at the native, bawled out, 'Shut that hole, you dirty nigger', and, drawing a revolver from his belt, shot at the unfortunate black. The poor fellow dropped from the cask bleeding at the shoulder. The proprietor ran to him to help, uttering curses in his native tongue; immediately an English Tommy remonstrated with the Aussie. Then the fun started. The place was very soon in darkness and I and my chum made a mad dive for the door. As we reached the safety of the street we could hear the crash of chairs and tables and the smashing of glasses and bottles mingled with the curses and oaths of drunken, fighting men . . .

After getting a skinful of drink the boys usually made their way back to camp via the railway sidings on one side of the town. Here by these railway sidings was the black spot of Suez, a bunch of houses the boys called the 'Rag'. Here lived the 'Bohemian ladies' of Suez. Girls of all nationalities lived here, their names and country printed on boards above the door. Dressed in their prettiest and flimsiest dresses they waited for Tommy. Black girls were there also, smiling and showing their pearly white teeth: these girls, of course, were the favourites of the Indian troops. Brown-skinned Arab girls, smothered in cheap rings, bracelets and beads, were also there, sitting, sipping coffee and smoking cigarettes. The houses were furnished only with a chair or two, a table, and a bed, the walls being adorned with an indecent picture or two.

The scenes at the 'Rag' in the evenings were almost unbelievable. Drunken Tommies danced with almost naked girls, no curtains or blinds were drawn to the windows, and every action of these soulless women and their drunken companions could be plainly seen. And so the immoral life went on and the half-crowns of Tommy kept accumulating in the locked iron box beside the bed, until the military police, promptly on the stroke of nine, cleared the whole place, Tommy returning to camp and the female vultures to count their ill-gotten money.

Returning to camp by the legitimate route was always very amusing. One could ride back to camp on a donkey's back for sixpence, and it was great fun to see the boys, absolutely too drunk to walk back to camp, being carried on the old donkey's back, first sliding off one side, and then the other, the old native who owned the donkey doing his best to keep Tommy mounted, and very often getting cursed for his trouble. Then on arrival at the camp no fare would be forthcoming until he had dug up some officer to help him get his sixpence.

George Ashurst, My Bit: A Lancashire Fusilier at War 1914–18, edited by
Richard Holmes (1987)

1915 Flanders Fields

John McCrae's 'In Flanders Fields' one of the most enduring of all the poems written during the Great War, was published anonymously in *Punch* on 6 December 1915. McCrae was a Canadian medical officer during the Second Battle of Ypres. His images have subsequently become part of our collective memory.

IN FLANDERS FIELDS

In Flanders fields the poppies blow
Between the crosses, row on row
    That mark our place; and in the sky
    The larks, still bravely singing, fly
Scarce heard amid the guns below.

We are the Dead. Short days ago
We lived, felt dawn, saw sunset glow,
    Loved and were loved, and now we lie
    In Flanders fields.

Take up our quarrel with the foe:
To you from failing hands we throw
    The torch; be yours to hold it high.
    If ye break faith with us who die
We shall not sleep, though poppies grow
    In Flanders fields.

John McCrae

1916 Dying Young for Kaiser and Vaterland

The brutality and inhumanity of war stood in great contrast to what I had heard and read about as a youth. I really wanted to go off to the Front at the beginning of the war because in school we were taught to be super patriots. This was drilled into us – in order to be men we should go off to war and, if necessary, bravely die for Kaiser and Fatherland.

When I had joined the army in the spring of 1916 I still carried presumptions that the war would be fought like the 1870 war between Germany and France. Man-to-man combat, for instance. But in the trenches friend and foe alike suffered from the effects of invisible machinery. It was not enough to conquer the enemy. He had to be totally destroyed. The fighting troops of the front lines saw themselves mired hopelessly in this hellish wasteland. Whoever lived through it thanked his good luck. The rest died as 'heroes'. It seemed quite unlikely to me in late 1916 that I should live through it. When you met someone you knew who belonged to a different outfit, he was greeted with the words, 'Well, are you still alive?' It was said humorously but meant in deadly earnest. For a young man who had a long and worthwhile future awaiting him, it was not easy to expect death almost daily. However, after a while I got used to the idea of dying young. Strangely, it had a sort of soothing effect and prevented me from worrying too much. Because of this I gradually lost the terrible fear of being wounded or killed.

Freiwilliger Reinhold Spengler, First Bavarian Infanterie Regiment, quoted in Lyn MacDonald, *1914–1918 – Voices and Images of the Great War* (1988)

1916 The Somme

Brigadier General Rees, General Officer Commanding 94th Infantry Brigade of 31 Division at the Somme, reports on the advance of the 31 Division on the left of the line, towards Serre, on the first day of the Somme, 1 July 1916:

They advanced in line after line, dressed as if on parade, and not a man shirked going through the extremely heavy barrage, or facing the machine-gun and rifle fire that finally wiped them out . . . [Rees] saw the lines which advanced in such admirable order melting away under the fire. Yet not a man wavered, broke the ranks, or attempted to come back. He has never seen, indeed could never have imagined, such a magnificent display of gallantry, discipline and determination.

The reports that he had from the very few survivors of this marvellous advance bear out what he saw with his own eyes, viz., that hardly a man of ours got to the German front line.

Tim Travers, *The Killing Ground* (1988)

1916

BEFORE ACTION

By all the glories of the day
  And the cool evening's benison,
By that last sunset touch that lay
  Upon the hills when day was done,
By beauty lavishly outpoured
  And blessings carelessly received,
By all the days that I have lived
  Make me a soldier, Lord.

By all of all man's hopes and fears,
  And all the wonders poets sing,
The laughter of unclouded years,
  And every sad and lovely thing;
By the romantic ages stored
  With high endeavour that was his,
By all his mad catastrophes
  Make me a man, O Lord.

I, that on my familiar hill
  Saw with uncomprehending eyes
A hundred of Thy sunsets spill
  Their fresh and sanguine sacrifice,
Ere the sun swings his noonday sword
  Must say good-bye to all of this; –
By all delights that I shall miss,
  Help me to die, O Lord.

W. N. Hodgson, 'Before Action' (published in *The New Witness*, 29 June 1916). Hodgson was killed a few days later.

1916 Battle of the Somme

Bert Steward was a nineteen-year-old rifleman in the 6th London Rifles at the battle of the Somme. He had no experience of machine-gun fire. A

237

guardsman he met at an estaminet one evening told him: 'When you go over the top, son, there's only one thing you can do. Walk a yard or two, then spin sideways as if you'd been hit, drop into the nearest shell-hole, and stay there. Believe me . . . it's your only chance, boy.' Then on 15 September he went over the top during the taking of the High Wood. It had been fought over, taken and retaken several times. There were no trees. Only earth and shell-holes. It was the first time tanks were used in battle. They would move ahead, it was claimed, and wipe out all the machine-guns.

Zero hour, and my corporal made a little gesture at me, and we got out of the ditch and started to walk. I never saw him again.

Imagine us then rather like overladen porters going slow over a shockingly ploughed field in a man-made thunder storm. Hailstones of a lethal kind zipped past our heads. From behind us the bombardment from our own guns, which I had seen massed wheel to wheel, went on. To left and right men were moving forward in uneven lines. My plan was to walk alone and not get bunched up with others. I kept away from them. I soon found this easier. On each side some had disappeared. I saw only one tank — in a ditch with a broken track, like a dying hippopotamus, with shells bursting round it. I kept walking. I walked about half a mile. I reached the shelter of an embankment. With this solid mass between me and the enemy I felt safe.

The next moment was the luckiest of my life. I had walked all the way through a hail of bullets. I had been a slowly-moving target for the machine guns. The bullets had all missed, though narrowly, for parts of my tunic were in ribbons. Then, just as I had reached safety, as I thought, what seemed like a hammer blow hit me on the top of my left shoulder. I opened my tunic. There was a clean round hole right through the shoulder. A bullet! But where from? Then I realised I was getting enfiladed by some machine-gunner to my right, on my side of the embankment. I threw myself down, but not before another bullet struck my right thigh.

In the embankment was the entrance to a dugout. I crawled into it. It was occupied by Germans. None of them spoke. They were all dead.

There was parcels from home strewn about, cigarettes, black bread, eatables, and one huge German, lying face downwards, made a good couch to sit on. Now I was joined by two friends, one less lucky, a young lad from Liverpool, with a bullet through the stomach.

Here we were, in front of our front line. About a hundred yards back I could see tin hats bobbing about. The remnants of the cast-irons were manning an improvised front line among the shellholes. Beyond them, I thought, was England, home and beauty.

I had taken High Wood, almost by myself, it seemed. I had no further territorial ambitions. Indeed, what I now had in mind was to go as quickly as possible in the opposite direction, as soon as possible. Leaving the dugout, I ran for it, zigzagging to escape bullets (two were enough) and so fast that I toppled head-first on top of a rifleman who was almost as scared as I was. After he had recovered he told me how I could work my way along the line of shellholes to a dressing station. I went, keeping my head down; I was taking no chances. I had two bullet holes. If they had been drilled by a surgeon they could not have been located more conveniently. I was incredibly lucky. But another might spoil everything. I crawled along.

The dressing station was a captured German underground hospital, with entrance big enough for an ambulance, built like a fortress, furnished with tiers of wooden bunks. It was crowded with wounded, now being sorted out by our adjutant.

'Those who can run follow me, nobody with a leg wound,' he said. 'We have to move fast,' I was the first to follow. In and out of shellholes we went – a rough but rapid journey in the right direction – until we reached a sunken lane where a horse-drawn hooded cart waited to take a dozen of us an hour's trot nearer home . . .

The Canadian doctor looked like any other in his white coat. He turned out to be a saint. 'You've been very lucky,' he said in a kindly way. Then he explained that one bullet, almost incredibly, had found a narrow gap between collar-bone and shoulder-blade, and that neither of the two had touched muscle or bone. 'How old are you and how long have you been in the trenches?' he asked and, when I told him, he wrote on a card and gave it to the nurse.

Later I looked up at the card pinned to the chart above my bed. It was marked with a big B. What did it mean? A nurse hurrying by answered my question. She smiled as she said – 'It means Blighty.'

Bert Steward, 'The Taking of High Wood', *The Guardian* (September 1990)

1916

LAMPLIGHT

We planned to shake the world together, you and I
Being young, and very wise;
Now in the light of the green shaded lamp
Almost I see your eyes

Light with the old gay laughter; you and I
Dreamed greatly of an Empire in those days,
Setting our feet upon laborious ways,
And all you asked of fame
Was crossed swords in the Army List,
My Dear, against your name.

We planned a great Empire together, you and I
Bound only by the sea;
Now in the quiet of a chill Winter's night
Your voice comes hushed to me
Full of forgotten memories: you and I
Dreamed great dreams of our future in those days,
Setting our feet on undiscovered ways,
And all I asked of fame
A scarlet cross on my breast, my Dear,
For the swords by your name.

We shall never shake the world together, you and I,
For you gave your life away;
And I think my heart was broken by the war,
Since on a summer day
You took the road we never spoke of: you and I
Dreamed greatly of an Empire in those days;
You set your feet upon the Western ways
and have no need of fame —
There's a scarlet cross on my breast, my Dear,
And a torn cross with your name.

May Wedderburn Cannan

PERHAPS . . .
To R. A. L.

Perhaps some day the sun will shine again,
And I shall see that still the skies are blue,
And feel once more I do not live in vain,
Although bereft of You.

Perhaps the golden meadows at my feet
Will make the sunny hours of spring seem gay,
And I shall find the white May-blossoms sweet,
Though You have passed away.

THE GREAT WAR FOR CIVILIZATION

Perhaps the summer woods will shimmer bright,
And crimson roses once again be fair,
And autumn harvest fields a rich delight,
Although You are not there.

But though kind Time may many joys renew,
There is one greatest joy I shall not know
Again, because my heart for loss of You
Was broken, long ago.

Vera Brittain

BREAK OF DAY IN THE TRENCHES

The darkness crumbles away –
It is the same old druid Time as ever.
Only a live thing leaps my hand –
A queer sardonic rat –
As I pull the parapet's poppy
To stick behind my ear.
Droll rat, they would shoot you if they knew
Your cosmopolitan sympathies.
Now you have touched this English hand
You will do the same to a German –
Soon, no doubt, if it be your pleasure
To cross the sleeping green between.
It seems you inwardly grin as you pass
Strong eyes, fine limbs, haughty athletes
Less chanced than you for life,
Bonds to the whims of murder,
Sprawled in the bowels of the earth,
The torn fields of France.
What do you see in our eyes
At the shrieking iron and flame
Hurled through still heavens?
What quaver – what heart aghast?
Poppies whose roots are in man's veins
Drop, and are ever dropping;
But mine in my ear is safe,
Just a little white with the dust.

Isaac Rosenberg

241

1916 The 'Lost Generation'

Britain is a collection of islands; and though, intellectually, the British know that air power and missiles have long ago abolished island status . . . the island mentality persists. It is sheer myopic insularity which inspires the great Casualty Myth. Its believers and perpetrators speak and write as though virtually every dead soldier on the Western Front between 1914 and 1918 wore khaki. [This belief] dates from the year 1916 . . . and in particular from awareness of the calamitous 1 July of that year, the worst day in the British Army's history.[1] The year as a whole cost the British army some 660,000 casualties, a figure which produced an enduring national trauma, already firmly lodged among some who possessed knowledge and influence, before the year was ended. Chief among them was the Secretary of State for War, Mr Lloyd George, who denounced the 'military Moloch' to Colonel Repington of The Times on 25 October 1916. To Lloyd George, loss on this scale (it implies about 200,000 dead) was something uniquely horrible. Horrible it certainly was but, regrettably, it was also commonplace – and that was something he was never able to reckon with. For example, as the year began, French losses (from a smaller population) already stood at about two million, compared with Britain's half million. According to one authority, even by March 1915, the Austro-Hungarian Army had lost over two million; the Russians lost that number in 1915 alone. The truth is that the only really exceptional thing about Britain's experience in 1916 was that she had been spared so long.

1. British Army losses on the first day of the Somme 1 July 1916:
Killed (or died of wounds):
Officers – 993
Other ranks – 18,247

John Terraine, The Smoke and the Fire: Myths and Anti-myths of War 1861–1945
(1980)

1916 Why are We Fighting? A View from the Ranks

Frederic Manning was born in Sydney, and worked in London as a journalist and author. He served in the Shropshire Light Infantry and his novel, Her Privates We (1930), was one of the most influential books about the experience of the Western Front, one of those works which contributed to the construction of popular memory of the Great War, over and above orthodox historiography and official records. In The Middle Parts of Fortune, he writes:

'We're fightin' for all we've bloody got,' said Madeley, bluntly.

'An' that's sweet fuck all,' said Weeper Smart. 'A tell thee, that all a want to do is to save me own bloody skin. An' the first thing a do, when a go into t' line, is to find out where t' bloody dressing-stations are; an' if a can get a nice blighty, chaps, when once me face is turned towards home, I'm laughing. You won't see me bloody arse for dust. A'm not proud. A tell thee straight. Them as thinks different can 'ave all the bloody war they want, and me own share of it, too.'

'Well, what the 'ell did you come out for?' asked Madeley.

Weeper lifted up a large, spade-like hand with the solemnity of one making an affirmation.

'That's where th'ast got me beat, lad,' he admitted. 'When a saw all them as didn't know any better'n we did joinin' up, an' a went walkin' out wi' me girl on Sundays, as usual, a just felt ashamed. An' a put it away, an' a put it away, until in th' end it got me down. A knew what it'd be, but it got the better o' me, an' then like a bloody fool, a went an' joined up too. A were ashamed to be seen walkin' in the streets, a were. But a tell thee, now, that if a were once out o' these togs an' in civvies again, a wouldn't mind all the shame in the world; no, not if I 'ad to slink through all the back streets, an' didn' dare put me nose in t' Old Vaults again. A've no pride left in me now, chaps, an' that's the plain truth a'm tellin'. Let them as made the war come an' fight it, that's what a say.'

'That's what I say, too,' said Glazier [. . .] 'Why should us'ns fight an' be killed for all them bloody slackers at 'ome? It ain't right. No matter what they say, it ain't right. We're doin' our duty, an' they ain't, an' they're coinin' money while we get ten bloody frong [francs] a week. They don't care a fuck about us. Once we're in the army, they've got us by the balls. Talk about discipline! They don't try disciplinin' any o' them fuckin' civvies, do they? We want to put some o' them bloody politicians in the front line, an' see 'em shelled to shit. That'd buck their ideas up.'

'I'm not fightin' for a lot o' bloody civvies,' said Madeley, reasonably. 'I'm fightin' for myself an' me own folk. It's all bloody fine sayin' let them as made the war fight it. 'twere Germany made the war.'

'A tell thee,' said Weeper, positively, 'there are thousands o' poor buggers, over there in the German lines, as don' know, no more'n we do ourselves, what it's all about.'

'Then what do the silly fuckers come an' fight for?' asked Madeley, indignantly. 'Why didn' they stay 't 'ome? Tha'lt be sayin' next that the Frenchies sent 'em an invite.'

'What a say is, that it weren't none o' our business. We'd no call to mix ourselves up wi' other folks' quarrels,' replied Weeper.

'Well, I don't hold wi' that,' said Glazier, judicially. 'I'm not fightin' for them bloody slackers an' conchies at 'ome; but what I say is that the Fritzes 'ad to be stopped. If we 'adn't come in, an' they'd got the Frenchies beat, 'twould 'a' been our turn next.'

'Too bloody true it would,' said Madeley. 'An' I'd rather come an' fight Fritz in France than 'ave 'im come over to Blighty an' start bashin' our 'ouses about, same as 'e's done 'ere.'

''e'd never 'ave come to England. The Navy 'd 'ave seen to that,' said Pacey.

'Don't you be too bloody sure about the Navy,' said Corporal Hamley, entering into the discussion at last. 'The Navy 'as got all it can bloody well do, as things are.'

Frederic Manning, *The Middle Parts of Fortune* (1929)

1916 'La Gloire'

Henri Barbusse published *Le Feu: Journal d'une Ecouade* in 1916. His descriptions of life and death in the trenches, his demolition of the pernicious ideal of 'La Gloire', outlast the actual narrative. This novel affected Siegfried Sassoon and Wilfred Owen in particular:

'They will say to you,' growled a kneeling man who stooped with his two hands in the earth and shook his shoulders like a mastiff, '"My friend, you have been a wonderful hero!"' I don't *want* them to say it!'

'Heroes? Some sort of extraordinary being? Idols? Rot! We've been murderers. We have respectably followed the trade of hangmen. We shall do it again with all our might, because it's of great importance to follow that trade, so as to punish war and smother it. The act of slaughter is always ignoble; sometimes necessary, but always ignoble. Yes, hard and persistent murderers, that's what we've been. But don't talk to me about military virtue because I've killed Germans.'

'Nor to me,' cried another in so loud a voice that no one could have replied to him even had he dared; 'nor to me, because I've saved the lives of Frenchmen! Why, we might as well set fire to houses for the sake of the excellence of life-saving!'

'It would be a crime to exhibit the fine side of war, even if there were one!' murmured one of the sombre soldiers.

The first man continued. 'They'll say those things to us by way of paying us with glory, and to pay themselves too, for what they haven't done. But military glory – it isn't even true for us common soldiers. It's for some, but outside those elect the soldier's glory is a lie, like every other fine-looking thing in war. In reality, the soldier's sacrifice is obscurely concealed. The multitudes that make up the waves of attack have no reward. They run to hurl themselves into a frightful inglorious nothing. You cannot even heap up their names, their poor little names of nobodies.'

'To hell with it all,' replies a man, 'we've got other things to think about.'

'But all that,' hiccupped a face which the mud concealed like a hideous hand, 'may you even *say* it? You'd be cursed, and "shot at dawn"! They've made around a Marshal's plumes a religion as bad and stupid and malignant as the other!'

The man raised himself, fell down, and rose again. The wound that he had under his armour of filth was staining the ground, and when he had spoken, his wide-open eyes looked down at all the blood he had given for the healing of the world.

Henri Barbusse, Le Feu (*Under Fire*) (1916), translated by Fitzwater Wray (1917)

1916

A POT OF TEA

You make it in your mess-tin by the brazier's rosy gleam;
You watch it cloud, then settle amber clear;
You lift it with your bay'nit and you sniff the fragrant steam;
The very breath of it is ripe with cheer.
You're awful cold and dirty, and a-cursin' of your lot;
You scoff the blushin' 'alf of it, so rich and rippin' 'ot,
It bucks you up like anythink, just seems to touch the spot:
  God bless the man that first discovered Tea!

Since I came out to fight in France, which ain't the other day,
I think I've drunk enough to float a barge;
All kinds of fancy foreign dope, from caffy and doo lay,
To rum they serves you out before a charge.
In back rooms of estaminays I've gurgled pints of cham;
I've swilled down mugs of cider till I've felt a bloomin' dam;
But 'struth! they all ain't in it with the vintage of Assam:
  God bless the man that first invented Tea!

I think them lazy lumps o' gods wot kips on asphodel
Swigs nectar that's a flavour of Oolong;
I only wish them sons o'guns a-grillin' down in 'ell.

Could 'ave their daily ration of Suchong.
Hurrah! I'm off to battle, which is 'ell and 'eaven too;
And if I don't give some poor bloke a sexton's job to do,
To-night, by Fritz's camp fire, won't I 'ave a gorgeous brew
    (For fightin' musn't interfere with Tea).
To-night we'll all be tellin' of the Boches that we slew,
    As we drink the giddy victory in Tea.

Robert Service

I DON'T WANT TO BE A SOLDIER

I don't want to be a soldier,
I don't want to go to war.
I'd rather stay at home,
Around the streets to roam,
And live on the earnings of a well-paid whore.
I don't want a bayonet up my arse-hole,
I don't want my bollocks shot away.
I'd rather stay in England,
In merry merry England,
And fuck my bloody life away.

Anonymous

MUNITION WAGES

Earning high wages? Yus,
    Five quid a week.
A woman, too, mind you,
    I calls it dim sweet.

Ye'are asking some questions —
    But bless yer, here goes:
I spends the whole racket
    On good times and clothes.

Me saving? Elijah!
    Yer do think I'm mad.
I'm acting the lady,
    But — I ain't living bad.

I'm having life's good times.
    See 'ere, it's like this:
The 'oof come o' danger,
    A touch-and-go bizz.

246

We're all here today, mate,
    Tomorrow – perhaps dead,
If Fate tumbles on us
    And blows up our shed.

Afraid! Are yer kidding?
    With money to spend!
Years back I wore tatters,
    Now – silk stockings, mi friend!

I've bracelets and jewellery,
    Rings envied by friends;
A sergeant to swank with,
    And something to lend.

I drive out in taxis,
    Do theatres in style.
And this is mi verdict –
    It is jolly worth while.

Worth while, for tomorrow
    If I'm blown to the sky,
I'll have repaid mi wages
    In death – and pass by.

                    Madeline Ida Bedford

1917

DULCE ET DECORUM EST

Bent double, like old beggars under sacks,
Knock-kneed, coughing like hags, we cursed through sludge,
Till on the haunting flares we turned our backs
And towards our distant rest began to trudge.
Men marched asleep. Many had lost their boots
But limped on, blood-shod. All went lame; all blind;
Drunk with fatigue; deaf even to the hoots
Of gas shells dropping softly behind.

Gas! GAS! Quick, boys! – An ecstasy of fumbling,
Fitting the clumsy helmets just in time;
But someone still was yelling out and stumbling,
And flound'ring like a man in fire or lime . . .

247

Dim, through the misty panes and thick green light,
As under a green sea, I saw him drowning.

In all my dreams, before my helpless sight,
He plunges at me, guttering, choking, drowning.

If in some smothering dreams you too could pace
Behind the wagon that we flung him in,
And watch the white eyes writhing in his face,
His hanging face, like a devil's sick of sin;
If you could hear, at every jolt, the blood
Come gargling from the froth-corrupted lungs,
Obscene as cancer, bitter as the cud
Of vile, incurable sores on innocent tongues, —
My friend, you would not tell with such high zest
To children ardent for some desperate glory,
The old Lie: Dulce et decorum est
Pro patria mori.

Wilfred Owen

Wilfred Owen was educated at the University of London, and served in
the Artists' Rifles. While recovering from shell-shock in Craiglockhart
Hospital, near Edinburgh, he met Robert Graves and Siegfried Sassoon.
He was killed only days before the Armistice. His poems rank among
the most original and moving of the war.

IN THE DORDOGNE

We stood up before day
and shaved by metal mirrors
in the faint flame of a faulty candle.

And we hurried down the wide stone stairs
with a clirr of spurr chains
on stone. And we thought
when the cocks crew
that the ghosts of a dead dawn
would rise and be off. But they stayed
under the window, crouched on the staircase,
the window now the colour of morning.

The colonel slept in the bed of Sully,
slept on: but we descended
and saw in a niche in the white wall

a Virgin and child, serene
who were stone: we saw sycamore:
three aged mages
scattering gifts of gold
But when the wind blew, there were autumn odours
and the shadowed trees
had the dapplings of young fawns.

And each day one died or another
died: each week we sent out thousands
that returned by hundreds
wounded or gassed. And those that died
we buried close to the old wall
within a stone's throw of Perigord
under the tower of the troubadours.

And because we had courage;
because there was courage and youth
ready to be wasted; because we endured
and were prepared for all the endurance;
we thought something must come of it:
that the Virgin would raise her child and smile;
the trees gather up their gold and go;
that courage would avail something
and something we had never lost
be regained through wastage, by dying,
by burying the others under the English tower.

The colonel slept on in the bed of Sully
under the ravelling curtains: the leaves fell
and were blown away: the young men rotted
under the shadow of the tower
in a land of small clear silent streams
where the coming on of evening is
the letting down of blue and azure veils
over the clear and silent streams
delicately bordered by poplars.

John Peale Bishop

John Peale Bishop, educated at Princeton, served with US 33rd Infantry
in France.

THE SILENT ONE

Who died on the wires, and hung there, one of two –
Who for his hours of life had chattered through
Infinite lovely chatter of Bucks accent:
Yet faced unbroken wires; stepped over, and went
A noble fool, faithful to his stripes – and ended.
But I weak, hungry, and willing only for the chance
Of line – to fight in the line, lay down under unbroken
Wires, and saw the flashes and kept unshaken,
Till the politest voice – a finicking accent, said:
'Do you think you might crawl through, there: there's a hole'
Darkness, shot at: I smiled, as politely replied –
'I'm afraid not, Sir.' There was no hole no way to be seen
Nothing but chance of death, after tearing of clothes
Kept flat, and watched the darkness, hearing bullets whizzing –
And thought of music – and swore deep heart's deep oaths
(Polite to God) and retreated and came on again,
Again retreated – and a second time faced the screen.

Ivor Gurney

Ivor Gurney won an open scholarship to the Royal College of Music, was always sensitive and moody and drawn to music and poetry. He served in France, was gassed and wounded and sent home. By 1918 serious signs of mental disturbance caused his committal to an asylum. He died in 1937, believing the Great War was still being fought.

1917 America enters the War

At the very lowest point of this terrible conflict, Germany took a step which was to bring the USA into the war – in January 1917 the German government declared it was once again to embark on a policy of unrestricted submarine warfare. They were taking the gamble that Britain would starve before America intervened. But President Wilson broke off diplomatic relations with Germany and in April the USA declared war:

It is a fearful thing to lead this great peaceful people into war, into the most terrible and disastrous of all wars, civilization itself seeming to be in the balance. But the right is more precious than peace, and we shall fight for the things which we have always carried nearest our hearts – for democracy, for the right of those who submit to authority to have a voice in their own governments, for the rights and liberties of small nations, for a universal dominion of right by such a concert of free peoples as shall bring peace and safety to all nations and make the world itself at last free. To such a task we can dedicate our lives and our fortunes, everything that we are and everything that we have, with the pride of those who know that the day has come when America is privileged to spend her blood and her might for the principles that gave her birth and happiness and the peace which she has treasured. God helping her, she can do no other.

Woodrow Wilson, US President, Address to Congress, asking for a Declaration of
War, 2 April 1917

NEXT TO OF COURSE GOD AMERICA I LOVE YOU

'next to of course god america i
love you land of the pilgrims and so forth oh
say can you see by the dawn's early my
country 'tis of centuries come and go
and are no more what of it we should worry
in every language even deafanddumb
thy sons acclaim your glorious name by gorry
by jingo by gee by gosh by gum
why talk of beauty what could be more beautiful than these heroic happy dead
who rushed like lions to the roaring slaughter
they did not stop to think they died instead
then shall the voice of liberty be mute?'

He spoke. And drank rapidly a glass of water

e. e. cummings

1917 Leprous Earth, Swollen and Blackened Corpses

An unnamed subaltern writes to *The Nation* in the hope of conveying some idea of what the Great War was really like for those who had to take part in it.

I have often heard it said that the curious thing about those who have been to the front is their complete indifference . . . The impression one has from them is that [war] is, on the whole, a dreary and unpleasant business, with its anxious moments and its bright moments, but not nearly such a hell as one really knows it to be.

In the case of the vast majority, however, this is an attitude, a screen -- I speak of educated, thinking men – and it is not granted to many who have not shared the same experiences to see behind this screen . . . [The] uninitiated [cannot] . . . realise or imagine even dimly the actual conditions of war. And a man who has been through it and seen and taken part in the unspeakable tragedies that are the ordinary routine, feels that he has something, possesses something, which others can never possess.

It is morally impossible for him to talk seriously of these things to people who cannot even approach comprehension. It is hideously exasperating to hear people talking the glib commonplaces about the war and distributing cheap sympathy to its victims.

Perhaps you are tempted to give them a picture of a leprous earth, scattered with the swollen and blackening corpses of hundreds of young men. The appalling stench of rotting carrion mingled with the sickening smell of exploded lyddite and ammonal. Mud like porridge, trenches like shallow and sloping cracks in the porridge – porridge that stinks in the sun. Swarms of flies and bluebottles clustering on pits of offal. Wounded men lying in the shell holes among the decaying corpses: helpless under the scorching sun and bitter nights, under repeated shelling. Men with bowels dropping out, lungs shot away, with blinded, smashed faces, or limbs blown into space. Men screaming and gibbering. Wounded men hanging in agony on the barbed wire, until a friendly spout of liquid fire shrivels them up like a fly in a candle. But these are only words, and probably only convey a fraction of their meaning to their hearers. They shudder, and it is forgotten . . .

Unnamed subaltern, letter published in *The Nation* (23 June 1917)

1917 Passchendaele

Passchendaele has become synonymous for slaughter. This third battle for the Ypres Salient was planned by Field Marshal Sir Douglas Haig so as to threaten German control of the Channel ports, which she was using for submarine warfare. Several in high office opposed the plan – among them the PM Lloyd George – fearing terrible casualties. It began with a bombardment of four and a half million shells which lasted ten days. The drainage system was destroyed and when the predicted rains came oceans of mud resulted. Ferocious fighting lasted from the end of July to early November, during which the Salient was extended by five miles at a cost of 300,000 British, 8,528 French and 260,000 German lives. Lloyd George ranked Passchendaele unsurpassed among the records of disaster wrought by human complacency:

And now we come to the battle which, with the Somme and Verdun, will always rank as the most gigantic, tenacious, grim, futile and bloody fights ever waged in the history of war. Each of these battles lasted for months. None of them attained the object for which they were fought. In each case it was obvious early in the struggle to every one who watched its course – except to those who were responsible for the strategic plan that wrought the grisly tragedy – that the goal would not be reached. Taken together they were responsible for the slaughter or mutilation of between 2,000,000 and 3,000,000 of brave men. The tale of these battles constitutes a trilogy illustrating the unquenchable heroism that will never accept defeat and the inexhaustible vanity that will never admit a mistake. It is the story of the million who would rather die than own themselves cowards – even to themselves – and also of the two or three individuals who would rather the million perish than that they as leaders should own – even to themselves – that they were blunderers. Hence the immortal renown and the ghastly notoriety of the Verdun, Somme and Passchendaele battlefields; the fame won by sustained valour unrivalled in the annals of war; the notoriety attained by a narrow and stubborn egotism, unsurpassed amongst the records of disaster wrought by human complacency.

Falkenhayn, Joffre, and Haig were trained soldiers who had worked hard to master their profession. But there is no profession where experience and training count less in comparison with judgment and flair. The intervals between great wars are fortunately so considerable, and in this age of restless invention the change in mechanism and therefore in methods is also so considerable and so rapid, that imagination, resource, initiative and flexibility are more essential to success in the vocation of the soldier than in any other.

The battle of the Flanders mud, better and more bitterly known as the Battle of Passchendaele, had been put into Sir Douglas Haig's tenacious brain as early as 1916. If it failed it was not for lack of the most elaborate and prolonged preparations. In July, 1917, he told the War Cabinet that he had been preparing for it the whole year.

David Lloyd George, *War Memoirs* (1938)

1917 *Three of the War's Greatest Poets Respond to the Catastrophes of 1917*

STRANGE MEETING

It seemed that out of battle I escaped
Down some profound dull tunnel, long since scooped
Through granites which titanic wars had groined.
Yet also there encumbered sleepers groaned,
Too fast in thought or death to be bestirred.
Then, as I probed them, one sprang up, and stared
With piteous recognition in fixed eyes,
Lifting distressful hands as if to bless.
And by his smile, I knew that sullen hall,
By his dead smile I knew we stood in Hell.
With a thousand pains that vision's face was grained;
Yet no blood reached there from the upper ground,
And no guns thumped, or down the flues made moan.
'Strange friend,' I said, 'here is no cause to mourn.'
'None,' said that other, 'save the undone years,
The hopelessness. Whatever hope is yours,
Was my life also; I went hunting wild
After the wildest beauty in the world,
Which lies not calm in eyes, or braided hair,
But mocks the steady running of the hour,
And if it grieves, grieves richlier than here.
For of my glee might many men have laughed,
And of my weeping something had been left,
Which must die now. I mean the truth untold,
The pity of war, the pity war distilled.
Now men will go content with what we spoiled,
Or, discontent, boil bloody, and be spilled.
They will be swift with swiftness of the tigress.
None will break ranks, though nations trek from progress.
Courage was mine, and I had mystery,
Wisdom was mine, and I had mastery:
To miss the march of this retreating world
Into vain citadels that are not walled.
Then, when much blood had clogged their chariot-wheels,
I would go up and wash them from sweet wells,
Even with truths that lie too deep for taint.
I would have poured my spirit without stint
But not through wounds; not on the cess of war.

Foreheads of men have bled where no wounds were.
I am the enemy you killed, my friend.
I knew you in this dark: for so you frowned
Yesterday through me as you jabbed and killed.
I parried; but my hands were loath and cold.
Let us sleep now . . . '

Wilfred Owen

DEAD MAN'S DUMP

The plunging limbers over the shattered track
Racketed with their rusty freight,
Stuck out like many crowns of thorns,
And the rusty stakes like sceptres old
To stay the flood of brutish men
Upon our brothers dear.

The wheels lurched over sprawled dead
But pained them not, though their bones crunched,
Their shut mouths made no moan.
They lie there huddled, friend and foeman,
Man born of man, and born of woman,
And shells go crying over them
From night till night and now.

Earth has waited for them,
All the time of their growth
Fretting for their decay:
Now she has them at last!
In the strength of their strength
Suspended – stopped and held.

What fierce imaginings their dark souls lit?
Earth! have they gone into you!
Somewhere they must have gone,
And flung on your hard back
Is their soul's sack
Emptied of God-ancestralled essences.
Who hurled them out? Who hurled?

None saw their spirits' shadow shake the grass,
Or stood aside for the half used life to pass
Out of those doomed nostrils and the doomed mouth,
When the swift iron burning bee
Drained the wild honey of their youth.

What of us who, flung on the shrieking pyre,
Walk, our usual thoughts untouched,
Our lucky limbs as on ichor fed,
Immortal seeming ever?
Perhaps when the flames beat loud on us,
A fear may choke in our veins
And the startled blood may stop.

The air is loud with death,
The dark air spurts with fire,
The explosions ceaseless are.
Timelessly now, some minutes past,
These dead strode time with vigorous life,
Till the shrapnel called 'An end!'

Isaac Rosenberg

'BLIGHTERS'

The House is crammed: tier beyond tier they grin
And cackle at the Show, while prancing ranks
Of harlots shrill the chorus, drunk with din;
'We're sure the Kaiser loves our dear old Tanks!'

I'd like to see a Tank come down the stalls,
Lurching to rag-time tunes, or 'Home, sweet Home',
And there'd be no more jokes in Music-halls
To mock the riddled corpses round Bapaume.

Siegfried Sassoon

1918 Western Front, 11 November 1918

By the middle of July 1918 it was obvious the tide had finally turned against the Central Powers. The major Allied counter-attack on the Western Front opened on 20 August and by the first week of September the Germans had retreated to the Siegfried Line. An Austro-Hungarian peace offer was made on 14 September (which was refused) and a German-Austrian request for an Armistice was sent to the USA on 4 October. The German war effort collapsed with naval mutiny spreading through Kiel, Hamburg, Bremen and north-western Germany and revolution breaking out in Munich. An Armistice was signed by Germany and the Allies on 11 November. The Great War, which killed

1.8 million Germans, 1.7 million Russians, 1.4 million French, 1.2 million Austrians and Hungarians, 950,000 British, 460,000 Italians, 325,000 Turks and 115,000 Americans and blinded, maimed or shell-shocked some 20 million others, was over. When the end came it seemed to many at the Front an anti-climax:

> November 11th. There had been so much talk of an armistice that a Brigade message in the morning telling us of its having been signed at 8 o'clock, and that hostilities were to cease at 11, fell somewhat flat. The event was anticlimax relieved by some spasmodic cheering when the news got about, by a general atmosphere of 'slacking off for the day', and by the notes of a lively band in the late afternoon. The men betook themselves to their own devices. There was a voluntary Service of Thanksgiving in the cinema which the Germans had built; the spacious building was quite full. The local civilians were overjoyed. They dug out some *drapeaux des Alliées* in astonishingly quick time. And they were hospitable with their poor means. They brewed an awful decoction of baked ground oats in place of coffee which had been unobtainable for a long time. To me the most remarkable feature of that day and night was the uncanny silence that prevailed. No rumbling of guns, no staccato of machine-guns, nor did the roar of exploding dumps break into the night as it had so often done. The War was over.

> Captain Llewelyn Evans, Royal Welch Fusiliers, in Captain J. C. Dunn, *The War the Infantry Knew 1914–1919 – A Chronicle of Service in France and Belgium* (1938)

What Was It All For?

Just as it might be argued that no poet captured so well as Rupert Brooke the very mood of the opening of the Great War in his sonnet sequence *1914*, no poet so brilliantly and satirically expressed the feelings of the survivors when regarding the War and its costs and seeking its justification as Ezra Pound:

from HUGH SELWYN MAUBERLEY
(Life and contacts)

These fought in any case,
and some believing,
    pro domo, in any case . . .

Some quick to arm,
some for adventure,
some from fear of weakness,
some from fear of censure,
some for love of slaughter, in imagination,
learning later . . .
some in fear, learning love of slaughter;
Died some, pro patria,
        non 'dulce' non 'et decor' . . .
walked eye-deep in hell
believing in old men's lies, then unbelieving
came home, home to a lie,
home to many deceits,
home to old lies and new infamy;
usury age-old and age-thick
and liars in public places.

Daring as never before, wastage as never before.
Young blood and high blood,
fair cheeks, and fine bodies;

fortitude as never before

frankness as never before,
disillusions as never told in the old days,
hysterias, trench confessions,
laughter out of dead bellies.

There died a myriad,
And of the best, among them,
For an old bitch gone in the teeth,
For a botched civilization,

Charm, smiling at the good mouth,
Quick eyes gone under earth's lid,

For two gross of broken statues,
For a few thousand battered books.

                    Ezra Pound, from *Hugh Selwyn Mauberley* (1920)

1917 The Arab Revolt

Thomas Edward Lawrence was an Arabist and archaeologist before
becoming a soldier. His intimate knowledge of desert-dwelling

tribesmen and their culture made him an ideal person to reanimate the Arab revolt against the Turks. Lawrence worked in collaboration with General Allenby and Emir Feisal, ensuring that the war in the desert played its part in the defeat of the Axis powers.

I had got among the first of them, and was shooting, with a pistol of course, for only an expert could use a rifle from such plunging beasts; when suddenly my camel tripped and went down emptily upon her face, as though pole-axed. I was torn completely from the saddle, sailed grandly through the air for a great distance, and landed with a crash which seemed to drive all the power and feeling out of me. I lay there, passively waiting for the Turks to kill me, continuing to hum over the verses of a half-forgotten poem, whose rhythm something, perhaps the prolonged stride of the camel, had brought back to my memory as we leaped down the hill-side:

For Lord I was free of all Thy flowers, but I chose the world's sad
    roses,
And that is why my feet are torn and mine eyes are blind with
    sweat.

While another part of my mind thought what a squashed thing I should look when all that cataract of men and camels had poured over.

After a long time I finished my poem, and no Turks came, and no camel trod on me: a curtain seemed taken from my ears: there was a great noise in front. I sat up and saw the battle over, and our men driving together and cutting down the last remnants of the enemy. My camel's body had laid behind me like a rock and divided the charge into two streams: and in the back of its skull was the heavy bullet of the fifth shot I fired . . .

To an Arab an essential part of the triumph of victory was to wear the clothes of an enemy: the next day we saw our force transformed (as to the upper half) into a Turkish force, each man in a soldier's tunic: for this was a battalion straight from home, very well found and dressed in new uniforms.

The dead men looked wonderfully beautiful. The night was shining gently down, softening them into new ivory. Turks were white-skinned on their clothed parts, much whiter than the Arabs; and these soldiers had been very young. Close round them lapped the dark wormwood, now heavy with dew, in which the ends of the moonbeams sparkled like sea-spray. The corpses seemed flung so pitifully on the ground, huddled anyhow in low heaps. Surely if straightened they would be comfortable at last. So I put them all in order, one by one, very wearied myself, and longing to be of these quiet ones, not of the restless, noisy, aching mob up the valley, quarrelling over the plunder, boasting of their speed and strength to endure God knew how many toils and pains of this sort; with death, whether we won or lost, waiting to end the history.

T. E. Lawrence, *The Seven Pillars of Wisdom* (1935)

XV

THE SPANISH CIVIL WAR

1936–1939 Spanish Civil War

Yet we were the casualties of our liberalism, of our decent aspirations. We wanted, desperately, to preserve something. The civil war in Spain revealed to us, not only the tragedy about to engulf the world, but our own national tragedy. Swiftly we knew that it was not a civil war in Spain, but a civil war in the world. Spain was a battle ground upon which all liberal principles were being raped and ravaged by the left and right. We could not throw our whole weight upon one side or the other because we did not believe in one side or the other.

R. W. Thomson, *An Echo of Trumpets* (1944)

The Spanish Civil War began as a revolt by Army chiefs at Mililla, in Spanish Morocco, against what they considered weak government in Madrid. It was, in fact, a backlash against the socialism and anti-clericalism of the Popular Front Republican Government of President Azana. The insurgents were led originally by General Sanjurjo, who was killed within two months, and then by General Franco.

The revolt spread to the garrison towns. Cadiz, Seville, Saragossa and Burgos declared for the insurgents, while the government held Madrid, Barcelona, Bilbao and Valencia. Franco's forces were soon joined by German and Italian 'volunteers' and Russia supplied the legitimate government with military advisers and equipment. By November Madrid was besieged.

An International Brigade of Anti-Fascists was formed and by February 1937 thousands of Americans, British and French were fighting in what had become an ideological war between the right and left.

In some ways the Spanish Civil War was a dry run for the conflict which broke out in 1939. The German air force assisted Franco's

261

eventual victory and learned valuable lessons about dive bombing.

There were four main stages to this war. For the first six months the rebel Nationalist forces (Fascists) triumphed in the west and south. In the north and east of Spain, Government support was strong, mainly from industrial workers, miners and Catalonians and Basques who hoped for eventual autonomy. At the end of 1936 Franco held nearly half of Spain – including the Portuguese frontier. The second stage was the attempt in 1937 by the Nationalists to advance from Teruel on Valencia and drive a wedge through Government territory and cut off Madrid. Madrid held out but Franco's forces took Bilbao. In the third phase Franco received considerably more help from Nazi Germany and Fascist Italy and severed Government territory with a six-month thrust to sea. They broke through in the Catalan front in December 1938. The collapse came in 1939 with a change in Russian policy reducing Government support considerably – Barcelona fell on 26 January and Madrid and Valencia were taken in March.

W. H. Auden served as a stretcher bearer on the Republican (Government) side. This poem, though obviously about the moment which brought forth the Spanish Civil War, also has a more general application. He asks how can we live with ourselves if we refuse to make fundamental choices? The political and military conflict in Spain is seen as a moment of choice between history stretching back to ancient times, and a future in which decency and justice may hold sway.

Stephen Spender worked in propaganda for the Government side. His poem discusses the validity of the 'final argument of rulers'.

SPAIN 1937

Yesterday all the past. The language of size
Spreading to China along the trade routes; the diffusion
    Of the counting-frame and the cromlech;
Yesterday the shadow-reckoning in the sunny climates.

Yesterday the assessment of insurance by cards,
The divination of water; yesterday the invention
    Of cart wheels and clocks, the taming of
Horses; yesterday the bustling world of the navigators.

Yesterday the abolition of fairies and giants;
The fortress like a motionless eagle eyeing the valley,
    The chapel built in the forest;
Yesterday the carving of angels and of frightening gargoyles.

The trial of heretics among the columns of stone;
Yesterday the theological feuds in the taverns
        And the miraculous cure at the fountain;
Yesterday the Sabbath of Witches. But today the struggle.

Yesterday the installation of dynamos and turbines;
The construction of railways in the colonial desert;
        Yesterday the classic lecture
On the origin of Mankind. But today the struggle.

Yesterday the belief in the absolute value of Greek;
The fall of the curtain upon the death of a hero;
        Yesterday the prayer to the sunset,
And the adoration of madmen. But today the struggle.

As the poet whispers, startled among the pines
Or, where the loose waterfall sings, compact, or upright
        On the crag by the leaning tower:
'O my vision. O send me the luck of the sailor.'

And the investigator peers through his instruments
At the inhuman provinces, the virile bacillus
        Or enormous Jupiter finished:
'But the lives of my friends. I inquire, I inquire.'

And the poor in their fireless lodgings dropping the sheets
Of the evening paper: 'Our day is our loss. O show us
        History the operator, the
Organizer, Time the refreshing river.'

And the nations combine each cry, invoking the life
That shapes the individual belly and orders
        The private nocturnal terror:
'Did you not found once the city-state of the sponge,

'Raise the vast military empires of the shark
And the tiger, establish the robin's plucky canton?'
        Intervene. O descend as a dove or
A furious papa or a mild engineer: but descend.'

And the life, if it answers at all, replies from the heart
And the eyes and the lungs, from the shops and squares of the city:
        'O no, I am not the Mover,
Not today, not to you. To you I'm the

'Yes-man, the bar-companion, the easily-duped:
I am whatever you do; I am your vow to be
        Good, your humorous story;
I am your business voice; I am your marriage.

'What's your proposal? To build the Just City? I will.
I agree. Or is it the suicide pact, the romantic
        Death? Very well, I accept, for
I am your choice, your decision: yes, I am Spain.'

Many have heard it on remote peninsulas,
On sleepy plains, in the aberrant fishermen's islands,
        In the corrupt heart of the city;
Have heard and migrated like gulls or the seeds of a flower.

They clung like burrs to the long expresses that lurch
Through the unjust lands, through the night, through the alpine
        tunnel;
        They floated over the oceans;
They walked the passes: they came to present their lives.

On that arid square, that fragment nipped off from hot
Africa, soldered so crudely to inventive Europe,
        On that tableland scored by rivers,
Our fever's menacing shapes are precise and alive.

Tomorrow, perhaps, the future: the research on fatigue
And the movements of packers; the gradual exploring of all the
        Octaves of radiation;
Tomorrow the enlarging of consciousness by diet and breathing.

Tomorrow the rediscovery of romantic love;
The photographing of ravens; all the fun under
        Liberty's masterful shadow;
Tomorrow the hour of the pageant-master and the musician.

Tomorrow, for the young, the poets exploding like bombs,
The walks by the lake, the winter of perfect communion;
        Tomorrow the bicycle races
Through the suburbs on summer evenings: but today the struggle.

Today the inevitable increase in the chances of death;
The conscious acceptance of guilt in the fact of murder;
        Today the expending of powers
On the flat ephemeral pamphlet and the boring meeting.

Today the makeshift consolations; the shared cigarette;
The cards in the candle-lit barn and the scraping concert,
        The masculine jokes; today the
Fumbled and unsatisfactory embrace before hurting.

The stars are dead; the animals will not look:
We are left alone with our day, and the time is short and
        History to the defeated
May say Alas but cannot help or pardon.

                                                            W. H. Auden

ULTIMA RATIO REGUM

The guns spell money's ultimate reason
In letters of lead on the spring hillside.
But the boy lying dead under the olive trees
Was too young and too silly
To have been notable to their important eye.
He was a better target for a kiss.

When he lived, tall factory hooters never summoned him
Nor did restaurant plate-glass doors revolve to wave him
        in.
His name never appeared in the papers.
The world maintained its traditional wall
Round the dead with their gold sunk deep as a well,
Whilst his life, intangible as a Stock Exchange rumour, drifted
        outside.

O too lightly he threw down his cap
One day when the breeze threw petals from the trees.
The unflowering wall sprouted with guns,
Machine-gun anger quickly scythed the grasses;
Flags and leaves fell from hands and branches;
The tweed cap rotted in the nettles.

Consider his life which was valueless
In terms of employment, hotel ledgers, news files.
Consider. One bullet in ten thousand kills a man.
Ask. Was so much expenditure justified
On the death of one so young and so silly
Lying under the olive trees, O world, O death?

                                                            Stephen Spender

1937 Shelling of Madrid

The fall of Madrid to Franco's forces bodied forth the defeat of Republicanism after a long and heroic resistance. The account by Ernest Hemingway is deceptive, very powerful indeed beneath its seemingly laconic surface quality.

Madrid: At the front, a mile and a quarter away, the noise came as a heavy coughing grunt from the green pine-studded hillside opposite. There was only a grey wisp of smoke to mark the Insurgent battery position. Then came the high inrushing sound, like the ripping of a bale of silk. It was all going well over into the town, so, out there, nobody cared.

But in the town, where all the streets were full of Sunday crowds, the shells came with the sudden flash that a short circuit makes and then the roaring crash of granite-dust. During the morning, twenty-two shells came into Madrid.

They killed an old woman returning home from market, dropping her in a huddled black heap of clothing, with one leg, suddenly detached, whirling against the wall of an adjoining house.

They killed three people in another square, who lay like so many torn bundles of old clothing in the dust and rubble when the fragments of the '155' had burst against the kerbing.

A motor car coming along the street stopped suddenly and swerved after the bright flash and roar and the driver lurched out, his scalp hanging down over his eyes, to sit down on the sidewalk with his hand against his face, the blood making a smooth sheen down over his chin.

Three times one of the tallest buildings was hit. Its shelling is legitimate, since it is a known means of communication and a landmark, but the shelling that traversed the streets seeking the Sunday promenaders was not military.

Yesterday I watched an attack against these positions where government tanks, working like deadly, intelligent beetles, destroyed machine gun posts in the thick underbrush while government artillery shelled the buildings and Insurgent trenches. We watched until dark but the infantry never advanced for an assault on these strong points.

But today, after fifteen minutes of the heaviest artillery fire, which with direct hit after direct hit, hid the five houses in one rolling cloud of white and orange smoky dust, I watched the infantry attack.

Behind a chalky-showing line of newly dug trenches, the men lay. Suddenly, one ran, bent low, to the rear. A half dozen followed and I saw one fall. Then four of these returned, and, bent forward like men walking along a dock in a heavy rain, the irregular line went forward. Some flopped to take cover. Others went down suddenly to stay as part of the view, a dark blue spot on the brown field. Then they were in the underbrush and out of sight and the tanks were moving ahead and shooting at the windows of the houses.

Below a sunken road there was a sudden flame and something burned yellow, with a black oily smoke rising. It burned for forty minutes, the flame mounting and then dying to mount again suddenly, and, finally, there was an explosion. Probably it was a tank. You couldn't see nor be sure because it was under the road, but other tanks passed it and, shifting to its right, went on firing into the houses and the machine gun posts in the trees. One at a time, men ran past the flame and into the woods along the slope close by the houses.

The machine gun and rifle fire made one solid crackling whisper in the air and then we saw another tank coming up with a moving shadow behind it that the glasses showed to be a solid square of men. It stopped and lurched and turned to the right, where the other foot soldiers had run one at a time bent double and where we had seen two fall. It passed into the woods and out of sight, its followers intact.

Then there was a great shelling again and we watched for the assault while the light failed and you could see nothing through the glasses but the plaster-shattered smoke of the houses where the shells were bursting. Government troops were within fifty yards of the houses when it was too dark to see. The outcome of the offensive designed to free Madrid from fascist pressure depends on the results of tonight's and tomorrow's action.

Ernest Hemingway, North American Newspaper Alliance dispatch (18 March 1937)
reprinted in *By-line* (1968).

The fall of Madrid also had enormous symbolic meaning; it signalled the end of the courageous struggle of Republicanism against Fascism. This is captured in Stephen Spender's poem:

FALL OF A CITY

All the posters on the walls
All the leaflets in the streets
Are mutilated, destroyed or run in rain,
Their words blotted out with tears,
Skins peeling from their bodies
In the victorious hurricane.

All the names of heroes in the hall
Where the feet thundered and the bronze throats roared,
Fox and Lorca claimed as history on the walls,
Are now angrily deleted
Or to dust surrender their dust,
From golden praise excluded..

All the badges and salutes
Torn from lapels and hands
Are thrown away with human sacks they wore
Or in the deepest bed of mind
They are washed over with a smile
Which launches the victors when they win.

All the lessons learned, unlearned;
The young, who learned to read, now blind
Their eyes with an archaic film;
The peasant relapses to a stumbling tune
Following the donkey's bray;
These only remember to forget.

But somewhere some word presses
On the high door of a skull, and in some corner
Of an irrefrangible eye
Some old man memory jumps to a child
— Spark from the days of energy.
And the child hoards it like a bitter toy.

Stephen Spender

(Ralph Fox and Federigo Garcia Lorca were English and Spanish poets, killed by the Nationalists.)

XVI

THE SECOND WORLD WAR

1939–1945 Second World War

Appeasement

As the decade of the 1930s gradually slipped by, one by one the sign-posts towards World War were passed one by one – Hitler's rise to power and denunciation of the the Versailles Treaty, Germany's leaving the League of Nations Disarmament Conference in 1933; the reintroduction of military service in Germany 1935; the military occupation of the Rhineland, the proclamation of the Berlin–Rome Axis in 1936; the Hossbach Minutes, in which Hitler's future intentions were stated in 1937; the Austrian *Anschluss* and publication of the Sudeten programme and the Munich crisis in 1938; the disappearance of Czechoslovakia, Britain's guarantees to Poland and Rumania and the Nazi–Soviet Non-Aggression Pact of 23 August 1939. W. H. Auden's poem evokes those terrible feelings of the time as peace slipped through our fingers:

> 'For the second time in our history, a British Prime Minister has returned from Germany bringing peace with honour. I believe it is peace for our time. . . . . . Go home and get a nice quiet sleep.'
>
> Neville Chamberlain, address from 10 Downing Street, London, 30 September 1938, after returning from the Munich Conference

SEPTEMBER 1, 1939

I sit in one of the dives
On Fifty-Second Street
Uncertain and afraid
As the clever hopes expire
Of a low dishonest decade:
Waves of anger and fear

Circulate over the bright
And darkened lands of the earth,
Obsessing our private lives;
The unmentionable odour of death
Offends the September night.

Accurate scholarship can
Unearth the whole offence
From Luther until now
That has driven a culture mad,
Find what occurred at Linz,
What huge imago made
A psychopathic god:
I and the public know
What all schoolchildren learn,
Those to whom evil is done
Do evil in return.

Exiled Thucydides knew
All that a speech can say
About Democracy,
And what dictators do,
The elderly rubbish they talk
To an apathetic grave;
Analysed all in his book,
The enlightenment driven away,
The habit-forming pain
Mismanagement and grief:
We must suffer them all again.

Into this neutral air
Where blind skyscrapers use
Their full height to proclaim
The strength of Collective Man,
Each language pours its vain
Competitive excuse:
But who can live for long
In an euphoric dream;
Out of the mirror they stare,
Imperialism's face
And the international wrong.

Faces along the bar
Cling to their average day:

The lights must never go out,
The music must always play,
All the conventions conspire
To make this fort assume
The furniture of home;
Lest we should see where we are,
Lost in a haunted wood,
Children afraid of the night
Who have never been happy or good.

The windiest militant trash
Important Persons shout
Is not so crude as our wish:
What mad Nijinsky wrote
About Diaghilev
Is true of the normal heart;
For the error bred in the bone
Of each woman and each man
Craves what it cannot have,
Not universal love
But to be loved alone.

From the conservative dark
Into the ethical life
The dense commuters come,
Repeating their morning vow;
'I *will* be true to the wife,
I'll concentrate more on my work.'
And helpless governors wake
To resume their compulsory game:
Who can release them now,
Who can reach the deaf.
Who can speak for the dumb?

All I have is a voice
To undo the folded lie,
The romantic lie in the brain
Of the sensual man-in-the-street
And the lie of Authority
Whose buildings grope the sky:
There is no such thing as the State
And no one exists alone;
Hunger allows no choice
To the citizen or the police;
We must love one another or die.

Defenceless under the night
Our world in stupor lies;
Yet, dotted everywhere,
Ironic points of light
Flash out wherever the Just
Exchange their messages:
May I, composed like them
Of Eros and of dust,
Beleaguered by the same
Negation and despair,
Show an affirming flame.

W. H. Auden

The Right to Live and to Live in Peace

Antoine de Saint-Exupéry, the French aviator and author, explained in a famous radio broadcast in the early months of the war, the very basic nature of the struggle with Germany. It was not an ideological conflict so much as a fight for the right of other nations to exist, and to exist harmoniously with each other.

We were human beings and thought that human beings were inspired in their behaviour by philosophies, religions, or doctrines. We believed that if human beings were ready to fight and die for a cause, it must be because this cause appealed to their idealism. We had forgotten that some motives for action have nothing to do with idealism and that a country may tend to expand as any blind organism does.

We had forgotten this, because for us civilization represented the conquest of mind over elementary urges. But over there, the mind was only a lackey charged with justifying the urges of the organism. Crusading pan-Germanism relies on Goethe or Bach. And thus Goethe or Bach, whom Germany today would leave to rot in a concentration camp or expel like Einstein, are used to justify mustard gas and the bombardment of open cities. But pan-Germanism has nothing to do with Goethe or Bach harnessed to its purposes. It has nothing to do with the ideology of people's rights, nothing to do with necessary Lebensraum. It is merely a question of space for its own sake. Pan-Germanism is the tendency toward expansion. It is a tendency found in all animal species. Every race tends to multiply and exterminate the others.

272

If there is any justification for Pan-Germanism, it is this — and this is not merely a witticism; we will encounter it in a veiled way in all Nazi writings. The argument runs: We Germans deserve to expand, to absorb our neighbours and use their goods for our aggrandizement, because a desire for expansion is a sign of vigour and we are the only ones who feel this appetite. Our superiority over our adversaries is contained in our wish to absorb them, whereas our degenerate adversaries are incapable of such a desire.

And so we know now that laying down our arms would mean confirming Germany's appetite. The monstrous Nazi–Soviet Pact has forever sealed off the route of expansion eastward. Who will feed their appetite tomorrow? Germany cannot be explained by means of reasoned ideologies. She does not follow definable goals. Germany's goals are nothing but a succession of tactical advances, of publicity stunts. The real aim of Germany is to expand.

That is why for us today it is not merely a question of fighting against Nazism, or for Poland, or for the Czechs, or for our civilization, but to fight in order to survive. Those who have left their farms, their shops, their factories, fight in order not to become mere fertilizer for German prosperity. They have gone out to gain the right to live and to live in peace.

Antoine de Saint-Exupéry, 'The Propaganda of Pan-Germanism', radio broadcast, 18 October 1939, translated by Norah Purcell

FAREWELL CHORUS

1

And so! the long black pullman is at last departing now,
After those undermining years of angry waiting and cold tea;
And all your small grey faces and wet hankies slide away
Backwards into the station's cave of cloud. And so Good-bye
To our home-town, so foreign now its lights no longer show;
And to old lives already indistinct as a dull play
We saw while staying somewhere in the Midlands long ago.

Farewell to the few and to the many; for to-night
Our souls may be required of us; and so we say Adieu
To those who charmed us with their ever ready wit
But could not see the point; to those whose polished hands
And voices could allay a little while our private pain
But could not stay to soothe us when worse bouts began;
To those whose beauties were too brief; Farewell dear friends.

To you as well whom we could never love, hard though
We tried, because our pity told us you were weak,
And because of pity we abhorred; to you
Whose gauche distress and badly-written postcards made us ache
With angrily impatient self-reproach! you who were too
Indelicately tender, whose too soft eyes made us look
(Against our uncourageous wish) swiftly away . . .

To those, too, whom we hardly knew, or could not know;
To the indifferent and the admired; to the once-met
And long remembered faces: Yes, Good-bye to you
Who made us turn our heads to look again, and wait
For hours in vain at the same place next day;
Who for a moment might have been the lost selves sought
Without avail, and whom we know we never shall find now.

Away, away! Yet now it is no longer in retreat
That we are leaving. All our will is drowned
As by an inner tidal-wave that has washed our regret
And small fears and exhausted implications out of mind.
You can't accompany our journey. Nor may we return
Except in unimpassioned recollections from beyond
That ever-nearer frontier that our fate has drawn.

2

And so let's take a last look round, and say Farewell to all
Events that gave the last decade, which this New Year
Brings to its close, a special pathos. Let us fill
One final fiery glass and quickly drink to 'the Pre-War'
Before we greet 'the Forties,' whose unseen sphinx-face
Is staring fixedly upon us from behind its veil;
Drink farewell quickly, ere the Future smash the glass.

Even while underneath the floor are whirling on
The wheels which carry us towards some Time-to-Come,
Let us perform this hasty mental rite (as one
Might cast a few imagined bays into the tomb
Of an unloved but memorable great man);
Soon the still-near will seem remotely far; there's hardly time
For much oration more than mere Good-bye, again:

To the delusive peace of those disintegrating years
Through which burst uncontrollably into our view
Successive and increasingly premonitory flares,
Explosions of the dangerous truth beneath, which no

274

Steel-plated self-deception could for long withstand . . .
Years through the rising storm of which somehow we grew,
Struggling to keep an anchored heart and open mind,

Too often failing. Years through which none the less
The coaxing of complacency and sleep could still persuade
Kind-hearted Christians of the permanence of Peace,
Increase of common-sense and civic virtue. Years which bade
Less placid conscientious souls indignantly arise
Upon ten thousand platforms to proclaim the system mad
And urge the liquidation of a senile ruling-class.
Years like a prison-wall, frustrating though unsound,

On which the brush of History, with quick, neurotic strokes,
Its latest and most awe-inspiring fresco soon outlined:
Spenglerian lowering of the Western skies, red lakes
Of civil bloodshed, free flags flagrantly torn down
By order of macabre puppet orators, the blind
Leading blindfolded followers into the Devil's den . . .

3

And so, Good-bye, grim 'Thirties. These your closing days
Have shown a new light, motionless and far
And clear as ice, to our sore riddled eyes;
And we see certain truths now, which the fear
Aroused by earlier circumstances could but compromise,
Concerning all men's lives. Beyond despair
May we take wiser leave of you, knowing disasters' cause.

Having left all false hopes behind, may we move on
At a vertiginous unmeasured speed, beyond, beyond,
Across this unknown Present's bleak and rocky plain:
Through sudden tunnels; in our ears the wind
Echoing unintelligible guns. Mirrored within
Each lonely consciousness, War's world seems without end.
Dumbly we stare up at strange skies with each day's dawn.

Could you but hear our final farewell call, how strained
And hollow it would sound! We are already far
Away, forever leaving further leagues behind
Of this most perilous and incoherent land
We're in. The unseen enemy are near.
Above the cowering capital Death's wings impend.
Rapidly under ink-black seas today's doomed disappear.

We are alone with one another, but our eyes
Meet seldom in the dark. What a relentless roar
Stuffs every ear, as though with wool! The winds that rise
Out of our dereliction's vortex, hour by hour,
To bring us word of the incessant wordless guns,
Tirades of the insane, thick hum of 'planes, the rage of fire,
Eruptions, waves: all end in utmost silence in our brains.
'The silence after the viaticum.' So silent is the ray
Of naked radiance that lights our actual scene,
Leading the gaze into the nameless and unknown
Extremes of this existence where fear's armour falls away
And lamentation and defeat and pain
Are all transfigured by acceptance; where men see
The tragic splendour of their final destiny.

David Gascoyne (New Year 1940)

1940 Dunkirk

Between 27 May and 4 June 1940, 200,000 British troops and 120,000 French troops were evacuated from the port of Dunkirk in northern France after the capitulation of the Belgian Army to the invading Germans in the north. There was in addition the fear of a German armoured thrust from the south which meant that the British Expeditionary Force and the French First Army were cut off. The allied troops were shipped back across the Channel in over eight hundred and fifty miscellaneous craft hurriedly assembled for the job. The incident has passed into national mythology, to be drawn upon whenever times seem particularly difficult. The Dunkirk Spirit has become an infallible British pick-me-up.

The picture will always remain sharp-etched in my memory – the lines of men wearily and sleepily staggering across the beach from the dunes to the shallows, falling into little boats; great columns of men thrust out into the water among bomb and shell splashes. The foremost ranks were shoulder deep, moving forward under the command of young subalterns, themselves with their heads just above the little waves that rode in to the sand. As the front ranks were dragged aboard the boats, the rear ranks moved up, from ankle deep to knee deep, from knee deep to waist deep, until they, too, came to shoulder depth and their turn.
Some of the big boats pushed in until they were almost aground,

taking appalling risks with the falling tide. The men thankfully scrambled up the sides on rope nets, or climbed the hundreds of ladders, made God knows where out of new, raw wood and hurried aboard the ships in England.

The little boats that ferried from the beach to the big ships in deep water listed drunkenly with the weight of men. The big ships slowly took on lists of their own with the enormous numbers crowded aboard. And always down the dunes and across the beach came new hordes of men, new columns, new lines.

On the beach was the skeleton of a destroyer, bombed and burnt. At the water's edge were ambulances, abandoned when their last load had been discharged.

There was always the red background, the red of Dunkirk burning. There was no water to check the fires and there were no men to be spared to fight them. Red, too, were the shell bursts, the flash of guns, the fountains of tracer bullets.

The din was infernal. The batteries shelled ceaselessly and brilliantly. To the whistle of shells overhead was added the scream of falling bombs. Even the sky was full of noise — anti-aircraft shells, machine-gun fire, the snarl of falling planes, the angry hornet noise of dive bombers. One could not speak normally at any time against the roar of it and the noise of our own engines. We all developed 'Dunkirk throat', a sore hoarseness that was the hallmark of those who had been there.

Yet through all the noise I will always remember the voices of the young subalterns as they sent their men aboard, and I will remember, too, the astonishing discipline of the men. They had fought through three weeks of retreat, always falling back, often without orders, often without support. Transport had failed. They had gone sleepless. They had been without food and water. Yet they kept ranks as they came down the beaches, and they obeyed commands.

While they were still filing back to the beach and the dawn was breaking with uncomfortable brilliance, we found one of our stragglers — a navy whaler. We told her people to come aboard, but they said that there was a motor-boat aground and they would have to fetch off her crew. They went in, and we waited. It was my longest wait, ever. For various reasons they were terribly slow. When they found the captain of the motor-boat, they stood and argued with him and he wouldn't come off anyway. Damned plucky chap. He and his men lay quiet until the tide floated them later in the day. Then they made a dash for it, and got away.

We waited for them until the sun was up before we got clear of the mole. By then, the fighting was heavy in-shore, on the outskirts of the town, and actually in some of the streets.

Going home, the dive bombers came over us five times, but somehow left us alone though three times they took up an attacking position. A little down the coast, towards Gravelines, we picked up a boatload of Frenchmen rowing off. We took them aboard. They were very much bothered as to where our 'ship' was, and said quite flatly that it was impossible to go to England in a thing like ours. Too, too horribly dangerous!

One of the rare touches of comedy at Dunkirk was the fear of the sea among French *poilus* from inland towns. They were desperately afraid to forfeit solid land for the unknown perils of a little boat. When, on the last nights of the evacuation, the little boats got to the mole many refused to jump in, despite the hell of exploding shells and bombs behind them.

David Divine, Dunkirk (1945)

DUNKIRK

To One who survived long enough to die of
wounds in an English Hospital.

Backs to the Sea!
O bitter the word 'Retreat'
and bitterer yet — 'Evacuate',
and nobody told the soldier why!
While Jerry's planes played merry hell
and laughed loud at our wounded pride:
Falling back with reluctant paces;
while Stukas spat death in our faces;
falling back — further back —
steadily back to the Sea . . . .
O God the crime!
(O blast the Sun!)
Pointing speechless guns
at contemptuous Huns
and five dud rounds
in our pouches . . . .

And nobody told us why!

My God,
How they cried,

how the wounded cried
as they staggered and sagged and died —
disarmed, in fierce anger and pride
on those lead-swept Dunes
in the Sun, on the way
to the Sea!

And nobody told them why!

God, how they cried
in their anger and pride,
in their impotence crucified!
Yea, loudly they cried as they'll cry anon
in the Day that will tell them why . . . .
when the scourge of Time
shall smite the crime,
the refuge of Lies
and the gilt-edged crime
that slew them
before their time!

O the crimson crime
that was yours and mine;
the crime that could dice
on the 'contract price'
of a Tank
and a Tommy Gun!
Spinning 'Put and Take'
for Judas's stake
and the profit
on Aeroplanes!

O despicable crime
that was yours and mine;
who could wine and dine
at home — so immune to the storm
in upholstered security;
while men fought with their fists
aye, with stones and sticks;
red mad in their anger and pride;
till they staggered and died
for the men that had lied,
on those lead-swept Dunes

in the Sun, on the way
to the Sea!

Tomorrow will tell them why!

Leon Atkins

1940

7 OCTOBER, 1940

One does not have to worry if we die:
Whoever dies, One does not have to bother
Because inside Her there is still another
And, that one wasted too, She yet replies
'Nothing can tire out Nature — here's another!'
    Fecundity par excellence is here,
    Lying in labour even on the bier.

Maternity's the holiest thing on earth
(No man who's prudent as well as wise
Concerns himself with what is in the skies);
Drain-deep below the slums another birth
    Sets angels singing — the other noise you hear
    May be the Warning, may be the All Clear.

Comfort ye My people! These reflections
Should help them die politely who must die,
And reconcile those left behind, who sigh
For loss of children or some near connections —
    Reflect! There is no need for grief nor gloom,
    Nature has ever another in Her womb.

Teeming and steaming hordes who helter-skelter
Stampede the city streets, to herd together
Angry and scared, in dark, in wintry weather —
Above ground still? Fear not, there's one deep shelter
    Open alike in Free and Fascist State,
    Vast, private, silent and inviolate.

Valentine Ackland

BLACK-OUT

Night comes now
Without the artistry of hesitation, the surprising

Last minute turn-aside into a modulation,
Without the rising
Final assertion of promise before the fall.
Darkness now
Comes by routine of cardboard shutter, rattle of curtain,
Comes like a sentence everyone's learnt to utter,
Undoubted and certain,
Too stupid to interest anyone at all.

Valentine Ackland

1940 Battle of Britain

The Battle of Britain was the war fought in the skies between the German Luftwaffe and the RAF in the months between July and October 1940. It was Hitler's intention to soften up Britain for invasion and began by attacking shipping, followed by airfields and finally the towns and cities. The Germans had 1,350 bombers and 1,200 fighters. The British RAF, using Spitfires and Hurricanes, was outnumbered three to one. On 15 September fifty-six German aircraft were destroyed. All told that summer 1,733 German planes were lost against British losses of 915. Hitler postponed the invasion, intending to deal with Russia first.

RECRUIT CENTRE

Here is the bombed house and the hard sea
breaking against our ranks, and here
the soldier eyes a star galaxy
thinking perhaps of some girl's hair.
Since I am such, and since I,
learning to move with more precision,
pathetic, speechless, a new toy,
have only memories against derision,
let me to-night take this, my mirror,
look into it, rub out the staring face,
taking instead your own, set where stars are
with swans riding the moon's race:
but I see the ship's lantern red in their wake
and know the spell altered, my magic too weak.

John Bayliss

REPORTED MISSING

With broken wing they limped across the sky
caught in late sunlight, with their gunner dead,
one engine gone — the type was out-of-date —
blood on the fuselage turning brown from red:
knew it was finished, looking at the sea
which shone back patterns in kaleidoscope,
knew that their shadow would meet them by the way,
close and catch at them, drown their single hope:

sat in this tattered scarecrow of the sky
hearing it cough, the great plane catching
now the first dark clouds upon her wing-base
patching the great tear, in evening mockery;
so two men waited, saw the third dead face,
and wondered when the wind would let them die.

John Bayliss

FOR JOHNNY

Do not despair
For Johnny-head-in-air;
He sleeps as sound
As Johnny underground.

Fetch out no shroud
For Johnny-in-the-cloud;
And keep your tears
For him in after years.

Better by far
For Johnny-the-bright-star,
To keep your head,
And see his children fed.

John Pudney

GIVE THEM THEIR LIFE . . .

Give them their life:
They do not know how short it grows;
So let them go
Young-winged, steel-fledged, gun-furious,
For if they live they'll live,
As well you know,
Upon the bitter kernels of their sweet ideals.

282

Give them their wings:
They cannot fly too high or far
To fly above
The dirty-moted, bomb-soured, word-tired world.
And if they die they'll die,
As you should know,
More swiftly, cleanly, star-defined, than you will ever feel.

H. E. Bates

PARACHUTE DESCENT

Snap back the canopy,
Pull out the oxygen tube,
Flick the harness pin
And slap out into the air,
Clear of the machine.

Did you ever dream when you were young
Of floating through the air, hung
Between the clouds and the gay
Be-blossomed land?
Did you ever stand and say,
'To sit and think and be alone
In the middle of the sky
Is my one most perfect wish'?

That was a fore-knowing;
You knew that some day
To satiate an inward crave
You must play with the wave
Of a cloud. And shout aloud
In the clean air,
The untouched-by-worldly-things-and-mean air
With exhilarated living.

You knew that you must float
From the sun above the clouds
To the gloom beneath, from a world
Of rarefied splendour to one
Of cheapened dirt, close-knit
In its effort to encompass man
In death.

David Bourne

1941 Tobruk

On 21 January 1941 the port of Tobruk in Libya (held by the Italians) was attacked by the 6th Australian and 7th British Armoured Divisions. It fell the next day and 25,000 prisoners were taken. The port was crucial to the Axis war effort against Egypt. Rommel seized Benghazi, and then drove on and attacked Tobruk in early April 1941 with one German and four Italian Divisions. British and colonial troops, supplied by the Royal Navy, held out for two hundred and forty days. They were finally relieved by the British 8th Army.

LANDSCAPE NEAR TOBRUK

This land was made for War. As glass
Resists the bite of vitriol, so this hard
And calcined earth rejects
The battle's hot, corrosive impact. Here
Is no nubile, girlish land, no green
And virginal countryside for War
To violate. This land is hard,
Inviolable, the battle's aftermath
Presents no ravaged and emotive scene,
No landscape à la Goya. Here are no trees
Uprooted, gutted farms; the unsalvaged scrap –
The scattered petrol-cans, the upturned
And abandoned truck, the fallen Heinkel; all
The rusted and angular detritus
Of war, seem scarcely to impinge
Upon the hard, resistant surface of
This lunar land: ephemeral
As trippers' leavings, paper-bags and orange-peel
Upon Ben Nevis. Sun and sand
Inhibit here the mind's habitual
And easy gestures; hand and eye
Perform their functions with a robot-cunning –
The sly and casual movements of
The shadowed thief. The soldiers camped
In the rock-strewn wadi merge
Like lizard or jerboa in the brown
And neutral ambient: stripped at gunsite,
Or splashing like glad beasts at sundown in
The brackish pool, their smooth

And lion-coloured bodies seem
The indigenous fauna of an unexplored,
Unspoiled country: harmless, easy to trap.
And tender-fleshed — a hunter's prize.

Jocelyn Brooke

TOBRUK 1941

His Company was in the second wave.
ADVANCE! Unfortunately something gave
him 'Gyppo Tummy', water melons p'raps,
and as a consequence occurred a lapse
of social etiquette if not the sin
of breaching military discipline.
Public Exposure! Desert Waste Defaced
By Private Soldier! Infantry Disgraced?

Then pulled his trousers up, pulled down his hat,
and checked his safety-catch. And after that
he caught the others up. To leave no doubt
in anybody else's mind about
the nature of the incident because
they might think he was shit-scared (which he was),
he started whistling *British Grenadiers*
as if he'd been a fighting man for years.

J. E. Brookes

Alexandria

The ancient capital of Ptolemaic Egypt has long-standing associations
with the British Army. Also, Napoleon used it as a base for his invasion
of Egypt in 1798–99 and British and French troops were used to quell
the uprising by nationalists under Arabi Pasha in 1882. Sir Garnet
Wolseley, Imperial Britain's great troubleshooter, defeated Arabi at Tel-
el-Kebir on 13 September 1882. Egypt was then occupied for sixty
years, and developed as the main naval base in the Eastern
Mediterranean. It was unusable as a port from June 1942 as a result
of the closeness of Rommel's armies.

ALEXANDRIA

To the lucky now who have lovers or friends,
Who move to their sweet undiscovered ends,
Or whom the great conspiracy deceives,
I wish these whirling autumn leaves:
Promontories splashed by the salty sea,
Groaned on in darkness by the tram
To horizons of love or good luck or more love —
As for me I now move
Through many negatives to what I am.

Here at the last cold Pharos between Greece
And all I love, the lights confide
A deeper darkness to the rubbing tide;
Doors shut, and we the living are locked inside
Between the shadows and the thoughts of peace:
And so in furnished rooms revise
The index of our lovers and our friends
From gestures possibly forgotten, but the ends
Of longings like unconnected nerves,
And in this quiet rehearsal of their acts
We dream of them and cherish them as Facts.

Now when the sea grows restless as a conscript,
Excited by fresh wind, climbs the sea-wall,
I walk by it and think about you all:
B. with his respect for the Object, and D.
Searching in sex like a great pantry for jars
Marked 'Plum and apple'; and the small, fell
Figure of Dorian ringing like a muffin-bell —
All indeed whom war or time threw up
On this littoral and tides could not move
Were objects for my study and my love.

And then turning where the last pale
Lighthouse, like a Samson blinded, stands
And turns its huge charred orbit on the sands
I think of you — indeed mostly of you,
In whom a writer would only name and lose
The dented boy's lip and the close
Archer's shoulders; but here to rediscover
By tides and faults of weather, by the rain
Which washes everything, the critic and the lover.

At the doors of Africa so many towns founded
Upon a parting could become Alexandria, like
The wife of Lot — a metaphor for tears;
And the queer student in his poky hot
Tenth floor room above the harbour hears
The sirens shaking the tree of his heart,
And shuts his books, while the most
Inexpressible longings like wounds unstitched
Stir in him some girl's unquiet ghost.

So we, learning to suffer and not condemn
Can only wish you this great pure wind
Condemned by Greece, and turning like a helm
Inland where it smokes the fires of men,
Spins weathercocks on farms or catches
The lovers at their quarrel in the sheets;
Or like a walker in the darkness might,
Knocks and disturbs the artist at his papers
Up there alone, upon the alps of night.

Lawrence Durrell

1941 Invasion of Russia

Rebuffed in the Battle of Britain, Hitler now turned his attention on Russia and German troops invaded Russia on 22 June 1941. British intelligence predicted that the Russian defence would collapse within ten days, American sources said three weeks. The Germans, too, were optimistic, as they were not equipped with winter clothing. Resistance was stiff and by December the Wehrmacht was fighting three hundred and sixty Russian divisions. The battle of Stalingrad began on 22 August 1942. After an eight-month siege the Germans captured Sebastopol and launched an assault against the Volga River centre for shipment of oil from the Caucasus. The battle lasted five months and the Russians lost 750,000 troops and Stalingrad's population was reduced from 500,000 to 1,500. German losses were heavy — 400,000, Roumanians 200,000, Italians 130,000 and Hungarians 120,000. 80,000 Axis troops surrendered in February 1943.

TWENTY YEARS OLD

Twenty years old was the man,
he bent where the forest-waters ran,
and, staring through the heat of day,
suddenly saw his hair was grey.

And there he swore a pitiless vow
to break the invader of his land.
Who will dare to blame him now
if battle-anger locks his hand?

Alexei Surkov, translated by Jack Lindsay

TRAGIC TALE

All things will change and come aright,
the capital will be rebuilt,
but the children screaming in the night
will leave unexpiated guilt.

There's no forgiveness for that fear
stamping their faces cut with pain.
O he must pay, and dearly pay,
and pay a hundredfold again.

And there will come at last a day
when none will credit he was here.
But a hundredfold he yet must pay
for the orphan's wail, the widow's tear.

Time will put out his fires; but time
will number still and still condemn
each face and fury of his crime:
Herod gone mad in Bethlehem.

And time will see our hopes fulfilled,
the witnesses will die at length,
but the image of the crippled children,
will never lose its awful strength.

Boris Pasternak (1941), translated by Jack Lindsay

IN THE SMALL STOVE

In the small stove a fire is beating;
from pinewood tears of resin rise
while the accordion's repeating
songs of your smile, songs of your eyes.

Your name the bushes murmur low,
near Moscow, in the snow-white field.
My voice would only have you know:
I live and love you and will not yield.

288

Snow and more snow. A desolate scene.
I long to reach you across the day.
A difficult distance lies between
and death is but four steps away.

Accordion, sing, despite, the storm;
call the stray, Happiness, home. I'm drenched,
dank in the dugout, chilled, yet warm
with love that never can be quenched.

Boris Pasternak (November 1941), translated
by Jack Lindsay

1941 Extermination Camps:
The Final Solution

All the thirty odd principal Nazi concentration camps were death
camps and millions of tortured, starved inmates perished in them.
Though the authorities kept records – each camp had its official
Totenbuch (death book) – they were incomplete and in many cases
were destroyed as the victorious Allies closed in. Part of one
Totenbuch that survived at Mauthausen listed 35,318 deaths from
January 1939 to April 1945. At the end of 1942 when the need of
slave labor began to be acute, Himmler ordered that the death rate in
the concentration camps 'must be reduced'. Because of the labor
shortage he had been displeased at a report received in his office that
of the 136,700 commitments to concentration camps between June
and November 1942, some 70,610 had died and that in addition 9,267
had been executed and 27,846 'transferred.' To the gas chamber, that
is. This did not leave very many for labor duties.

But it was in the extermination camps, the *Vernichtungslager*, where
most progress was made toward the 'final solution'. The greatest and
most renowned of these was Auschwitz, whose four huge gas
chambers and adjoining crematoria gave it a capacity for death and
burial far beyond that of the others – Treblinka, Belsec, Sibibor and
Chelmno, all in Poland. There were other minor extermination camps
near Riga, Vilna, Minsk, Kaunas and Lwow, but they were
distinguished from the main ones in that they killed by shooting
rather than by gas.

For a time there was quite a bit of rivalry among the S.S. leaders as
to which was the most efficient gas to speed the Jews to their death.
Speed was an important factor, especially at Auschwitz, where toward
the end the camp was setting new records by gassing 6,000 victims a

day. One of the camp's commanders for a period was Rudolf Hoess, an ex-convict once found guilty of murder, who deposed at Nuremberg on the superiority of the gas he employed:

The 'Final Solution' of the Jewish question meant the complete extermination of all Jews in Europe. I was ordered to establish extermination facilities at Auschwitz in June 1941. At that time there were already in the General Government of Poland three other extermination camps: Belzec, Treblinka and Wolzek . . .

I visited Treblinka to find out how they carried out their extermination. The camp commandant at Treblinka told me that he had liquidated 80,000 in the course of half a year. He was principally concerned with liquidating all the Jews from the Warsaw ghetto.

He used monoxide gas and I did not think that his methods were very efficient. So when I set up the extermination building at Auschwitz, I used Zyklon B, which was a crystallized prussic acid which we dropped into the death chamber from a small opening. It took from three to fifteen minutes to kill the people in the death chamber, depending upon climatic conditions.

We knew when the people were dead because their screaming stopped. We usually waited about half an hour before we opened the doors and removed the bodies. After the bodies were removed our special commandos took off the rings and extracted the gold from the teeth of the corpses.

Another improvement we made over Treblinka was that we built our gas chambers to accommodate 2,000 people at one time, whereas at Treblinka their ten gas chambers only accommodated 200 people each.

William L. Shirer, *The Rise and Fall of The Third Reich* (1959)

PIGTAIL

When all the women in the transport
had their heads shaved
four workmen with brooms made of birch twigs
swept up
and gathered up the hair

Behind clean glass
the stiff hair lies
of those suffocated in gas chambers
there are pins and side combs
in this hair

THE SECOND WORLD WAR

The hair is not shot through with light
is not parted by the breeze
is not touched by any hand
or rain or lips

In huge chests
clouds of dry hair
of those suffocated
and a faded plait
a pigtail with a ribbon
pulled at school
by naughty boys.

The Museum, Auschwitz, 1948.
Tadeusz Różewicz, translated by Adam Czerniawski

I SAW A BROKEN TOWN

I saw a broken town beside the grey March sea,
Spray flung in the air and no larks singing,
And houses lurching, twisted, where the chestnut trees
Stand ripped and stark; the fierce wind bringing
The choking dust in clouds along deserted streets,
Shaking the gaping rooms, the jagged, raw-white stone.
Seeking for what in this quiet, stricken town? It beats
About each fallen wall, each beam, leaving no livid, aching place
    alone.

March, 1941, after the bombing of Wallasey,
Mabel Esther Allan

HARVEST

In open country the September fields
Now face the death of harvest, and their powers
Through ruthless loss redouble their ability,
But here, the blackened dust of London shields,
With artificial pomp of bedded flowers,
The helpless shame of its outworn sterility.

There death is rich in promised life, but here,
When our bright masqueraders freeze and sicken,
We have no power to give them fresh fertility.
Thus, through the smiling scorn of this dread year,
We stand inert and see our comrades stricken,
Our hands unarmed, ashamed of our futility.

ECHOES OF WAR

We watch afar and mark the hideous pace
At which the Reaper moves; like corn our pride
Bows its plumed head to dark humility,
Nor have we vision to discern some place
Where, from the furrowed grave of hopes that died,
Point the bright blades of immortality.

Mary Désirée Anderson

THE BLACK-OUT

I never feared the darkness as a child,
For then night's plumy wings that wrapped me round
Seemed gentle, and all earthly sound,
Whether man's movement or the wild,
Small stirrings of the beasts and trees, was kind,
So I was well contented to be blind.

But now the darkness is a time of dread,
Of stumbling, fearful progress, when one thinks,
With angry fear, that those dull amber chinks,
Which tell of life where all things else seem dead,
Are full of menace as a tiger's eyes
That watch our passing, hungry for the prize.

Over all Europe lies this shuddering night.
Sometimes it quivers like a beast of prey,
All tense to spring, or, trembling, turns at bay
Knowing itself too weak for force or flight,
And in all towns men strain their eyes and ears,
Like hunted beasts, for warning of their fears.

Mary Désirée Anderson

THRENODE FOR YOUNG SOLDIERS KILLED IN ACTION

For all the young and the very lovely
    Who will come no more to an earthly home,
For all such virgin trees cut by death's axe —
    How can I for such a sacrifice atone?
Could my silver lakes of tears be enough?
    The long threnodes my tinsel nightingales sing?
No not enough! oh not nearly enough!
    I would find a more splendid offering.

292

For all the talented and the gallant
  Who will tread no more any earthly place,
For unknown painters and poets burnt by death's flames —
  How can I perform sufficient penance?
What of long fastings and a crown of thorns?
  Could prayers and sackcloth ever suffice?
No not enough! oh not nearly enough!
  Only my life would be fair sacrifice.

Olivia Fitzroy

TOAST

All the way back from the air field
Along the jolting road,
Past the paddy fields
And the mud-covered water-buffalo,
I have been pretending to myself
That I am not thinking about letters.
At the door of Regulating I pause,
It is a creed with me never to look for a letter,
If there is one for me it will find me.
Today, feeling bad-tempered, I defy my creed
But there is no letter.
I walk up to the mess.
Irrationally I can feel hot tears in my eyes.
I concentrate on the thought of toast for tea,
Hot toast and lots of butter,
Even jam.
It is something to look forward to for almost ten minutes.
No one answers when I speak,
They are deep in their letters.
I pour milk into my tea and wait for the toast.
They laugh over their letters, and read excerpts,
From a sister in Australia,
From a friend in hospital,
From a friend in France,
I think hard about the toast.
There is no jam but meat paste
And a soft-looking paw-paw which I don't like.
The toast is as good as I know it will be
I crunch it slowly
And the butter runs on to my fingers

ECHOES OF WAR

And I try not to listen to Wren shop,
To the details of the friend's illness,
To the delinquencies of the dhobi.
I am a little afraid, for when the toast is finished
There will be nothing to look forward to,
And so it was yesterday
And so it will be tomorrow.

Olivia Fitzroy

KILLED IN ACTION

His chair at the table, empty,
His home clothes hanging in rows forlorn,
His cricket bat and cap, his riding cane,
The new flannel suit he had not worn.
His dogs, restless, with tortured ears
Listening for his swift, light tread upon the path.
And there – his violin! Oh his violin! Hush! hold your tears.

For N. J. de B.-L.
Crete, May, 1941

Juliette de Bairacli-Levy

GARDEN IN THE SKY

There is a monstrous garden in the sky
Nightly they sow it fresh. Nightly it springs,
Luridly splendid, towards the moon on high.
Red-poppy flares, and fire-bombs rosy-bright
Shell-bursts like hellborn sunflowers, gold and white
Lilies, long-stemmed, that search the heavens' height . . .
They tend it well, these gardeners on wings!

How rich these blossoms, hideously fair
Sprawling above the shuddering citadel
As though ablaze with laughter! Lord, how long
Must we behold them flower, ruthless, strong
Soaring like weeds the stricken worlds among
Triumphant, gay, these dreadful blooms of hell?

O give us back the garden that we knew
Silent and cool, where silver daisies lie,
The lovely stars! O garden purple-blue
Where Mary trailed her skirts amidst the dew
Of ageless planets, hand-in-hand with You
And Sleep and Peace walked with Eternity . . .

But here I sit, and watch the night roll by.
There is a monstrous garden in the sky!

Written during an air-raid. London, midnight, October 1941
Margery Lawrence

1942 Soldier's Food, Operation 'Torch'

Anglo-American Landings, Tunisia, November 1942

Our soldiers at the front learned quickly how to keep their stomachs filled during emergencies. Ordinarily, the soldier's food was prepared for him in army mess kitchens, but at the front many things could happen. Small parties went out for days at a time and had to carry their own rations. On the battle front, kitchen trucks came up only at night and sometimes not even then. With our mobile armies on the move it wasn't always possible for kitchen trucks to be in the right place at the right moment, and as a consequence every soldier learned how to feed himself. Every vehicle from jeep to tank had a few spare cans of rations hidden away somewhere.

Soldiers cooked their own meals when on the move. They made a fire in one of two ways, each involving the use of gasoline: For a short fire they dug a hole about the size of a man's hand, poured gasoline into it, sprinkled sand over the gasoline, and then threw in a match. The sand kept the gas from burning too quickly. On a small fire like that they could heat a canteen or cup of coffee. For a bigger fire, they filled a small can with gasoline and buried it even with the surface of the ground. They piled rocks around to set their cooking utensils on, and then tossed a match at the gas.

I never saw a real skillet, pan or stewpot. The soldiers made their own utensils out of those famous five-gallon gasoline tins. I don't believe there's anything in the world that can't be made out of a five-gallon gasoline tin.

The soldiers also learned not be lax about keeping their mess kits clean, for they found out by bitter experience that a dirty mess kit was the quickest way to violent nausea through poisoning. To wash their mess kits they scoured them with sand and then polished them with toilet paper — the best dishrag I've ever found.

Despite their primitive forms of cooking, the soldiers did eat well. They got either British or American rations, or a mixture of the two. Soldiers who were traveling actually preferred the British 'compo' to our own famous C ration. The reason being that the C ration has so little variety that after three meals a man could hardly look a C can in the face.

The British compo was more diverse. It had such things as sausage, puddings, chocolate bars, salt, jam, butter, and cheese. It even included toilet paper.

Although a general order was issued against buying food from the Arabs, in order to avoid using up their supply, we bought it anyhow. Mess sergeants scoured the country and came back with eggs, sheep and chickens. You might say we lived partly off the country.

Of course ridiculous prices were paid to the Arabs, which infuriated the Europeans in North Africa because it ran up the prices for them too. But the Americans' attitude was usually expressed something like this: 'Well, money means nothing to us here, and from the looks of most of the Arabs a few extra francs won't hurt them.'

We had more eggs right at the front than anywhere else in the whole European and African theaters of war. The love of Americans for eggs has become almost a legend. Along the roads over which our motor convoys were passing constantly, Arabs stood by the score, even out on the limitlesss desert, holding up eggs for sale. The natives paid one franc for an egg. Mess sergeants paid three francs when buying in bulk, and individual soldiers paid five francs an egg.

Ernie Pyle, *Here is Your War – The Story of G.I. Joe* (1945)

1942 *Aspects of life on the Home Front*

NOTES ON LIFE AT HOME, FEBRUARY, 1942

What sounds fetched from far the wind carries tonight,
Do you hear them? Out where the sheep are
Huddles on wintry hill this cold night,
Under the lea of the hill folded;
There on the hard earth the wind goes
Massively over them, burdened with all that has colded
A thousand hearts, emptied a million hearts,
Slain twice and thrice a million. Over it blows
And like a flood pours into the house, under the doors,
Rushing like blood out of the dying veins, over the living it pours
And so, like a cunningly-channelled flood, empties away, departs
Leaving us dirtied with litter of not our own casualties, not our own
    hearts.

Valentine Ackland

FLASHBACK

I remember waking
from a sort of sleep,
khaki-clad and rigid on the canvas bed,
gas mask already slung
like an obscene shoulder-bag;
torch in one hand, tin hat in the other,
and the blasted buzzer shaking
the waking brain to jelly,
mercilessly dragging the tired body up
out of exhausted oblivion.

First out tonight.
Feet into rubber boots,
stumble down the darkened corridor,
burst through the black-out into the noisy yard
where the cars stand patiently,
their burden of stretchers
outlined against a blazing sky.

Fumble for the lock of the old Ford –
'Put out that bloody torch!'
squeeze in behind the wheel, wait for the men;
three bearers pile in the back
loud with their cockney curses,
the leader beside me
'Now lads, remember there's a lidy in the car'.

Pull the starter, oh God make her go!
She goes. Across the yard,
double declutch at the gate, and out –
roaring down the now invisible road,
masked sidelights only –
roaring down to disaster;
where the bomb-ploughed houses wait
with their harvest of casualties.

Valentine Ackland

PICTURE FROM THE BLITZ

After all these years
I can still close my eyes and see
her sitting there,
in her big armchair,
grotesque under an open sky,

framed by the jagged lines of her broken house.
Sitting there,
a plump homely person,
steel needles still in her work-rough hands;
grey with dust, stiff with shock,
but breathing,
no blood or distorted limbs;
breathing, but stiff with shock,
knitting unravelling on her apron'd knee.

They have taken the stretchers off my car
and I am running
under the pattering flack
over a mangled garden;
treading on something soft
and fighting the rising nausea —
only a far-flung cushion, bleeding feathers.

They lift her gently
out of her great armchair,
tenderly,
under the open sky,
a shock-frozen woman trailing khaki wool.

Lois Clark

THE 'MONSTROUS REGIMENT'

What hosts of women everywhere I see!
I'm sick to death of them — and they of me.
(The few remaining men are small and pale —
War lends a spurious value to the male.)
Mechanics are supplanted by their mothers;
Aunts take the place of artisans and others;
Wives sell the sago, daughters drive the van,
Even the mansion is without a man!
Females are farming who were frail before,
Matrons attending meeting by the score,
Maidens are minding multiple machines,
And virgins vending station-magazines.
Dames, hoydens, wenches, harridans and hussies
Cram to congestion all the trams and buses;
Misses and grandmas, mistresses and nieces,
Infest bombed buildings, picking up the pieces.

THE SECOND WORLD WAR

Girls from the South and lassies from the North,
Sisters and sweethearts, bustle back and forth.
The newsboy and the boy who drives the plough:
Postman and milkman — all are ladies now.
Doctors and engineers — yes, even these —
Poets and politicians, all are shes.
(The very beasts that in the meadows browse
Are ewes and mares, heifers and hens and cows . . .)
All, doubtless, worthy to a high degree;
But oh, how boring! Yes, including me.

Alice Coats

LAMENT OF A DESERT RAT

I've learnt to wash in petrol tins, and shave myself in tea
Whilst balancing the fragments of a mirror on my knee
I've learn to dodge the eighty-eights, and flying lumps of lead
And to keep a foot of sand between a Stuka and my head
I've learnt to keep my ration bag crammed full of buckshee food
And to take my Army ration, and to pinch what else I could
I've learnt to cook my bully-beef with candle-ends and string
In an empty petrol can, or any other thing
I've learnt to use my jack-knife for anything I please
A bread-knife, or a chopper, or a prong for toasting cheese
I've learnt to gather souvenirs, that home I hoped to send
And hump them round for months and months, and dump them in the
    end
But one day when this blooming war is just a memory
I'll laugh at all these troubles, when I'm drifting o'er the sea
But until that longed-for day arrives, I'll have to be content
With bully-beef and rice and prunes, and sleeping in a tent.

N. J. Trapnell

GERMAN P.O.W. CAMP

Here where the flies are thickest,
and the jagged strands of wire
enclose with coil and palisade
is a zoo grotesque,
where trained, potential killers
are without their fangs
and pace the cage in twos and threes,
dragging boredom with each step.

On the ground, baked hard as teak,
the motley bivouacs are strewn,
ground-sheet, silken parachute,
torn canvas, dusty blanket,
anything that serves
as parasol and parapluie.
Observe the prisoners,
blond arrogance of hair,
the athlete in their stance,
and hear their marching songs,
drum-like in cadence
and as mellow maudlin
as the feel of wine,
making an outlaw flag
wave in the heart,
hysteria its nationality.
These traits in time of war
when all virility is at high price,
almost compel an urge to fraternise.
But then an inner voice recalls –
Dachau, the death, despair and darkness,
Rotterdam, rased flat by bombs,
Paris, festering with pompous uniforms
and the malignant swastika,
and England's scars.
In a trice I have become
the gaoler once again,
confident with hate
and quick to penalise.

Tunisia
Alan White

1942 A Minor Mass Execution in the Ukraine, 5 October 1942

. . . My foreman and I went directly to the pits. I heard rifle shots in quick succession from behind one of the earth mounds. The people who had got off the trucks – men, women and children of all ages – had to undress upon the order of an S.S. man, who carried a riding or dog whip. They had to put down their clothes in fixed places, sorted according to shoes, top clothing and under-clothing. I saw a heap of shoes of about 800 to 1,000 pairs, great piles of under-linen and clothing.

Without screaming or weeping these people undressed, stood around in family groups, kissed each other, said farewells and waited for a sign from another S.S. man, who stood near the pit, also with a whip in his hand. During the fifteen minutes that I stood near the pit I heard no complaint or plea for mercy . . .

An old woman with snow-white hair was holding a one-year-old child in her arms and singing to it and tickling it. The child was cooing with delight. The parents were looking on with tears in their eyes. The father was holding the hand of a boy about 10 years old and speaking to him softly; the boy was fighting his tears. The father pointed to the sky, stroked his head and seemed to explain something to him.

At that moment the S.S. man at the pit shouted something to his comrade. The latter counted off about twenty persons and instructed them to go behind the earth mound . . . I well remember a girl, slim and with black hair, who, as she passed close to me, pointed to herself and said 'twenty-three years old.'

I walked around the mound and found myself confronted by a tremendous grave. People were closely wedged together and lying on top of each other so that only their heads were visible. Nearly all had blood running over their shoulders from their heads. Some of the people were still moving. Some were lifting their arms and turning their heads to show that they were still alive. The pit was already two-thirds full. I estimated that it contained about a thousand people. I looked for the man who did the shooting. He was an S.S. man, who sat at the edge of the narrow end of the pit, his feet dangling into the pit. He had a tommy gun on his knees and was smoking a cigarette.

The people, completely naked, went down some steps and clambered over the heads of the people lying there to the place to which the S.S. man directed them. They lay down in front of the dead or wounded people; some caressed those who were still alive and spoke to them in a low voice. Then I heard a series of shots. I looked into the pit and saw that the bodies were twitching or the heads lying already motionless on top of the bodies that lay beneath them. Blood was running down their necks.

The next batch was approaching already. They went down into the pit lined themselves up against the previous victims and were shot.

Testimony given by Hermann Graebe, engineer at German construction firm in the Ukraine, to Nuremberg tribunal. *Nazi Conspiracy and Aggression*, US Government Printing Office, Washington (1946).

Eastern Front

IN WOODS NEAR THE FRONTLINE

Soundless and almost weightless
yellow the birchleaf falls,
and an old waltz *Autumn's Dream*
on an accordion calls.

The bass-tones sigh complaining
as if in a dream they sigh,
The soldiers sit there and listen,
my comrades, and so do I.

We went with the step of this waltz
in spring to the swaying square.
We fell in love with our girls
and drew them close, to its air.

We glanced into kindled eyes
across the entwining tune;
and with it we wandered in sorrow,
lonely under the moon.

And now in the frontline woods,
again with its beat we were spelled.
All listened and all were silent,
for something precious it held.

And everyone thought of his love
and a spring that returns no more;
and everyone knew that the road
to his love ran on through the war.

Well, friends, if our turn is nearing,
let's see that the steel doesn't break.
Our hearts must learn not to falter,
our hands must learn not to shake.

Let the difficult hour be haloed
with lights of the trysts we recall.
If we come to a hole in the ground,
it's only once, and that's all.

If we come through the smoke and the fire
of death, we shall know it is true:
The fighter has conquered his fear.
And what we must do, we shall do.

THE SECOND WORLD WAR

It's time that we went, my friends,
for the hour is growing late:
by all that our yesterdays lived for,
by all that our morrows await.

by all who are stricken like leaves,
by the land where our spirits were bred —
accordion, turn from the dancing
and strike up a march-tune instead.

M. Isakovsky (1942), translated by Jack Lindsay

THE SOLDIERS AT LAURO

Young are our dead
Like babies they lie
The wombs they blest once
Not healed dry
And yet — too soon
Into each space
A cold earth falls
On colder face.
Quite still they lie
These fresh-cut reeds
Clutched in earth
Like winter seeds
But they will not bloom
When called by spring
To burst with leaf
And blossoming
They sleep on
In silent dust
As crosses rot
And helmets rust.

Italy, January 1943,
Spike Milligan

SICILIAN TOWN: AUGUST 1943

What was your crime, you little mountain town?
Why is that mother picking through those stones?
The entrails of the church stare to the sky;
The Military Police say: 'Out of Bounds,'

'No halting on the Road': the people stare
Blank-eyed and vacant, hollow-eyed and numb.
You do not seem to hate us: we are they
Who blew your town to dust with shell and bomb.

'Water not drinkable': 'One Way Street';
The road machine runts rubble from the track.
Was this a house, home of two lovers' joys,
Reduced by chemists' blast to pristine rock?

The moody mountain frowns, aloof, detached.
What was your crime, you little mountain town?
Just that you lay upon the Armies' route;
Two tracks met here by whim in ancient time.

N. T. Morris

1943 Leningrad

After the Nazi invasion, Leningrad was blockaded for thirty months.
The successful Russian offensive was mounted on 15 January 1944.
After five days fighting Leningrad was relieved. 600,000 citizens
survived – estimated deaths during the blockade vary between 600,000
to 900,000.

DAWN IN BESIEGED LENINGRAD

Diamonds, Sparkling. Gifts that cannot ease
the agonies of a town where all the faces
are branded deep with hunger, death, disease.
What use then are these opalescent spaces,
this garden-glint, this crystal light of trees?
They should be shrouded, like a shrouded mirror
in homes where death makes glittering things a horror.

How may we shroud them? There's no warming mists
curling to blur with clouds the aery dome.
Unmelting snow, like Ural amethysts,
has found on boughs its settled shining home.
No southern rose was like the sunset-rose.
All round a fiercely-tender beauty glows.

And when, above the streets, the morning star
climbs up the sky to warn us of the dawn
and throbs and beams in lucid strength afar,
such a sharp iciness from earth is drawn

the universe seems gasping to behold
how souls themselves are frozen by the cold.

The lightest touch is needed to explode
my memory's mine-fields. All night long I lay
fearing the charge and trembling. Down the road
of dangers yet I goad my spirit, astray
among the crouching deaths, but keep the track:
no timid yieldings now, no turning-back

in panic. Steadily I press ahead,
so that my pen, dipped deep in blood, may write
its message with an ink so richly red
a year may pass and still the fires be bright,
a life may pass, and still the words be fed
with fervours like the blood my wounds have bled.

I'll wage a bitter war, for which I'll borrow
each righteous weapon that our wrath commands:
the children's tears, the aging people's sorrow,
the lonely grave in far-off desert-sands.
For victory's sake we shall not even spare
our deepest, our most intimate despair.

Vera Inber, translated by Jack Lindsay

VERGISSMEINICHT
Elegy for an 88 Gunner.

Three weeks gone and the combatants gone,
returning over the nightmare ground
we found the place again and found
the soldier sprawling in the sun.

The frowning barrel of his gun
overshadows him. As we came on
that day, he hit my tank with one
like the entry of a demon.

And smiling in the gunpit spoil
is a picture of his girl
who has written: *Steffi, Vergissmeinicht.*
in a copybook Gothic script.

ECHOES OF WAR

We see him almost with content,
abased and seeming to have paid,
mocked by his durable equipment
that's hard and good when he's decayed.

But she would weep to see today
how on his skin the swart flies move,
the dust upon the paper eye
and the burst stomach like a cave.

For here the lover and the killer are mingled
who had one body and one heart;
and Death, who had the soldier singled
has done the lover mortal hurt.

Home, Tripolitania, 1943
Keith Douglas

CONVOY EPISODE

No sound save swishing sea is heard
Above the throb of engines. Ships
To starboard silently pursue
Their course; a single seagull dips
Astern, and dusk and the grey gloom
Steal ever closer from the dim
Horizon . . . Mute, be-duffeled men
Stand grouped around their guns, as grim
As gravestones, peering eastward for
That shape which spells a welcome chance
Of action . . . Heroes? No — beneath
Each muffled frame a heart a-dance
And stomach sickly strained
With apprehensive tension.
                      Then . . .
'Aircraft in sight!' The air at once
Is full of sound, alive again,
The pom-poms pumping death, swift red
Tracked tracer tears the sky,
Staccato clatter marks the quick
Fed Bren; green beaded streams let fly
From other guns, ship shakes as shells
Are hurled from major armament —
Exhilarating cordite fumes

Escape as every charge is spent.
The Heinkel hesitates, then twists
And disappears beneath the swell . . .
A cheer . . .
　　　　'Cease fire' . . .
　　　　　　A happy crew
Collects the case of every shell
Expended – souvenirs, as were
The boxing programmes years ago –
The thrill of victory the same
And joy of contest. Well they know
The penalty for aiming low.

John Wedge

AIR RAID

'Aircraft! Stand still you bloody fool.'
Too late. He's seen the movement and glittering in the sun.
The Messerschmidt swoops down with flame-tipped guns.
Around your sprawling form the deadly bullets splatter,
And lying tense fearful of the hideous chatter,
You feel Death's haunting figure stalking near,
Sweat, cold about your body, tingling with fear.

And now the plane has turned to its patrol.
You rise and fingers trembling light a cigarette.
One man lies groaning, arm smashed by a cannon-shell.
You pad a splint and bandage the jagged hole;
Now for the morphine, tell him not to fret,
He's bloody lucky he got off so well.

Charles Robinson

1944 Invasion

D Day 6 June 1944

The invasion of the French mainland had long been planned. On 6 June
1944, 176,000 Allied troops landed at Omaha Beach, Utah Beach and
other beaches along the Normandy coast. Allied forces crossed the
Loire on 11 August and the US 7th Army landed in Southern France on
15 August and moved up the Rhine Valley. The US 3rd Army under

General George S. Patton reached the Seine on 19 August and the Allied armies annihilated the German 7th Army at Falaise Gap from 13 to 20 August. On 20 August the French retook Marseille and Paris was liberated on 25 August. Four years of German occupation were over.

NAMING OF PARTS

To-day we have naming of parts. Yesterday,
We had daily cleaning. And to-morrow morning,
We shall have what to do after firing. But to-day,
To-day we have naming of parts. Japonica
Glistens like coral in all of the neighbouring gardens
        And to-day we have naming of parts.

This is the lower sling swivel. And this
Is the upper sling swivel, whose use you will see
When you are given your slings. And this is the piling swivel,
Which in your case you have not got. The branches
Hold in the gardens their silent, eloquent gestures,
        Which in our case we have not got.

This is the safety-catch, which is always released
With an easy flick of the thumb. And please do not let me
See anyone using his finger. You can do it quite easy
If you have any strength in your thumb. The blossoms
Are fragile and motionless, never letting anyone see
        Any of them using their finger.

And this you can see is the bolt. The purpose of this
Is to open the breech, as you can see. We can slide it
Rapidly backwards and forwards; we call this
Easing the spring. And rapidly backwards and forwards
The early bees are assaulting and fumbling the flowers:
        They call it easing the Spring.

They call it easing the Spring; it is perfectly easy
If you have any strength in your thumb: like the bolt,
And the breech, and the cocking-piece, and the point of balance,
Which in our case we have not got; and the almond-blossom
Silent in all of the gardens and the bees going backwards and
        forwards,
        For to-day we have naming of parts.

Henry Reed

THE SECOND WORLD WAR

SOLDIERS IN TRAINING

From far away, a mile or so,
The wooden scaffolds could be seen
　　On which fat felons swung;
But closer view showed these to be
Sacks, corpulent with straw and tied
　　To beams from which they hung.

The sergeant halted his platoon.
'Right lads,' he barked, 'you see them sacks?
　　I want you to forget
That sacks is what they are and act
As if they was all Jerries – wait!
　　Don't move a muscle yet!

'I'm going to show you how to use
The bayonet as it should be done.
　　If any of you feel
Squeamish like, I'll tell you this:
There's one thing Jerry just can't face
　　And that thing is cold steel.

'So if we're going to win this war
You've got to understand you must
　　Be brutal, ruthless, tough.
I want to hear you scream for blood
As you rip out his guts and see
　　The stuff he had for duff.'

The young recruits stood there and watched
And listened as their tutor roared
　　And stabbed his lifeless foe;
Their faces were expressionless,
Impassive as the winter skies
　　Black with threats of snow.

　　　　Vernon Scannell, from *Bayonet Training*

INVASION SPRING

Where purple cuckoo-clappers quake
within their green translucent shrine,
and cobra-headed ferns awake,
the sullen mighty tanks recline.

Young shepherds sleep beside their flock,
or watch the stormy skies all night,
where brown owls with soft voices mock
great bands of darker birds in flight.

Like old calm shepherds of the fell
these know and call their lambs by name —
Susannah, Charmer, Cheyenne Belle,
Calamity and Texas Dame.

All Sussex flows with silver blood
from wounded white anemones,
while flowers in dark remembered mud
lie drowned among the waiting trees.

Here light words die as soldiers dream
beneath green hedges in the sun,
and see their twentieth April gleam,
who dare not hope for twenty-one.

Ruth Tomalin

1944 Battle of the Bulge

On 24 November 1944 Strasbourg fell to the Allies, but the Germans launched a counter-offensive in the Ardennes on 16 December (brilliantly planned by von Rundstedt) which took a very heavy toll, especially of US forces in Belgium. The conflict lasted well into January 1945 — and the Allied offensive against Germany was put back by many weeks. German losses were heavy, 220,000 men (with 110,000 prisoners of war), 600 tanks and assault guns.

THE MINE EXPERT

I have my share of duties, some distasteful, some heartwarming;
of them all, disarming mines is the most non-habit-forming.

The Army tried to make it habitual with me;
they sent me to a mine school (Tullahoma, Tennessee);
they sent me to another near the stones on Salisbury Plain,
then packed me up to practice with the knowledge I had gained.

I knew the cunning devices, every single working part.
I gloried in the knowledge (disarming is an art).
The human mind is superior to insensate bits of steel,
but I never could suppress the qualms that I would feel.

THE SECOND WORLD WAR

Solicitous of my safety, the Army trained me well;
I learned my avocation, or I would not be here to tell
of a game that is so thrilling, played with hands that dare not shake,
about a sport that's so demanding, you're allowed not one mistake.

I have my share of duties, some distressing, some heartwarming;
of them all, disarming mines is the most non-habit-forming.

THOUGHTS WHILE SETTING ANTIPERSONNEL MINES

A P mines are tricky to set;
steady hand are required and skill.
But I take no pride in this devious work
and I sorrow for what I may kill.

I set them to fell the plodding man,
not the bounding deer.
Would that I knew a way to keep
the innocent far from here

THE GOOD SOLDIER

First he oiled his rifle.
Next he cared for his feet,
then slowly opened a ration
and forced himself to eat.

MAROON MUD AND DOG-TAGS

A corpse in the road, a column of tanks
in a clanking, grinding fury,
maroon mud and dog-tags —
nothing to bury.

RETREAT

The boy in front of me faltered,
broke stride and slumped to the snow.
'I can't go on, Lieutenant,
leave me here and go.
I'll catch up with the column
after a little rest;
and if I don't, Lieutenant,
it will be for the best.'

A boot to his rump, the answer,
sharp slaps upon his cheek.
'Sergeant, help me with this man!'
We got him to his feet.
We trotted him back to his place in line
and he walked the snowy way.
We kicked and cursed when he faltered —
and the man is alive today!

THE POET

With clinical eye and mind alert
he watched the ebb and flow,
saw in live bodies beyond all hurt
dead eyes; saw blood on snow.

He walked with death ever near
beneath an indifferent sky,
knew the sickening taste of fear,
watched the valiant die,

watched the cowardly live on,
knew anguish at broken trees,
saw the mine-slain forest fawn
and proud men on their knees.

He recorded minutely in memory
all that came to pass,
then, ill of soul, wrote poetry
as a sick cat eats grass.

Dale R. Carver, 424th US Infantry

1945 The Second World War Ends

The war comes to an end. In the Pacific massive military operations
conclude with the US invasion of the Philippines under General
MacArthur, who enters Manila on 4 February. Over a thousand
bombers drop tons of explosives on Berlin. Dresden is bombed to
oblivion with an estimated death toll of 135,000. A hundred US B-24s
bomb Tokyo on 9 March with more than 124,000 deaths. By the end of
April Russian forces reach the suburbs of Berlin. Hitler commits suicide
on 30 April, Germany unconditionally surrenders on 8 May and the air
war against Japan intensifies. On 6 August an atomic bomb is dropped

on Hiroshima and on 9 August an atomic bomb is dropped on Nagasaki. Japan asks for peace on 10 August 1945. Formal Japanese surrender is signed on USS *Missouri*, 2 September 1945.

The Second World War killed an estimated 54.8 million people, most of them civilians. Fifty-seven nations were involved. Russian military losses totalled 7,500,000, Germany's 2,900,000, Japan's 1,500,000, the USA's 290,000, France's 247,000 and Britain's 398,000. An estimated 14,000,000 died in the Nazi policy of genocide.

6 AUGUST 1945

In the Enola Gay
five minutes before impact
he whistles a dry tune
Later he will say
that the whole blooming sky
went up like an apricot ice
Later he will laugh and tremble
at such a surrender
for the eye of his belly
saw Marilyn's skirt's
fly over her head for ever

On the river bank
bees drizzle over
hot white rhododendrons
Later she will walk
the dust, a scarlet girl
with her whole stripped skin
at her heel, stuck like an old
shoe sole or mermaid's tail

Later she will lie down
in the flecked black ash
where the people are become
as lizards or salamanders
and, blinded, she will complain:
Mother you are late, so late

Later in dreams he will look
down shrieking and see
ladybirds
ladybirds

Alison Fell

ECHOES OF WAR

THE DAY AFTER

Who will be next to break this terrible silence,
While the doom of war still shivers over these
Unwilling either to die or to be defeated, –
In the agony of death still torn, contorted,
Torn between saving face and body, both
Mutilated almost beyond recognition?
The face fights on long after
The body's overwhelmed and hacked to pieces.
Every scar of it's their fault; yet I am dumb;
In the blind eyes of pity the good and the evil
Are equals when they're gasping in the sand,
Helpless. The reality so blinds
Our senses that it seems less than a dream,
Yet we shall live to say 'Twice in a lifetime
We saw such nakedness that shame
Itself could not look on, and of all the feelings,
Hate, anger, justice, vengeance, violence, –
Horror alone remained, its organ voice
Searching us with a sickening clarity.'
And now the word comes in of those two cities
With all their living burden
Blown to the wind by power
Unused except by God at the creation, –
Atomised in the flash of an eye.
Who else but God or the instrument of God
Has the power to pass such sentence?
Here the road forks, to survival or extinction,
And I hold my tongue through the awful silence,
For if God had nothing to do with it,
Extinction is the least price man can pay.

Edward Lowbury

THREE DAYS: THE WAR ENDS

A pleasant way to finish the war off
At the convalescent Depot at Salerno,
Scrounging, on the Education Staff –
Run Quiz, Tombola, Brains' Trust in the N.A.A.F.I.,
Give left-wing lectures on the post-war world.

Plenty of cheap, good spirits in the Sergeants' Mess,
And sea and time enough to swim off hangovers.

Armistice, Italy, was a fine day.
We were awed and excited, suddenly free.
Finito Tedesci, Finito Boum Boum. And no fear now
To be sent up through squalid transit-camps
To front-line mountains, snow and mud and bang.
Sang the RED FLAG again, several times this time –
Alex had brought it off before Montgomery –
And a muscular Glaswegian R.S.M.
Thumped on the bar and glinted through black brows:
'It's victorry for the lads. I'm glad. I'm glad
It's victorry for the worrkers back at home'
We left the mess and went swimming, drunk in the moonlight.

V.E. Day was a different matter, stale.
Started drinking in the morning, went on all day,
We'd expected this so long, and O.K. this was it,
We were rancid with expectation.
And Churchill wireless-spoke, fatigued. What was it?
Submarine bases, Ireland? What about demobilisation?
And a red-cap sergeant, who nobody trusted,
Lay groaning under a table: 'Four bleeding years!
Churchill! Four bastard years and a half!
Churchill! etc., etc., etc.,'
True but tedious, we thought.

Next day got up with brass-sick mouth.
We went about our duties, sullenly.

V.J. Day I spent in Halifax, Yorks.,
Wilfred Pickles' home-town, R.E. Depot.
They had the gall to get us on parade
For a major to tell us the war was over.
It wasn't we weren't pleased the new invention
Had finally finished things off. And no fear now etc.
But there wasn't much celebration, there wasn't much beer in the
    town,
And the locals wouldn't have a lot to do with us.
They'd had time to get used to soldiers, all through the war.

                                                    Martin Bell

HIROSHIMA

Hi-ro-shi-ma
Hi-ro-shi-ma
Shrine of tinkling bells
and beauty blossoming,
petalled in paper houses
with an artist's landscape,
brush and soft pen . . .
all gold and pale rose-mist
(With bamboo leaves).

Within your heart, delicate,
like a bird's wing,
there is an unborn cry.
I feel it here,
still . . .
a pang within my breast,
this sorrow torn
from the tomb of Science
and derelict destruction.

I can see
that mushroom hanging,
hovering ominously
even on a clear, bright
summer's day —
Amid the clapping voices
of children,
and soft, unspoken words
like silk and sake:

Amid the chatter of rice-tables,
square, low,
and cushions:
Amid the tap of tiny women
in kimonos,
their black hair framing
moon faces and with
large eyes . . .
that do not accuse me.

Mary Beadnell

THE FALLEN

(V.J. Day, August 15, 1945)

Have no self-pity now for loneliness;
Permit no tear, no sad, recalling sigh
For these, the dead, who counted all things less
Than honour, and the courage so to die:
Remembering that age too seldom gives
What youth has dreamed: our hopes are mostly vain
And fortunate indeed is he who lives
Forever young, beyond the reach of pain.
Yours is the sorrow, heart that still must beat,
Yours is the heavy burden of the day,
Yours the long battle now against defeat.
Be not less steadfast in the fight than they;
Nor shun the throng: their spirits linger there,
Whose laughter rang so gaily on the air.

Vera Box

XVII

AMERICAN INVOLVEMENT
IN THE EAST

1950-1953 Korean War

At the end of the Second World War, Korea was divided into Soviet (North Korean) and US (South Korean) zones of occupation. This was followed by a perpetual war. As James Cameron wrote: 'From 1945 to 1950 both sides shouted about invasion and at last, on June 25th, it came to pass . . .' The United Nations authorized member nations to go to South Korea's aid.

James Cameron visited the front:

Bit by bit the front materialized, the tanks squatted on the flats of the river-beds, the road grew dense with traffic, and soon, where it ran in a kind of cutting between wooded slopes, were the groups of men, like picnickers, crouching on the verge with automatic guns, huddling in the dust of the passing wheels among a litter of ration-cans ('The Ripe Flavor of Nutty Home-Grown Corn Enriched with Body-Building Viadose') or heads buried under the hood of a jeep. The air was alive with a tinny whispering from field-telephones and the radios of tanks, a thin erratic chattering like insects, the ceaseless indiscriminate gossip of an army. Up and down the road, weaving through the traffic, bare-legged Koreans humped loads of food or mortar ammunition on their porters' framework of wood, like men with easels on their backs.

The artillery became abruptly louder and more personal, cracking horribly from the sides and behind. The planes flew overhead as though on rails. The war was all on one side — no combat, no visible encounter of any kind; so far no reply at all to all this ironclad effort. The guns were fighting the silence; the convoy was grinding into a vacuum; the men were advancing into empty space. It could have been an elaborate and over-realistic exercise — except for the hills around, and the roadblocks behind, and the fact that it was this kind of empty country that had driven us backwards a hundred and fifty miles already, and still had us hemmed in: a yielding wall of irresistible no-man's-land.

The village where the North Koreans had been until an hour ago was half a mile up the road, or had been; there was nothing much left. It had been rocketed, what remained was a heap of ashes, a few mud walls, with one or two North Koreans sprawled among the debris in unreal tangled postures, with calcined limbs projecting in impossible attitudes. The only visible body that still bore the semblance of a man remained sitting upright in a pile of still redly glowing cinders; for a startling moment he looked not like a dead Korean but like a living yogi. The rest were carrion. It had not long happened, but already in the heat of the day the smell was unendurable. The marching men hurried past, gagging . . . .

A little way down, by a cluster of roofless homes, there was an old man, one of the typical old men of Korea, with a placid Buddha face; in some curious way he had let the battle catch up with him and he was done for. He sat beside a dry-stone wall, and then he lay. He had not been hit, or damaged in any way; it seemed he had been minding his own business when the war accumulated suddenly around him, and he was unable to cope with it — the noise, the burning, the fuss. We stopped a passing GI and borrowed a new water-bottle, but the water dribbled down among the hairs of the old man's beard, spaced out far apart like white wires, and he died without any confusion or excitement at all; it was the most composed and deliberate action I had seen that day, and certainly the most graceful.

James Cameron, *Point of Departure* (1967)

1965–1973 Vietnam War

'The people of South Vietnam have chosen to resist North Vietnamese aggression. At their request the United States has taken its place beside them in this struggle.'

(President Lyndon B. Johnson, 11 February 1965)

The origins of the Viet Nam War are obscure. They go back to the Japanese conquests of South-east Asia in the 1930s, which were succeeded by anticolonial war against the French. The French were defeated at Dien Bien Phu in 1954, and the aftermath of the conflict involved the division of Viet Nam along the 17th parallel.

The South was always troubled by corruption and suppression and in 1958 a Communist-led assault began from the north of Viet Nam. The USA sent in 2,000 'military advisers' to support the South and a full-scale civil war soon developed. By 1965 the military situation had deteriorated severely and the USA became more heavily involved. By the end of 1968, 550,000 US troops were involved in Viet Nam. The situation worsened and it became a war the USA could not win. It was America's longest war, with 350,000 casualties, and a war which created extremely bitter controversy at home. It destroyed the political career of US President L. B. Johnson.

GREEN BERET

He was twelve years old,
and I do not know his name.
The mercenaries took him and his father,
whose name I do not know,
one morning upon the High plateau.
Green Beret looked down on the frail boy
with the eyes of a hurt animal and thought,
a good fright will make him talk.
He commanded, and the father was taken away
behind the forest's green wall.
'Right kid tell us where they are,
tell us where or your father − dead.'
With eyes now bright and filled with terror
the slight boy said nothing.
'You've got one minute kid', said Green Beret,
'tell us where or we kill father'
and thrust his wrist-watch against a face all eyes,
the second-hand turning, jerking on its way.
'OK boy ten seconds to tell us where they are'
In the last instant the silver hand shattered the
sky and the forest of trees.
'Kill the old guy' roared Green Beret
and shots hammered out
behind the forest's green wall
and sky and trees and soldiers stood
in silence, and the boy cried out.
Green Beret stood
in silence, as the boy crouched down
and shook with tears,
as children do when their father dies.

'Christ,' said one mercenary to Green Beret,
'he didn't know a damn thing
we killed the old guy for nothing.'
So they all went away,
Green Beret and his mercenaries.

And the boy knew everything.
He knew everything about them, the caves,
the trails, the hidden places and the names,
and in the moment that he cried out,
in that same instant,
protected by frail tears
far stronger than any wall of steel,
they passed everywhere
like tigers
across the High Plateau.

Ho Thien

XVIII

THE FALKLANDS CONFLICT

1982 Falklands War

Walking into the hotel was the fulfilment of a dream, a fantasy that had filled all our thoughts for almost three months. 'We never doubted for a moment that the British would come,' said the proprietor . . . It was like liberating an English suburban golf club.

Max Hastings, The Standard (6 October 1983)

The Falkland Islands – two large islands and about two hundred smaller ones – have been under British rule since the 1830s. Argentine governments had disputed British claims to the Falkland Islands for some time. The crisis which was to lead to the war began inauspiciously enough when a number of Argentine scrap merchants landed on South Georgia, an administrative dependency of the Falkland Islands. These landings were technically illegal, but seemed hardly the stuff of which international conflicts are made. But then, without warning, the Argentine invaded on 2 April 1982.

The British governement was criticized for underestimating the Argentine intentions, and for having withdrawn an armed survey vessel, HMS *Endurance*, from service in the South Atlantic. A British Task Force sailed, and Britain was at war. It was a costly war, fought in the glare of press and radio coverage. The British lost by air attack or missiles HMSs *Sheffield*, *Ardent*, *Antelope*, and *Sir Galahad*, as well as the supply ship, *Atlantic Conveyor*. Other shipping was severely damaged. At Goose Green there was a ferocious battle, and at Bluff Cove British troops were strafed from the air before anti-aircraft defences were set up or troops even disembarked.

The Argentine forces surrendered on 13 June 1982.

1982

DAWN ATTACK

Steam rises off of their bodies,
Their faces are tired and drawn.
Their feet still hurt from the marching they've done,
And their clothes are muddy and torn.
They drink their tea or have a last smoke,
As they wait for the first light of dawn.

'On your feet lads', whispers the Sergeant,
'Come on we're out on the right!'
They quietly pick up their weapons,
The ones they've been cleaning all night.
Then silently follow him into the mist,
Until the last man's out of sight.

The whistle and crump of mortars is heard,
The Artillery thunders away.
An explosion close by, but we're safe in the trench,
It was probably only a stray.
The radio's dead, what's wrong on the right?
We stand there and silently pray.

Then suddenly all becomes quiet,
'The mist's clearing', our Captain said.
'Come on lads, it's time to move forward'.
In my stomach a feeling of dread,
Then we move out, on the right, to the valley,
To pick up our wounded and dead.

Steam rises off of their bodies,
Their faces no longer look drawn.
There's no pain in their feet from the marching they did,
Though their clothes are still muddy and torn.
Now they've drunk their last drink and had their last smoke,
And they'll never again see a dawn.

R. J. Latham, 9th Parachute Squadron, Royal Engineers

GOTCHA DRAMA

The Sun headlines were *Gotcha*
and seventeen year olds
acted out a bare-bones play.

324

THE FALKLANDS CONFLICT

They envied those there —
the regulars who'd signed up
into the real thing.

It would all be finished
before they had a run
at the Argies, alas.

They buried the *Belgrano*,
sank it over and over
in a London classroom —

Cheering, holding up their papers
to calls of *Gotcha*,
and walked on waves, no surrender.

Katherine Gallagher

TEA-TIME IN PORTSMOUTH 1982

The news comes pouring as she runs from school.
'We made some cakes. There's fifteen pence to pay.
We had an awful dinner. It was yuk!
I got a star in history today.

You know that girl with glasses and long hair,
Who said this year they're going to Italy?
They won't be going now. She's been away.
Her Dad was on the *Sheffield*. What's for tea?'

Margaret Hothi

NO HEROES

There were no heroes here
Amongst the men who tramped through
Rutted, quaking moor,
Or crawled, cat-silent,
Over skittering scree
To prove the way.

No heroes fought the blazing fires
Which sucked the very blood from
Ship and man alike.
Or braved knife cold
Without a thought
To save a life.

No heroes they, but ones who loved
Sweet life and children's laugh,
And dreamt of home
When war allowed.
They were but men.

David Morgan, Sea Harrier pilot, Royal Navy

MY FAMILY

Did you see us on the telly, Mum?
When we sailed away –
Laughing, waving, cheering
Like in films of yesterday.

Did you read it in *The Sun*, Pop?
How we pasted them first time.
You told me all about your war.
What do you think of mine?

Did you get the letters home, dear?
How I missed you and was sad.
Did you give my love to Tracy?
Does she miss her funny Dad?

Did you see us on the hillside?
Could you spot which one was me?
Were the flowers very heavy
For a grown up girl of three?

Paul D. Wapshott, formerly Parachute Regiment

XIX

THE GULF WAR

1991 The Gulf War

'We have before us the opportunity to forge for ourselves and for future generations a new world order, a world where the rule of law, not the law of the jungle governs the conduct of nations.'

George Bush, US President, broadcast, 15 January 1991

Iraq invaded the neighbouring state of Kuwait on 2 August 1990. All diplomatic and peaceful methods of negotiating a withdrawal failed and Kuwait was forced to endure Iraqi occupation despite a United Nations deadline which expired on 15 January 1991. Vast forces — American, British, French and others — assembled waiting, it seemed, for the terrible Armageddon which was to follow the expiry of the UN deadline. Fears were aroused about the Iraqi war machine, that the country had nuclear capability, that they would use nerve gas, that they possessed super long-range guns, that their Republican Guard would fight to the death. It was the first war watched on the world's televisions like a spectator sport, from early preliminaries, through diplomatic negotiations and opening salvoes to on-the-spot accounts of massive bombardments, deployment of 'smart' bombs, Scud missiles launched on Israel and the bombing of Baghdad. Late-twentieth-century techno-logical war it may have been, but the Gulf War still featured scenes as ancient as war itself — Saddam's torture chambers, the Kuwaitis' revenge on the Palestinians, the horrors endured by the Kurds, the burning of oilfields as the ultimate scorched-earth policy — all these scenes rehearsed barbarity as ancient as human history.

An Army Fights on Its Stomach

It is as if a city of half a million Americans had picked up and moved to Saudi Arabia.

Meeting the awesome task of sending so many people half-way around the world, feeding, clothing and sheltering them, has won Major-General William Pagonis a nickname of which he is quite proud: The Grand Mover.

Now, as the ground war looms, he is facing the challenge of moving hundreds of thousands of troops and their supplies to the front.

As the US Army's chief logistician in the Gulf, General Pagonis is compared by other officers to Milo Minderbinder, the supply genius of Joseph Heller's *Catch-22*, who bartered, traded and wheedled what he needed to keep his forces happy and up to scratch.

On a less whimsical note, President Bush has recognised General Pagonis's skills by recommending him for promotion from major-general to lieutenant-general.

Keeping America's forces poised for combat is expensive and difficult. In the past six months, the general's staff has served 90 million meals, delivered 160 million gallons of water and pumped 100 million gallons of petrol.

General Pagonis had a staff of five working from the boot of a car when he arrived in Saudi Arabia in early August. Now his team has grown to 16,000 working round the clock.

He is supported by 4,000 men and women at the Defense Personnel Support Centre (DPSC) in Philadelphia, Pennsylvania, who spend their days at computers or on telephones seeking contractors, filling orders and ensuring the right items are sent to the right place at the right time.

Once goods have arrived in Saudi Arabia by ship or plane, more than 2,000 lorries distribute them. Each vehicle makes an average, one-way haul of about 230 miles every day across the eastern province of the vast desert kingdom.

By the end of last month, the DPSC had dispatched food worth £347.5 million, medical supplies costing £209 million, and clothing and other textiles worth £414 million in support of the Gulf operation.

Subsistence items – as the military refers to food – included 7.6 million Meals Ready to Eat (MREs), not the dinner of choice for American Servicemen, who have nicknamed them Meals Rejected by Ehthiopians. More popular among the troops are the Meal Ordered Ready to Eat (MORE) selections prepared under a private contract. They included chicken breast, spaghetti, beef pot roast, sukiyaki with rice and lasagne.

Another firm has been awarded a contract to deliver 14 million 'lunch bucket' meals such as beef stew, chili and beans, pasta and chicken.

A treat for the American soldier could be one of the 12 million heat-resistant Hershey chocolate bars already shipped to the desert. Staples such as sugar, flour and coffee, so far totalling almost 15lb million, have also been sent.

The supply of medical goods sent to the Gulf costs an average of £1.2 million a day. Along with 2.2 million tubes of lip salve, 715,000 cans of foot powder and 558,000 bottles of sunscreen are more sobering items such as 790,000 atropine injectors containing an antidote to chemical agents and 60,000 pyridostigmine bromide tablets, an anti-nerve gas drug.

America's troops have received 3.2 million pairs of desert camouflage trousers, 376,000 pairs of goggles to protect against sand, wind and dust, 1.4 million pairs of tan desert boots and 1.34 million chemical suits.

The comforts of home include mail delivery, a huge operation involving almost 300 tons of mail a day to men and women scattered from warships in the Red Sea to outposts on the Saudi–Kuwait border.

Much of the post is from children and well-wishers and is addressed simply to: 'Any soldier, Saudi Arabia'. One recipient of such a letter in the Marines has successfully proposed marriage to the young woman who sent it.

A staff of 350 sorts and delivers the mail from distribution centres in Dhahran, Riyadh and Bahrain. 'We use everything available short of Bedouins and camels,' said Major Michael Whitaker, commander of postal services in the Gulf.

Patricia Wilson, *Daily Telegraph* (12 February 1991)

Something Evil has Visited Kuwait City

What kind of people would do this? That's what we kept asking ourselves in Kuwait City yesterday. Day had been turned into night, so thick was the canopy of smoke, the nation's oil wells burning gold and orange along the black-fringed horizon. Hieronymus Bosch courtesy of the Iraqi Army.

They had even used the modern equivalent of a torture wheel. All day, Kuwaiti men, young and old, approached our car with their terrible stories. 'They twisted my son on a pole and broke his legs with pieces of wood,' a stooped old man said. 'They thought he was in the resistance. Now they have taken him away, with all the others, as a human shield.'

Then there was Heather Rennison, an English woman married to a Kuwaiti. 'A cousin of my mother-in-law was arrested. She was only 19 and they had found two-way radios in her bedroom. Three days later they came to her home to ask her parents for clothes and blankets. So her parents thought she would be all right. Then the Iraqis hanged her and dumped her body outside her home. There were burns from electricity on her arms and legs. Of course, the Iraqis kept the clothes and blankets.'

Perhaps one needed to walk the pavements of Kuwait City yesterday to understand the extent of what the Iraqis did, that it really does amount to a war crime. 'I will show you the mosque where they shot 11 men on Friday,' a bearded man shouted to us from his car.

The Abdullah Othman mosque stands in the Palestinian Hawali quarter. The bearded man pointed to a yellow wall. 'The Iraqis said that all those at prayer would be taken away – kidnapped – and 11 men stayed in the mosque and refused to go. So they brought them here, blindfolded them, made them stand with their backs to the wall and shot them in the face.' The bullets that had hit the worshippers' heads were embedded in the yellow wall. 'Don't be surprised,' the man said. 'I had two neighbours who the Iraqis thought were in the resistance. So they pushed them into the drains, closed the grille, poured petrol on them and set them on fire. Their families buried them later – you can't leave bodies in drains.'

The figure of 5,000 Kuwaiti men abducted in the last hours before Iraq's retreat seems fantastic until you find – as I did yesterday – that the first three families who offered lifts to various locations in Kuwait City had all lost sons as hostages. The young men had simply been ordered into Iraqi Army buses as they walked to work. Three thousand men and women murdered here, the Kuwaitis also tell you. Who could do this?

It is comforting, in trying to come to terms with a reign of terror, to search for some logical reason, historical hatred perhaps, or some aberrant unit of the Iraqi secret police. But this would be fanciful. What is one to think when one walks, as I did yesterday, through the smoking embers of the National Museum, fired by the Iraqis on Tuesday? Or the gutted interior of the parliament? Or the still burning library in the Seif Reception Palace – its magnificent golden clock tower smashed by a tank shell – where I found, lying on a chair, the remains of a book published by the government of India, entitled *The Collected Works of Mahatma Gandhi*? What kind of people burn museums and libraries?

Outside the museum, Kuwait's collection of historic wooden boats had been burned to cinders. The 'Islamic house' lay in ruins. The walls of the Emir of Kuwait's Dasman Palace had been torn down with explosions and bulldozers. The Iraqis had used tanks to shoot at the parliament. The great hotels had been systematically fired. The Iraqis had even planted explosives in the bedrooms of the Meridian Hotel. It was like a medieval army which conquered, looted and then burned even on an individual level.

Boat owners found their yachts stolen or deliberately sunk in the marinas. Shopkeepers found their stores burned if they could not be looted. At an abandoned anti-aircraft gun on the coast – where the Iraqis mined the lovely beaches against a non-existent American amphibious landing – I came across piles of brand new women's shoes, made in France, none of them matching, all wrapped inside Iraqi army blankets along with body-building magazines. Why did they do this, these soldiers? Why had they stolen, too, an exhibition display of women's eye shadow? There were cartridge cases across the forecourt of the great museum, bullet-holes in the cracked walls of the building that once contained Kuwait's finest – and long ago looted – national treasures. What was he thinking, this soldier, when he opened fire at a museum?

The seafront restaurants have been torn down, the high, glass-covered landmark water towers machine-gunned. At al-Ahmadi, the Iraqis set off explosives every hour at the two oil farms, each containing 20 tanks. The fine old British 'White House' there was burned down along with the control room that operates the oil pipelines.

I suppose one sensed in Kuwait yesterday that something very wicked, at times evil, had visited this city. Not just an occupation army, not even the Iraqi Ba'ath Party apparatus, but something which intrinsically links dictatorship and corruption. 'Down with the dirty Fahd, Sabah and Hosni [Mubarak]', said a blood-red graffito on the wall of one of the burned palaces. 'Long live Saddam Hussein.' In the little, looted museum of Kuwaiti peasant art, I found a poster of Saddam stapled to the wall. 'Most victorious of all Arabs, the great leader Saddam Hussein – God bless him,' the caption said.

Whoever uttered such prayers? Colonel Mustapha Awadi, of the Kuwaiti resistance movement, offered to show me. In a bleak housing estate in the suburb of Quwain, he took me to a school – the Iraqis used schools as interrogation centres – and in a classroom I found 16 young Iraqi soldiers. They sat on the floor, legs crossed, moustachioed, miserable, ordinary men with tired, dirty faces and grimy uniforms. 'They were happy to surrender,' the colonel said. 'See? We have even given them food and tea. I promise they will be handed over unharmed to the Kuwaiti Army.'

Two of the men had been wounded in the face – their bandages were fresh – and they all smiled when I greeted them and when they heard me tell the colonel in Arabic that I would mention their presence to the Red Cross. One could not help but feel sorry for these defeated teenagers with their sad smiles. So what kind of men had raped Kuwait?

Robert Fisk, Independent (28 February 1991)

INDEX

INDEX

Fortinbras xi
Fort Sumter 175
Franco, General 261
Franco–Prussian War x–xi, 197
Franz Ferdinand, Archduke of
  Austria 220
Frederick I, Holy Roman Emperor
  50
Frederick II, the Great 50, 123,
  132
French, Sir John 231
French Revolution 140
Froissart, Sir John 57, 59
'from Hugh Selwyn Mauberley'
  257
Froude, James Anthony 85

Gallagher, Katherine 325
Gallic Wars 27
Gallic War, The 28
Gallipoli 233
'Garden in the Sky' 294
Gardner, Brian 215
Gascoyne, David 276
Gates, General 139
Gaunt, John of 65
Gentleman's Magazine, The 136
George II 124
'German P.O.W. Camp' 299
German unification 219
Geronimo 195
Gestes des Chiprois, Les 52
'Gettysburg Address' 188
Gettysburg, battle of 176, 186
Gibney, Thomas 155
'Give Them Their Life . . .' 282
Glendower, Owen 55
Globe and Laurel, Journal of the
  Royal Marines 168
Glover, Michael 202
Goethe, Johann Wolfgang 141
'Good Soldier, The' 311
Good Soldier Švejk, The 92, 224
Gordon, General Charles 203
'Gotcha Drama' 324
Gough, Viscount 161
Graebe, Hermann 301
Grant, James 200
Grant, Ulysses Simpson,
  President of the USA 176, 194
Grant Camp 192
  massacre 193
Graves, Robert 248
Gravesend 109
Great War, The 219–60
'Green Beret' 321
Grenville, Sir Richard 85
Greville, Fulke 83
Grey, Sir Edward 219
Grimmelshavsen, Johann Jakob
  Christoffel von 92
Guillemard, Robert 143
Gujarat, battle of 162
Gulf War 327–32
Gurney, Ivor 250

Haig, Field Marshall Sir Douglas
  252
Hakluyt, Richard 84
Hamilton, Charles James 124
Hamlet xi
Hamlet xi
Hampshire Regimental Journal 134
Handel, George Friderich 123
Hannibal 24
Hapsburg succession 123
Harold II 40
Harper's Weekly 205
'Harvest' 291
Harwich 109
Hasek, Jaroslav 92, 223
Hastings, battle of 40
Havelock, General Sir Henry 170
Hawke, Admiral Edward 134
Hay, Ian 233
Headlam, C.E.S. 18
Hearst, William Randolph 205
Heights of Abraham 124
Hemingway, Ernest 267
Henry V 57, 59, 61
Henry V 61, 62
Henry VI 65
Henry VI, Part Three 68, 70
Henry VII 70
Henry VIII 72
Henry Tudor 65, 70
*Here is Your War — The Story of
  G.I. Joe* 296
Hermann 31, 32
Hermann und die Fürsten 33
Hermannsschlacht, Die 32
Herodotus 13, 15
Her Privates We 242
Hinmaton-Yalakit: Thunder
  Rolling in the Mountains 195
'Hiroshima' 316
*Historical Papers Relating to the
  Jacobite Period* 126
*Historical Records of the Royal
  Marine Forces* 139
Histories 13
Histories, Book VII 15
History of a Campaign that Failed
  177
History of the Conquest of Peru 77
*History of England from the
  Accession of James II* 117
*History of England from the Fall of
  Wolsey to the Defeat of the
  Spanish Armada* 85
History of Herodotus, Book VI 14
History of Rome, Book 21, 26
Hobbes, Thomas vii
Hodgson, W.N. 237
Holinshed, Raphael 56, 61, 71
Holwell, John Zephaniah 130
Homer viii, 3, 7
Hood, Thomas 150
'Horatius' 11
Hossbach Protocol 269
Hothi, Margaret 325

Housman, A.E. 232
Howard of Effingham, Lord 89
Howe, Admiral Richard 141
Hundred Years War 56–64
Hungarian revolt 163
'Hunting of the Cheviot, The' 55
Hystapes, Darius 13

'I Don't Want to be a Soldier' 246
Iliad, The ix, 3, 5, 7
Illustrated London News 201
Inber, Vera 305
Independent 332
Indian Wars 191–6
Indus Valley viii
'In Flanders Fields' 235
Ingham, Bernard xi
Inkerman, battle of 168
International Brigade of Anti-
  Fascists 261
'In the Dordogne' 248
'In the Small Stove' 288
Invasion of the Crimea, The 165
'Invasion Spring' 309
'In Woods Near the Frontline'
  302
Isabella, Queen of England 57
Isakovsky, M. 303
Isandhlwana 201
'I Saw a Broken Town' 291

Jackson, Stonewall 186
Jackson, T. Sturges 142
Jacobite rebellion 123, 126–7
Jalalabad 159
James II 118
James IV 72
Jameson Raid 208
Jerusalem, fall of 48
Jewish Revolt 33
Jewish War 35
Joan of Arc 57, 62
Johnson, Lyndon B., President of
  USA 320, 321
Johnstone, James ('Chevalier de
  Johnstone') 127
Joseph, Chief 195
Josephus, Flavius 35
Joubert, General 210
*Journal of the Society of Army
  Historical Research*
Journals of John Knox, The 137
Journals (Rowland Davies) 120
Journals (Florentia Sale) 160
Juan, Don, of Austria 77

Kabul, retreat from 159
Kadikoi 164
Kauravas ix
Khalil, Sultan-al-Ashraf 50
Khartoum, siege of 203
Khyber Pass 159
'Killed in Action' 294
Kincaid, Sir John 147
Kinglake, Alexander William 165

INDEX

ACKNOWLEDGMENTS

The Author would like to thank: the Librarian and staff at Bournemouth Polytechnic, especially the Inter-Library Loan department, for their splendid help in locating texts, often when only skimpy details could be provided, as well as acknowledging the massive role inevitably played by The London Library in any such project; Mrs Sue Court for superb secretarial assistance; Professor John Mackenzie at the University of Lancaster, who gave considerable guidance with various stages of the research for this volume; Tracey Smith, Managing Editor at Bloomsbury Publishing Limited, who was endlessly encouraging throughout this undertaking; and the custodians and staff of various museums, especially The Imperial War Museum and British county regimental museums, who attempt to maintain some kind of official public memory of those terrible and massive conflicts which have shaped and conditioned what we are.

Please Note: Every effort has been made to trace the copyright holders in this book. The Publishers apologize if any material has been included without permission and would be pleased to hear from anyone who has not been consulted.

The Author and Publisher wish to thank the following for permission to use copyright material:

Penguin Books Ltd for an excerpt from Thucydides, *The Pelopennesian War*, translated by Rex Warner; Cornell University Press for an excerpt from *Poema de mio Cid*, translated by Lesley Byrd Simpson; Hutchison and Company for an excerpt from *The Song of Roland*, translated by D. D. R. Owen; Eyre Methuen for an excerpt from Bertolt Brecht's *Mother Courage*, translated by Eric Bentley; Harper Collins for sections from *The Diary of Samuel Pepys*, edited by Robert Latham; Houghton

Mifflin Company for sections from *A Diary from Dixie*, edited by Ben Ames Williams; Frederick Warne for an excerpt from *Rorke's Drift — A Victorian Epic*, by Michael Glover; Leo Cooper Ltd. for sections from *Young Winston's Wars — the Original Dispatches of Winston S. Churchill*; Macmillan Publishing Co. Inc, for an excerpt from *The Good Soldier Švejk* by Jaroslav Hasek, translated by Cecil Parrott; Alan Sutton and Company for an excerpt from *My Bit — A Lancashire Fusilier at War 1914—18*, by George Ashurst; Michael Joseph for an excerpt from Lyn MacDonald's *1914—18: Voices and Images of the Great War*; The *Guardian* for an excerpt from *The Battle of the Somme*, by Bert Steward; Sidgwick and Jackson for an excerpt from *The Smoke and the Fire — Myths and Anti-myths of War 1861—1981*, by John Terraine; Random Century Group for *Strange Meeting* by Wilfred Owen; Oxford University Press for *The Silent One*, by Ivor Gurney; Routledge for an excerpt from *The Killing Ground* by Tim Travers; George Sassoon for *Blighters* by Siegfried Sassoon; Faber and Faber for *Spain 1937* and *1 September 1939* by W. H. Auden; Faber and Faber for *Ultima Ratio Regum* by Stephen Spender; Harper Collins for an excerpt from *By Line* by Ernest Hemingway; David Higham Associates for *Bombing Casualties in Spain*, by Herbert Read; Faber and Faber for *Elegy on Spain* by George Barker; Oxford University Press for *Farewell Chorus* by David Gascoyne; David Higham Associates for an excerpt from *Dunkirk* by David Divine; Secker and Warburg for excerpts from *The Rise and Fall of the Third Reich*, by William L. Shirer; Virago Press for *I Saw a Broken Town*, by Mabel Esther Allan; Laurence Pollinger for *Garden in the Sky* by Margery Lawrence; Oxford University Press for *Vergissmeinnicht*, by Keith Douglas; the author, Dale R. Carver, for *The Mine Expert, Thoughts While Setting Anti-personnel mines, Retreat*, and *The Poet*; Robson Books, for *Bayonet Training*, by Vernon Scannell; Ewan McNaughton Associates, Syndication Agents for the *Daily Telegraph*, for *An Army Fights on its Stomach* by Patricia Wilson; and The *Independent* for *Something Evil has Visited Kuwait City*, by Robert Fisk.